American SPEAK OUT

Elementary
Split Coursebook 2

with DVD/ROM and MP3 Audio CD

Pearson

Frances Eales • Steve Oakes

Catalogue Publication Data

Authors: Frances Eales, Steve Oakes; Louis Harrison
American Speakout Elementary Split Coursebook 2
with DVD-ROM and MP3 Audio CD
First published
Pearson Educación de México, S.A. de C.V., 2017
ISBN: 978-607-32-4205-9
Area: ELT
Format: 21 x 29.7 cm Page count: 144

Managing Director: Sergio Fonseca ■ **Innovation & Learning Delivery Director:** Alan David Palau ■ **Regional Content Manager - English:** Andrew Starling ■ **Publisher:** A. Leticia Alvarez ■ **Content Support:** Isabel Moreno ■ **Editorial Services Manager:** Asbel Ramírez ■ **Art and Design Coordinator:** Juan Manuel Santamaria ■ **Design Process Supervisor:** Aristeo Redondo ■ **Layout:** Andrés Morales ■ **Cover Design:** Ana Elena García ■ **Photo Research:** Beatriz Monsiváis ■ **Photo Credits:** Pearson Asset Library (PAL)

Contact: soporte@pearson.com
This adaptation is published by arrangement with Pearson Education Limited

Pearson Education Limited
Edinburgh Gate
Harlow
Essex CM20 2JE
England
and Associated Companies throughout the world.

Used by permission and adapted from
Speakout 2ND EDITION Elementary Students' Book
ISBN: 978-1-2921-1592-4
and
Speakout 2ND EDITION Elementary Workbook
ISBN: 978-1-4479-7676-9
First published, 2015

First published, 2017

ISBN PRINT BOOK: 978-607-32-4205-9

Impreso en México. *Printed in Mexico.*

1 2 3 4 5 6 7 8 9 0 - 20 19 18 17

D.R. © 2017 por Pearson Educación de México, S.A. de C.V.
Avenida Antonio Dovalí Jaime #70
Torre B, Piso 6, Colonia Zedec Ed. Plaza Santa Fe
Delegación Álvaro Obregón, México, Ciudad de México, C. P. 01210

Esta obra se terminó de imprimir en julio de 2017
en los talleres de Reproducciones Fotomecánicas, S.A. de C.V.
Durazno1, Col. Las Peritas, C.P. 16010,
México, Ciudad de México.

www.PearsonELT.com

Pearson

Pearson Hispanoamérica

Argentina ■ Belice ■ Bolivia ■ Chile ■ Colombia ■ Costa Rica ■ Cuba ■ República Dominicana ■ Ecuador ■ El Salvador ■ Guatemala
■ onduras ■ México ■ Nicaragua ■ Panamá ■ Paraguay ■ Perú ■ Uruguay ■ Venezuela

Acknowledgments

The Publisher and authors would like to thank the following people and institutions for their feedback and comments during the development of the material: **Hungary:** Tom Boyle; **Poland:** Lech Wojciech Krzeminski, Piotr Swiecicki; **Spain:** Bernadette de Mornay, Carmen Gómez Benítez, Liam Tweed; **U.K.:** Lilian Del Gaudio Maciel, Niva Gunasegaran.

Text acknowledgments

We are grateful to the following for permission to reproduce copyright material: Extracts on page 70 adapted from Tour D'Afrique The Silk Route Bike Tour, http://tourdafrique.com/. Reproduced with permission from Tour D'Afrique; Extracts on page 70 adapted from "Riding The Silk Road with Tour D'Afrique", The Adventure Blog by Nate Cavalieri, 6 July 2012, http://theadventureblog.blogspot. hu/2012/07/riding-silk-road-with-tour-dafrique.html. Reproduced with permission from Nate Cavalieri.

Illustration acknowledgments

Fred Blunt pgs 31, 81, 86, 101, 106, 111, 129, 132, 134, 135, 141, 142, 147, 150, 166, 168; **Stephen Cheetham** (Handsome Frank) pgs 10; **Peter Grundy** pgs 53, 121; **Lyndon Hayes** pgs 165, 168; **Kerry Hyndman** pgs 41, 71, 73; **Joanna Kerr** pgs 50, 54, 80, 136, 137, 165; **Harry Malt** pgs 135, 150; **Vicky Woodgate** pgs 137; In house pgs 14, 16, 39, 46, 50, 72, 96, 145, 161, 166.

Photo acknowledgments

The Publisher would like to thank the following for their kind permission to reproduce their photographs:

(Key: b-bottom; c-centre; l-left; r-right; t-top)

123RF.com: Andrei Shumskiy 7b (icon), 17b (icon), 27b (icon), 37b (icon), 47b (icon), 57b (icon), 67b (icon), 77b (icon), 87b (icon), 97b (icon), 107b (icon), 117b (icon); **Alamy Images:** maximimages.com 10/5, British Retail Photography 12, Tim Gainey 17cr, M. Timothy O'Keefe 17r, Mike Booth 19, Ben Molyneux People 20 (c), Blend Images 20 (e), Hasloo 20 (g), ACORN 1 22 (f), Tim Gainey 22 (e), Jan Wlodarczyk 22 (d), Jonathan Vandevoorde 23tr, M. Timothy O'Keefe 24-25 (background), Sergio Pitamitz 32tl, Mary Evans Picture Library 35 (d), Galyna Andrushko 37r, Andreas von Einsiedel 37l, Keith Morris 40b, Zuma Press 40c; OJO Images Ltd 43l, Galyna Andrushko 44 (f), Foodfolio 47l, Art Directors & TRIP 50 (i), Helen Sessions 50 (d), Kumar Sriskandan 53tl, Maksym Yemelyanov 60bl, Oleksiy Maksymenko Photography 61c, Idealink Photography 68 (b), Jamie Pham 68 (c), imageBROKER 69b, blickwinkel 70 (e), Alex Fairweather 70 (b), ONTHEBIKE.PL 67cl, 71l, Rolf Richardson 72b, Paul Rushton 74b, AGF Srl 77r, PhotoEdit 77cr, National Geographic Image Collection 78-79 (a), AGF Srl 84-85, Dorothy Alexander 87l, dbimages 87r, Wendy Connett 88-89t, F1online digitale Bildagentur GmbH 88b, Stuart Forster India 92b, Wild Places Photography / Chris Howes 94-95 (background photo), Chuck Eckert 97cr, Design Pics Inc 102b, Chuck Eckert 103b, Keith Morris 103t, Cultura Creative 107cr, BSIP SA 109b, Sally and Richard Greenhill 112 (b), Desintegrator 113 (d), David Lee 114 (a), Leon Werdinger 118 (e), Buzz Pictures 124r, Eureka 124tr, Wavebreakmedia Ltd UC6 153/p, Archimage 156/e, David Bagnall 156/c, Gary Roebuck 156/g, Alex Segre 156/d, Jim West 160/c, Randy Duchaine 162c, Randy Duchaine 166bl, **APN:** Kevin Farmer 28t; **BBC Photo Library:** 14tl, 47r, 54l; **BBC Worldwide Ltd:** 7r, 24 34l, 44b, 74l, 94l, 97r, 104r, 107r, 114bl, 114br; **Copyright Cascade News Limited:** 167r; **Corbis:** 10/4, Kate Kunz 20 (b), Lucidio Studio Inc 21tr, Catherine Karnow 33tr, Paule Seux / Hemis 37t, Ariel Skelley 42r, Great Stock 44 (a), SOPA RF / Maurizio Rellini 44-45 (background), Jack Clark / AgStock Images 47t, Sam Diephuis 57t, Jon Hrusa 57r, John Turner 57l; Stephane Cardinale 58cr, Blend 60tl, Fancy 60bc, Ocean 61tr, Louise Gubb 64b, 64-65, Blend Images / Jose Luis Pelaez Inc 99bl, Sayre Berman 107cl, David Raymer 108 (a), Image Source 109 (d), Jeremy Horner 118 (d), Brandon Todd 120l, Fancy 153/h, Juice 153/j, Creative / Flirt 159/e, f, Ryan Pyle 162tr, Ryan Pyle 166tr, **DK Images:** William Reavell 9 (a); **Fotolia.com:** Paul Brighton 9 (b), Sebastian Duda 9 (d), filipbjorkman 9 (New Zealand), 9 (Peru), Kiddaikiddee 9 (France), 9 (Thailand), Vector Icon 9 (Egypt), Ronald Hudson 10/3, Ilyarexi 11l, Les Cunliffe 13r, sborisov 23tc, etiennevoss 35 (a), Picsfive 39, 50 (c), 50 (g), Jiri Hera 50 (f), dizain 59(t), Daddy Cool 59(l), filipefrazao 62(t), Dudarev Mikhail 68(t), Dirima 69(t), Christopher Meder 69bc, micromonkey 69t, gaelj 70(t), chbaum 70 (a), FOTOALEM 70 (c), Vladimir Wrangel 70 (d); jovannig 72(t), pigprox 73(t), hstiver 75(t), Elnur 81(t), Artens 88(t), connel_design 89(t), Md .Ehtesham Khaled 90(t), EvrenKalinbacak 90c, Lisa F. Young 99(t), Den100bl, NinaMalyna 102t, Elena Petrova 104 (a), pichart99thai 104 (c), denio109 107l, tibor13 108(t), wayne_0216 109(t), Bits and Splits 110(t), Laurent Renault 111(t), baibaz 114(t), Timmary 114(t), Kaspars Grinvalds 115(t), Netzer Johannes 118(t), olly 123(t), fovito 124c (inset), 152/l, 153/a, 153/i, Bilan 3D 152/j, Claudio Divizia 152/c, corepics 153/q, Sakkmesterke 153/n, annawin 154/c, 155/f, David Hughes 155/c, Iriana Shiyan 155/h, Giovanniluca 157/t, M.studio 157/u, algre 160/o, andreamuscatello 160/n, Yuri Bizgaimer 160/j, Daniel Boiteau 160/p, Calado 160/m, Christopher Dodge 160/i, fisherman3d 160/b, il-fede 160/g, Markus Mainka 160/h, villy_yovcheva 160/f, elophotos 162l, Tilio & Paolo 167tl, **Getty Images:** Lester Lefkowitz 7cl, Damon Hyland 8tr, Andrew Hetherington 13b, 21tl, iStock / 360 / MasterLu 22-23c (background), Mitchell Funk 23tl, Subir Basak 27r, Future Light 27t, Photodisc 27cl, Rob Lewine 29b, arabianEye 30bl, Subir Basak 34c, Sunil Kumar 34-35 (background), AFP 40t, iStock 43r, Digital Vision 44 (b), iStock / 360 / luamduan 44 (e), Moment 44 (c), Travelpix Ltd 44 (d), iStock 48l, Photolibrary 48r (a), The Image Bank 49r (b), Rick Gershon 57cl, ONOKY 57cr, Dave J Hogan 58cl, isifa 58r, Lonely Planet Images / Michael Coyne 67r, LightRocket / Frank Bienewald 68 (a), iStock / sturti 72t, Robert Daly 77l, Photographer's Choice / Charriau Pierre 77t, Photodisc 79 (c), AFP / Tiziana Fabi 81 (d), Jeremy Sutton-Hibbert 84l, iStock / Peter Kim 87cl, Moment 87t, iStock / Peter Kim 90b, iStock / 360 / adventtr 97l, Photos.com / 360 / Jupiterimages 97cl, iStock / 360 / K-SquaredDesigns 98, Fuse 99br, Photodisc / Tim Robberts 99tl, Purestock 99r, Moment 100t, iStock /360 /jerbarber104-105 (background), The Image Bank 107t, Image Source 108 (c), The Image Bank 113 (e), Cliff Leight 117l, Stockbyte 117r, iStock 118 (c), Christopher Kimmel 118 (b), The Image Bank 118 (a), Thomas Northcut 122, Esch Collection 123t, Stephen Frink 124-125t (background), Mark Kostich 124cr, James R.D. Scott 124tl, Vetta 20 (d), 124br, ziggymaj 152; The Image Bank 159/a, **Pearson Education Ltd:** Tsz-shan Kwok 10/2, Gareth Boden 20 (f), 33b, Terry Leung. Pearson Education Asia Ltd 61tl, Jon Barlow 154/g, 154/j, Coleman Yuen 157/i; **Pearson Education Ltd.:**152/a;152/h, Pearson Education Ltd.159b/a-r; **Pearson Asset Library:** Millena 10 (background), Palo_ok. 48(t), Joey Chan. Pearson Education Asia Ltd.49(t), P72. 50(t), NADKI 51(t), wavebreakmedia 52(t), Photo.Lux 54(t), 55(t), Glayan 58(tl), holbox 58(tc), Andresr 63(tr), Ehrman Photographic 64(t), hlongwangchao 78(t), alessandro0770 84(t), PrimePhoto 85(t); **PhotoDisc:** 35 (c); **Photolibrary.com:** Mel Yates 156/h; 159tl, Corbis 159/h-i, Creatas 159/g, **Photoshot Holdings Limited:** 21bl; **Plainpicture Ltd:** Folio Images 67t; Christine Basler 97t, **Press Association Images:** Abaca USA 120r; **Reuters:** Ajay Verma (INDIA) 17t; **Rex Features:** Photofusion 7cr, Hotsauce / Brian J. Ritchie 58l, 24 / 7 MEDIA 59tl, Aflo 59tr, ZUMA 100r; Guy Bell 102-103t (background), Eye Candy 112 (a), Mike Forster 117cl, 24 / 7 MEDIA 152/f, Startraks Photo 153/c, 24 / 7 MEDIA 72c, **Robert Harding World Imagery:** Sakis Papadopoulos 54-55; imageBROKER 71r, **Science Photo Library Ltd:** Maximilian Stock Ltd 114-115 (background); **Shutterstock.com:** Khakimullin Aleksandr 8(t), Syda Productions 8(tl), AndresR 9(t), Tiggy Gallery 9(e), Travellight 9(c), PhotonCatcher 10(t), Wildly Wise 10/1, Chuckstock 11(t), Feng Yu 11br, Baranq 12(t), Vacclav 12(tl), Shutterdivision 12(tr), Motorolka 13(t), Sorbis 13c, Helga Esteb 14(t),14(br), Jstone 15(t), ajkkafe 17l, Germanskydiver 17cl, Maradon 333 18(t), StockLite 18t, wavebreakmedia 18c, Brocreative 18b, Monkey Business images 19(t), Milos 4U 20(t), Monkey Business Images 20 (a), Rawpixel.com 22(t), David Evison 22(c), MJTH 22tr, Vidux 22(a), windu 22(b), Nacho Such 24(t), Maridav 25(t), Gyorgy Barna 27cr, PSV 27l, frescomovie 28(t), wavebreakmedia 29(t), Syda Productions 30(t), Dragon Images 30cl, Tyler Olson 30t, LDprod 31(t), Master1305 32(t), melis 33(tl), CandyBox Images 33bc, Voraorn Ratanakorn 34(t), gualtiero boffi 35(t), danymages 35(b), smspsy 37(tr), Patrick Wang 37cl, Cardaf 38(t), Anyaivanova 38, Photographee.eu 39(t), Michael Dechev 40(t), Kekyalyaynen 41(t), Freedom_Studio 42(t), PEPPERSMINT 45(t), MNStudio 47cr, smereka 47cl, Jiri Miklo 49l, Chris Baynham 50 (j), terekhov igor 50 (h), monticello 50 (a), s-ts 50 (b), victoriaKh 50 (e), Sergio Martinez 51 (a), Preto Perola 51 (b), MNStudio 52, Iakov Filimonov 53tr, Vasilyev Alexandr 58(t)Alla Simacheva 58(tc), Yuri Chen 58(tr), Maros Bauer 59(tl), Iryna Tiumentseva 61(t), mimagephotography 63(tl), Akarat Phasura 68(cr), holbox 69tc, mhatzapa 60tr, Oksix 60br, Best Photo Studio 61br, Brocreative 61bl, beemanja 67cr, CandyBox Images 67l, Valeriy Lebedev 69r, My Good Images 71(t), DmitriMaruta 73b, estherpoon 74(t), leungchopan 74-75 (background), Olesya Feketa 79 (b), Niyazz 80(t), scyther5 82(t), Lacrifa 83(t), charnsitr 87(cr), llaszlo 90t, weltreisendertj 91(t), Juan A. Valino Garcia 92(t), michaelheim 93(tl), Shanti Hesse 93(tr), EviJanku 94(t), TaiChesco 98(t), Andy Dean Photography 98l (inset), zlikovec 100(t), Sergey Uryadnikov 100br, THONGPARN INTHIRACH 101(t), Photo travel VlaD 102(t), elwynn 103(t), Minerva Studio 104(t), Lester Balajadia 104(b), Balazs Kovacs Images 104(d), egd 104(e), Olaf Naami 104(f), prudkov 105(t), wavebreakmedia 108 (b), Thomas M Perkins 109 (e), NotarYES 110t, Photographee.eu 112(t), Lisa S 112(c), Monkey Business Images 113(t), Shutterstock 114(c), 114(d), 114(e), Redko Evgeniya 114(f), Liv Friis-Larsen 114(b), Vartanov Anatoly 117cr, Seleznev Oleg 117t, Steve Photography 119(t), Eniko Balogh 120(t), RG2 121(t), stefanolunardi 122(t), Martin Novak 123tc (foreground), Willyam Bradberry 124(t), Scott E Read 124bl, Isabelle Kuehn 125(t), Ovchynnikov Oleksii 128, 152/k, Aarrows 152/g, AntonBurakov 152/b, Design56 152/e, Manifeesto 152/d, Rob Wilson 152/i, LifetimeStock 153/d, Phovoir 153/e, Shutterstock 153/g, 153/o, Margarita Borodina 153/m, Crystal Kirk 153/b, Markus Gann 153/f, Dmitry Kalinovsky 153/k, Alexander Raths 153/l, Ana Bokan 154/e, Franck Boston 154/d, Goodluz 154/a, 154/f, Monkey Business Images 154/b, Denis Nata 154/i, Max Topchii 154/h, Beata Becla 155/e, Andriy Bondarev 155/g, colorvsbw 155/j, Ariadna De Raadt 155/b, Semmick Photo 155/k, Artazum and Iriana Shiyan 155/a, Diane Uhley 155/i, Chuck Wagner 155/d, Adisa 156/n, Dean Bertoncelj 156/m, Carole Castelli 156/b, Dotshock 156/i, Anton Gvozdikov 156/f, Dmitry Kalinovsky 156/k, Monkey Business Images 156/l, I. Pilon 156/a, YanLev 156/j, Byggarn.se 157/b, Ekaterina Lin 157/e, Yulia Davidovich 157/y, Dionisvera 157/d, eelnosiva 157/r, Fotogiunta 157/w, Gavran333 157/l, Gregory Gerber 157/s, Jiri Hera 157/q, Jessmine 157/k, joesayhello 157/z, mtsyri 157/n, Jovan Nikolic 157/j, Noraluca013 157/p, M. Unal Ozmen 157/v, Ravl 157/g, Valentina Razumova 157/c, Smit 157/a, Danny Smythe 157/f, 157/h, Abel Tumik 157/x, Yellowj 157/m, Zurbagan 157/o; Jeffrey J Coleman 159/n, Elwynn 159/j, Ondine C 159/b-d, Andrey_Popov 159/k-m, Natursports 160/a, Julian Rovagnati 160/e, alexdrim 160/k,Tateyama 160/l, leoks 164, **SuperStock:** Blue Jean Images 7t, Corbis 7l; BlueMoon Stock 20 (h), UpperCut Images 92t, **The Kobal Collection:** Universal / McBroom, Bruce 77cl, Atlas Entertainment 80 (a), Warner Bros. / D.C. Comics / James, David 80 (b), Miramax / Universal / Bailey, Alex 81 (c), Paramount Classics / Geller, Nicolas 81 (e), Danjaq / Eon Productions 82 (f), Dreamworks / 20th Century Fox 82 (d), Film 4, Ingenious Film Partners, Potboiler Productions 82 (e), New Line Cinema 82 (a), Warner Bros 82 (b), Working Title Films 82 (c) 20th Century Fox Animation / Blue Sky Studios 83 (g), Fido Film AB 83 (h).

Every effort has been made to trace the copyright holders and we apologize in advance for any unintentional omissions. We would be pleased to insert the appropriate acknowledgment in any subsequent edition of this publication.

CONTENTS

LISTENING/DVD	SPEAKING	WRITING
listen to people talk about how they like to travel	talk about vacations	
listen to a conversation with a traveler	plan and talk about a long journey	check and correct information about a vacation
understand directions	give directions	
Going Local: Hong Kong: watch an extract from a travel show about Hong Kong	describe part of a town/city you know	write a short travel article about a town/city
	talk about what people are doing	improve your use of pronouns; write comments on a picture
listen to people talk about actors	talk about what you wear	
listen to conversations about movies	ask for and give recommendations	
Robert Peston Goes Shopping: watch an extract from a TV show about shopping trends	talk about a survey on trends	write a summary of a survey
	talk about transportation in different cities	
listen to a man talk about traveling for free	talk about types of transportation	
listen to a woman talk about her problems getting to work	apologize for being late	write a story using linkers
Airport: watch an extract from a documentary about a day at Heathrow airport	deal with problems when flying	write a website entry about problems when flying
listen to a radio interview with lottery winners	talk about your future plans/wishes	
	make predictions about situations	improve your use of linkers and write a short story
	make and respond to suggestions for a day out	
Wild Weather: watch an extract from a documentary about the wettest place in Europe	describe unusual weather	write a message forum notice about your city
listen to a radio show about colds and flu	talk about what to do when you don't feel well	
	talk about ways of reducing stress	make your stories more interesting with adverbs
listen to situations where people offer to help	offer to help someone	
Horizon: Sugar Versus Fat: watch a clip from a documentary about fat and sugar	talk about diets	write some advice for a health forum
listen to people talking about their experiences	ask and answer questions about life experiences	write an email using linkers
	describe how you feel about different situations	
listen to phone conversations	make telephone calls and say telephone numbers	
Shark Therapy: watch a clip from a documentary about sharks	talk about an exciting or frightening experience	write a story about an exciting or frightening experience

COMMUNICATION BANK page 143 AUDIO SCRIPTS page 147

7 vacations

SPEAKING
7.1 Talk about how you like to travel
7.2 Plan and talk about a long journey
7.3 Give directions in the street
7.4 Describe part of a town/city you know

LISTENING
7.1 Listen to people talk about how they like to travel
7.3 Understand directions
7.4 Watch an extract from a travel show about Hong Kong

READING
7.2 Read an article about a bike tour across Asia

WRITING
7.2 Check and correct information about a vacation
7.4 Write a short travel article about a town/city

How was your last vacation?

INTERVIEWS

vacation or trip | holiday

7.1 TRAVEL PARTNERS

G comparatives
P word stress; sentence stress
V travel adjectives

A

B

C

D

VOCABULARY
TRAVEL ADJECTIVES

1 A Work in pairs. Do you enjoy traveling? Do you ever go abroad? What places/things can you see in the pictures? Make a list of adjectives to describe them.

Market: hot, busy …

B Match the adjectives in column A with their opposites in column B.

A	B
hot	noisy
fast	empty
crowded	boring
expensive	cheap
comfortable	cold
interesting	uncomfortable
quiet	slow

S7.1

C WORD STRESS Listen and underline the stressed syllable in each adjective. Then listen again and repeat.

crowded

D Work in pairs and take turns. Student A: Choose one of the pictures A–D. Describe it using four adjectives from Exercise 1B. Student B: Guess the picture.

SPEAKING

2 A Do the travel quiz below. Circle your answers.

B Work in pairs and compare your answers. Are you good travel partners? Why/Why not?

TRAVEL QUIZ

Going on vacation this year? Do the quiz and find your perfect travel partner!

1 I like traveling …
a) by plane **b)** by train **c)** by car

2 I like staying in …
a) a hotel **b)** a self-catering apartment **c)** a tent

3 I prefer …
a) relaxing on a beach **b)** doing something athletic
c) going sightseeing

4 I like going on vacation …
a) in spring **b)** in summer **c)** in winter

5 When I'm on vacation I like eating …
a) local dishes **b)** the food I usually eat **c)** fast food

6 In the evenings I like …
a) going for a walk **b)** going to a restaurant
c) going to a nightclub

7 My perfect vacation is …
a) a weekend **b)** a week **c)** a month

athletic — sporty

LISTENING

S7.2

3 A Listen to two people doing the quiz. Answer the questions.

1 How many of their answers are the same?

2 Are they good travel partners?

B Listen again. Write man (M) and woman (W) next to the answers in the quiz in Exercise 2A.

C Work in pairs and discuss. Is the man or the woman a good travel partner for you? Why/Why not?

GRAMMAR

COMPARATIVES

4 A Look at audio script S7.2 on page 154 and complete the sentences.

1 Planes are fast ______ ______ trains.

2 Summer's hot ______ ______ spring.

3 A hotel's ______ expensive ______ an apartment.

S7.3

B SENTENCE STRESS Underline the stressed words in the sentences above. Listen and check. Notice the pronunciation of *than* /ðən/. Then listen again and repeat.

C Complete the table.

	Adjective	Comparative	Rule
short adjectives	fast	fast *er*	Use adjective + -________
long adjectives	comfortable	________ comfortable	Use ______ + adjective
irregular adjectives	good/bad	better/worse	

▶ page 128 LANGUAGEBANK

5 A Write comparative sentences. Use the adjectives in parentheses.

1 shoes, sneakers (comfortable) for traveling
Sneakers are more comfortable than shoes for traveling.

2 autumn, spring (romantic)

3 traveling by car, traveling by bus (bad) on a hot day

4 cafés, restaurants (cheap) in my city

5 an e-book, a book (good) on vacation

6 museums, art galleries (interesting)

7 city, beach (nice) for a day out

8 a cheap hotel, a good hotel (easy to find)

B Work in pairs and compare your answers.

6 A Choose two places you know, e.g. cities, cafés, nightclubs. Which one do you like more? Write two sentences about each place using comparatives.

I like Krakow more than Warsaw because it's smaller and cheaper.

B Talk to other students and tell each other about your places. Which place would you like to visit?

A: I like Krakow more than Warsaw.
B: Why?
A: Because it's smaller and more beautiful.

SPEAKING

7 A Write notes about a good or bad vacation you went on. Think about the questions below and use the pictures to help.

- Where and when did you go?
- Who did you go with?
- Where did you stay? Was it good?
- What did you do? Did you enjoy it?
- Where did you eat? Did you like the food?
- Was it hot?
- Did you like it more than your town/city? Why/Why not?

B Work in pairs. Ask and answer the questions above. What's similar about your vacations?

7.2 THE LONGEST BIKE RIDE

G superlatives
P weak form: *the*
V places

VOCABULARY
PLACES

1 A Work in pairs. Look at pictures A–E. Which of the things in the box can you see?

a mountain a hill a river a lake a forest a village a market a famous building a desert

A

B

C

D

E

B Work in pairs. Look at the words in the box in Exercise 1A and write an example for each word. Use your country if possible.

A mountain: Monte Cervino (Italy)

The Silk Route Bike Tour: is it the greatest journey in the world? The company calls it "the longest, hardest, highest, hottest, coldest bicycle tour in the world". In eighteen weeks you travel over 7,000 miles through seven different countries and have the most exciting ride of your life.

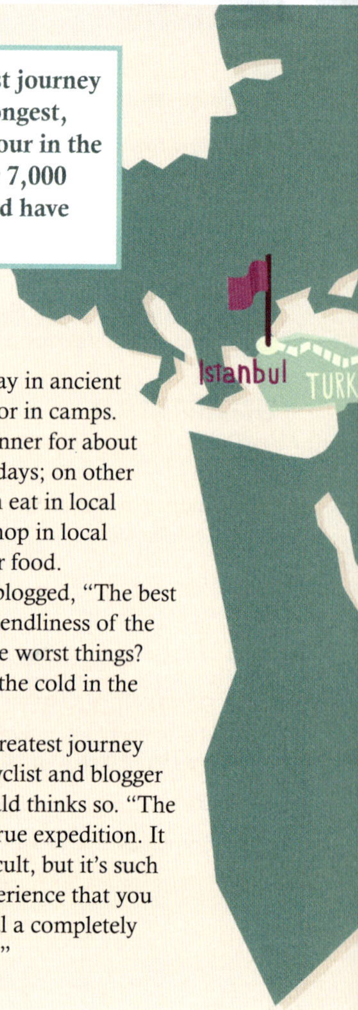

"A thousand years ago people went by camel and did about fifteen miles a day," says Nate Cavalieri, one of the Silk Route Tour staff. "But on a bike you do fifteen miles in an hour." And along the way you see some of the most beautiful places in the world.

From Shanghai, you go across Asia, through Iran and arrive in Istanbul, Turkey, at the end. You travel across the deserts of China and cycle the Pamir Highway to over 1,5091 feet, across the "Roof of the World" in the mountains of Tajikistan. On the way, there are villages, markets and ancient buildings.

At night, you stay in ancient roadside hotels or in camps. A chef cooks dinner for about half of the 133 days; on other days cyclists can eat in local restaurants or shop in local markets for their food.

One cyclist blogged, "The best thing was the friendliness of the people." And the worst things? "The snow and the cold in the Pamirs."

So is it the greatest journey in the world? Cyclist and blogger Miles MacDonald thinks so. "The Silk Route is a true expedition. It is long and difficult, but it's such an amazing experience that you arrive in Istanbul a completely changed person."

READING

2 A Read the introduction to the article about the Silk Route Tour and answer the questions.

1 What is the Silk Route Tour?
2 How many countries does it travel through?

B Work in pairs. What else would you like to know about the Silk Route Tour? Write three questions using the words in the box to help.

countries sleep people food bikes price

Which countries does it visit?

3 A Read the article. Did you find the answers to your questions?

B Read the article again. Are sentences 1–6 true (T) or false (F)?

1 The Silk Route Tour travels through seven countries in eighty weeks.
2 A bicycle is faster than a camel.
3 The tour starts in Istanbul and ends in Shanghai.
4 Cyclists stay in hotels and camps.
5 They take turns cooking dinner every evening.
6 One cyclist thought the snow and the hills were the best things.

C Would you like to go on the Silk Route Tour? Why/Why not?

The Silk Route Bike Tour

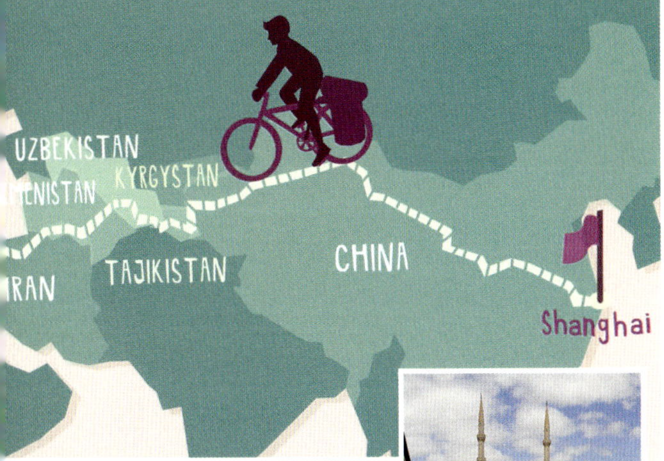

Istanbul, Turkey

Pamir Mountains, Tajikistan

GRAMMAR
SUPERLATIVES

4 A Complete the sentences with words from the article above.

1 Is it the _________ journey in the world?

2 You see some of the _________ _________ places in the world.

3 The ________ thing was the friendliness of the people.

B Underline other examples of superlatives in the introduction. Then complete the table below.

	Adjective	Superlative	Rule
short adjectives	great	*the greatest*	Use ________ + adjective + - ________
long adjectives	exciting	________	Use ________ + ________ + adjective
irregular adjectives	good bad	________ ________	

C WEAK FORM: *the* Listen to the pronunciation of *the* in the sentences in Exercise 4A. Then listen and repeat.

▶ page 128 LANGUAGEBANK

5 A Make questions about the Silk Route Tour.

1 What / cold / place you visited?
What was the coldest place you visited?

2 What / hot / place?

3 What / friendly / place?

4 What / far / distance you traveled in one day?

5 What / beautiful / building you saw?

6 What / amazing / experience of the journey?

B Match answers a)–f) with questions 1–6.

a) "It was Turpan, China."
"For me, the Gobi Desert: 122 degrees Fahrenheit!"

b) "The Blue Mosque. I took 100 pictures."
"The Bibi-Khanym Mosque."

c) "Meeting locals everywhere."
"Arriving in Istanbul."

d) "About 93 miles, in western China."
"I don't remember … at least 62 miles."

e) "The mountains in Kyrgyzstan."
"The desert at night. There was snow!"

f) "Iran; the people there were so kind."
"Everywhere, really."

C Listen to a conversation with a Silk Route Tour cyclist. Underline the answers he gives in a)–f).

SPEAKING

6 A Work with other students. Plan a long journey to another country. Choose five places to visit: The most exciting, the most beautiful, the highest, etc.

First we go to … , then we visit the oldest/most famous … in …

B Tell the class about your journey. Ask and answer questions about each journey.

A: Where do you sleep at night?
B: In small hotels.

C Discuss. Which journey is the most interesting?

WRITING
CHECKING AND CORRECTING

7 A Read the student's homework below. Find and correct ten mistakes with:

• spelling • simple past • singular/plural
• comparatives/superlatives

On Saturday, we went by bus across the ~~dessert~~ *desert*. We meet a lot of peoples. The peoples in the villages was friendlyer than in the city. At night, we staid in a camp. It was not very comftable, but it was more cheaper than the hotels. We buyed all our food in markets.

B Write four sentences about your last vacation.

In the U.K., use centigrade to measure temperature.

7.3 CAN YOU TELL ME THE WAY?

G giving directions
P sentence stress: correcting
V places

VOCABULARY
PLACES

1 A Work in pairs and look at the pictures and the information. Why is Liverpool famous? What can a tourist do there?

LIVERPOOL'S CULTURE BEAT

Think Liverpool and you probably think about the Beatles and world-class football. But did you know that Liverpool has the most museums and art galleries in the U.K. outside of London? And a fantastic variety of restaurants, shops, bars, cafés – and a beautiful waterfront.

DON'T MISS LIVERPOOL ON YOUR NEXT TRIP TO THE U.K.!

B Look at the map on page 73. In the box below check (✓) the places you can find on the map.

a road/street a park a block stop lights
a corner a pedestrian street a parking lot
an intersection

C Work in pairs. Cover this page and take turns. Student A: Point at one of the places above on the map. Student B: Say the place.

FUNCTION
GIVING DIRECTIONS

2 A Match directions 1–8 with diagrams A–H.

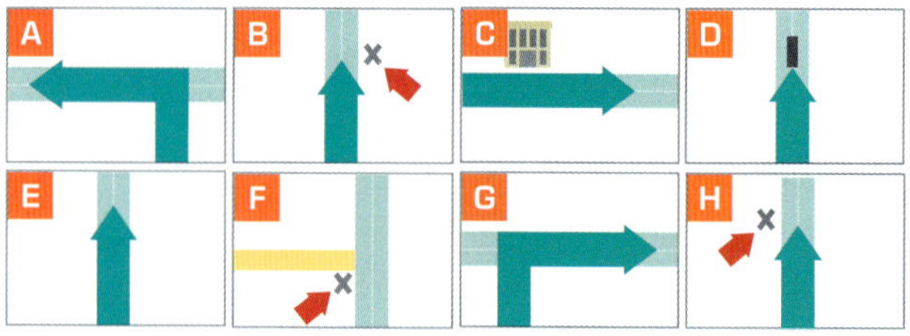

1 Turn right. *G*
2 Turn left.
3 Go straight.
4 Go past the movie theater.
5 Stop at the traffic lights.
6 It's on the corner.
7 It's on the right.
8 It's on the left.

7.6 **B** Listen and check. Then listen and repeat.

7.7 **3 A** Look at the map and find "Start here". Listen to a woman asking for directions.

1 The Air and Space Museum 2 The Capitol

7.8 **B** Listen again. How does the woman ask for directions? Complete the conversations.

W: Excuse me.
M: Yes.
W: [1]_____ you [2]_____ me [3]_____ _____ _____ _____ the Air and Space Museum?
M: Yeah. You go straight on this pedestrian street.
W: Excuse me. [4]_____ _____ Capitol [5]_____ here?
M: Uh. Let me think. Yes, the Capitol is at one end of The National Mall.

C Listen again and underline the stressed words in the woman's sentences. Then listen and repeat.

7.9 **D** Number the directions to the Capitol in order. Then listen again and check.

a) Then turn left. The name of the street is 3rd Street.
b) The next street is a diagonal.
c) Go straight here for three blocks. *1*
d) Then turn left on 1st Street. The Capitol is on the right.
e) Go straight for a short block.
f) Go past the East Building of the National Gallery of Art on the left.
g) Go left at the corner. I think it's Pennsylvania Avenue.

▶ page 128 LANGUAGEBANK

4 Work in pairs. Student A: Look at page 146. Student B: Look at page 144.

bars / block / stop lights
parking lot / an intersection

pubs / square / traffic lights
car park / a crossroad

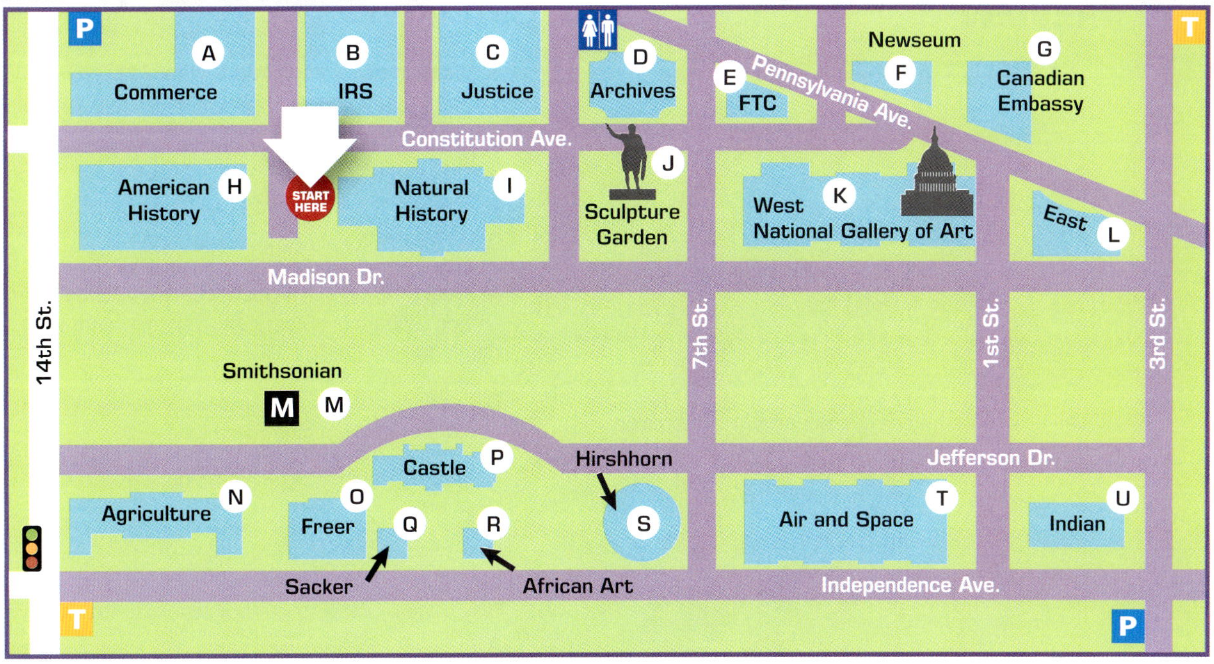

KEY: P parking lot T taxi public bathrooms pedestrian street

LEARN TO

CHECK AND CORRECT DIRECTIONS

5 A Read the extracts. How does the woman check the directions? Underline the phrases she uses.

M: You go straight on this pedestrian street. Can you see those sculptures?

W: Yes.

M: Well turn right at the corner after the Sculpture Garden.

W: Turn right ?

M: Yes. Then you go past some grass, that's the center of The National Mall, and you come to the intersection of 7th street and Jefferson Drive. On your right, you'll see a large cylindrical building. That's the Hirshhorm Museum. You can't miss it.

W: OK.

M: There are always a lot of walking tours there. Turn left on Jefferson Drive, and it will be on your right side with a large pointed silver sculpture on top.

W: Thanks. So, it's right at the corner after the Sculpture Garden and then past some grass, and then it's on the left, on Jeff … ?

M: Jefferson Drive.

W: Jefferson Drive. Right, thanks.

M: No problem.

S7.10

B STATEMENT STRESS: correcting Look at the conversation extracts below. Listen and underline the stressed words in B's answers.

1 **A:** Turn left.
B: No, turn right.

2 **A:** So it's on Jefferson Street.
B: No, it's on Jefferson Drive.

3 **A:** So it's in Pennsylvania Street.
B: No, it's in Pennsylvania Avenue.

4 **A:** So it's past the traffic lights.
B: No, past the park.

C Listen again and repeat B's answers.

> **American Speak out TIP**
> When you want to correct a mistake, you can use stress. Remember to say the correct word higher, LOUDER and l o n g e r.
> *Is it fifty-two High Street?*
> *No, it's **thirty**-two.*

D Work in pairs and take turns. Student A: Look at page 143. Student B: Look at page 144.

SPEAKING

6 Work in pairs. Student A: Choose a starting point on the map and give directions to one of the places. Student B: Listen and follow the directions. Check you understand everything.

public bathrooms — public toilets

7.4 HONG KONG

DVD PREVIEW

1 A Work in pairs. Look at the page and answer the questions.

1 Which of the things in the box can you see on the page?

a skyscraper	karaoke	a train
a shopping mall	a bamboo steamer	

2 What can you see/do in Hong Kong?

3 Which activities are popular in Hong Kong a) for tourists b) for locals c) for both?

B Read the text and underline the correct alternative.

1 Carmen is a *new/business/travel* journalist.

2 She has *two/three/four* questions.

3 She gets information from *local people/guidebooks and tourists*.

Going Local: Hong Kong

In *Going Local*, journalists go to cities around the world and try to see the city through the eyes of a local person. In this program, travel journalist Carmen Roberts is in Hong Kong. She has three questions or challenges* and she travels around the city to find the answers. There are two rules: no guidebooks and no tourists — so Carmen can only ask local people for help. Join Carmen as she leaves the skyscrapers, shopping malls and tourist places and tries to get to the heart of Hong Kong.

*a challenge = a difficult but exciting activity or task

DVD VIEW

2 A Work in pairs and read Carmen's three challenges. Which do you think is the easiest thing to find in Hong Kong?

1 Find the best milk tea in Hong Kong.

2 Find a shop where you can buy locally made goods.

3 Where do locals go to have fun?

B Watch the DVD. Which was the easiest thing to find? What problems did Carmen have with the challenges?

C Look at the program extracts below. Watch the DVD again and correct the mistakes.

1 The tea is really, really strong, but it's also very hot. *sweet*

2 It's quite refreshing actually when it's a warm day here in Hong Kong.

3 I found a place to go, but when do I get there?

4 Look at the rows and rows and rows of bamboo baskets, as far as the eye can see.

5 How long does it take you to finish one?

6 What do you do for friends?

7 There's a place like right next door actually called Blue MR or something.

8 Pick a song that you can definitely hear, a classic.

3 Work in pairs and answer the questions.

1 For you, what is the most interesting thing to do or to see in Hong Kong?

2 Can you think of two other challenges to give Carmen?

3 Do you think Hong Kong is a good place to visit? Why/Why not?

train / shopping mall — tram / shopping centre

American Speakout a city challenge

4 A Work in pairs and read the questions. Check (✓) one question you would like to answer for a town/city you know.

1 Where do locals go to have fun?
2 Where is there a walk that tourists don't know about?
3 Where can you find great street food?
4 Where can you see something tourists never see?
5 Where can you take the best picture in the town/city?

B Answer the questions below about your challenge. Write notes not full sentences.

- Where is it?
- What can you find or see there?
- When is the best time to go there?
- Why do you like it?

7.11

C Listen to a man talk about a place in his city. Which challenge in Exercise 4A does he speak about?

D Listen again. Which questions in Exercise 4B does he answer?

E Listen again and check (✓) the key phrases you hear.

KEYPHRASES

It's in the [north/south/west/east] of Massachusetts.
It's [near/next to …]
There are lots of …
It's got lots of …
You can [find/see/eat/…]
It's [the best place to/one of the best places to] …
Most tourists don't know about it.
Tourists [don't usually/often] go there.
It's really [interesting/delicious/fun/quiet/beautiful/…]

5 A Work in groups. Student A: Answer the question you chose in Exercise 4A. Use the key phrases to help. Other students: Ask some questions about the place.

B Which place or experience was the most interesting for you?

writeback a travel article

6 A Work in pairs and read the article. Which question in Exercise 4A does it answer? Which of the three places would you most like to visit?

My Boston

Boston is the capital and largest city in the U.S. state of Massachusetts. It was one of the first cities founded by British immigrants. Tourists love its famous sites: Fenway Park, the New England Aquarium, and the Boston Common. Summer is the best time of the year to visit this enchanting place.

But where do you go to escape the tourists? Here are three ideas:

1 **Forest Hills Cemetery** – This peaceful cemetery offers pleasant lake views with a twist. The cemetery features the typical, concrete headstones alongside a tiny village of concrete houses, which represent the homes of people who are buried there.

2 **Christian Science Mapparium** – Located within the Mary Baker Eddy Library, your senses and love of travel will delight while marveling inside the 30 ft. diameter sphere. The stained glass globe will fascinate you, as will the light show.

3 **Bodega** – A true discount shopper's delight! Hidden behind a fake Snapple machine, inside what looks like a typical corner store is a collection of designer label footwear, with special sales several times a year.

B Read the article again. For each place, which questions does the writer answer?

Where is it?
What can you see or do there?
When is a good time to visit?

C Write a website article about two or three places in your town/city which are away from the tourist centres. Use the ideas and phrases from Exercise 4 and the article above to help. Write 100—150 words.

7.5 LOOKBACK

V TRAVEL ADJECTIVES

1 A Complete the travel adjectives.

1 f__st
2 c__ld
3 sl__w
4 cr__wd__d
5 ch__ __p
6 __mpty
7 b__r__ng
8 c__mf__rt__bl__
9 n__ __sy
10 __nt__r__st__ng
11 h__t
12 q__ __ __t
13 __xp__ns__v__
14 __nc__mf__rt__bl__

B Work in pairs. Which adjectives in 1A describe …

… the building you are in now?
… your last weekend?
… your last vacation?
… your favorite café or restaurant?
… your favorite type of car?

G COMPARATIVES

2 A Look at the two ways of traveling from Moscow to Beijing. Write six sentences comparing them. Use adjectives from Exercise 1A.

China Airlines flight: $1,130, Business class, seven hours twenty minutes, two meals, two movies

Trans-Siberian Railway: $590 second class, seven days, four beds per compartment, restaurant on train

The train is cheaper than the plane.

B Work in pairs and discuss. Which way of traveling from Moscow to Beijing is better: The train or the plane? Why?

V PLACES

3 Work in pairs. Look at the words in the box below and find one place:

1 where you can swim.
2 with a lot of trees.
3 where people live.
4 where you can buy things.
5 that's hot in the day and cold at night.
6 that is high.
7 that tourists often visit.
8 that usually has a name.

a mountain	a village	a desert	a lake	a hill
a market	a river	a forest	a famous building	

G SUPERLATIVES

4 A Complete the quiz with superlatives of the adjectives in parentheses.

City quiz

1 *The friendliest* (friendly) city in the world is:
a) Rio de Janeiro **b)** Cairo **c)** Kuala Lumpur

2 The world's ____________ (big) city is:
a) Seoul **b)** Mexico City **c)** Tokyo

3 ____________ (good) place to live is:
a) Zurich **b)** Vancouver **c)** Melbourne

4 ____________ (safe) city in the world is:
a) Vienna **b)** Singapore **c)** Dublin

5 ____________ (beautiful) city is:
a) Cape Town **b)** Sydney **c)** Prague

6 ____________ (popular) tourist destination in the world is:
a) Spain **b)** the U.S. **c)** France

7 ____________ (fast)-growing cities in the world are in:
a) China **b)** Africa **c)** India

8 ____________ (busy) shopping street in the world is in:
a) London **b)** Hong Kong **c)** Shanghai

Key 1a 2c 3b 4a 5a 6c 7b 8a

B Work in pairs and do the quiz. Then check your answers in the key.

F GIVING DIRECTIONS

5 A Put the words in order. Start with the underlined words.

1 there / restaurant / here / Is / a / near?
2 corner / turn / Go / left / straight / at / the / and
3 bank / turn / Go / the / and / right / past
4 left / on / It's / the
5 the / at / Stop / intersections
6 way / you / to / tell / the / Can / me / supermarket? / the
7 the / The / station / on / right / police / is
8 it / miss / can't / You

B Work in pairs and take turns. Student A: Think of a place near where you are now. Give directions. Student B: Guess the place.

A: Go out of the main entrance and turn left …

UNIT 8

HAVING A GREAT TIME p78

WHAT A DIFFERENCE! p80

WHAT DO YOU RECOMMEND? p82

CHANGING TRENDS p84

SPEAKING
8.1 Talk about what people are doing
8.2 Describe people's appearance
8.3 Ask for and give recommendations
8.4 Talk about a survey on trends

LISTENING
8.2 Listen to people talk about actors
8.4 Watch an extract from a program about changing shopping trends

READING
8.1 Read research about language people use on social networking sites

WRITING
8.1 Improve your use of pronouns; Write comments on a picture
8.4 Write a summary of a survey

What was the last movie you saw?

INTERVIEWS

8.1 HAVING A GREAT TIME

G present continuous
P weak forms: prepositions and articles
V verbs + prepositions

1 **Researchers from Penn University looked at over fifteen million Facebook messages, and tried to answer some questions: Do men and women use different words in their messages? How is the language of a younger and older person different? They found some surprising things.**

2 The researchers studied messages from over 75,000 people. They looked at the language in the messages and also the most popular topics for messages.

3 They found some big differences between men and women. Women use more adjectives and phrases for feelings, for example: "excited", "wonderful", "love you" and <3, the emoticon for a heart. They often talk about family and friends.

4 Men talk about sports, computers, game consoles and videos (Xbox and YouTube are popular). They also often use swear words. It's interesting that men use "my wife" and "my girlfriend" more than women. Women often put "amazing" in front of "husband" or "boyfriend".

5 And what about age? It isn't surprising that thirteen- to eighteen-year-old kids talk about school a lot ("school", "homework", "English") but people from twenty-three to twenty-nine speak about work ("at work", "new job", "office"). Older people are more interested in family and friends and their favorite words are "son", "daughter", "my kids" and "friends".

6 So, let's see how the research works for us. Look at these messages from two friends. What can you say about the writers?

> "Wonderful birthday! Katya brought me breakfast in bed this morning and now Yuri is cooking dinner (tomato pasta). I'm lucky to have such a lovely family."

> "I'm having a great time here in Brazil with my girlfriend. We're relaxing by the swimming pool, AND Brazil won the soccer game last night! Life is perfect. Thinking about you all in the office! See you next week."

READING

1 **Work in pairs and discuss. Which alternative is true for you?**

1 I take photos with *my camera/my cell/my camera and cell*.
2 My favorite subjects are *people/places*.
3 I put my pictures *online/in a book*.
4 I write comments on the pictures in *English/my language*.

2 **A** **Read the introduction to the article (paragraph 1) and choose the best title.**

Your age, your personality
Women talk more than men
Your words, your identity

B **Work in pairs. Match the people in A to the language in B.**

A People	B Words people use
1 women	a) "daughter"
2 men	b) "at work"
3 teenagers	c) "homework"
4 people in their 20s	d) "<3" (= ♥)
5 people from 30 to 65	e) "YouTube"

C **Read paragraphs 2—5 and check your ideas.**

D **Read paragraph 6 and answer the writer's question. Check your answer on page 145.**

E **Work with other students. Do you agree with the research? Is it true for you or your friends?**

GRAMMAR

PRESENT CONTINUOUS

3 **A** **Complete the table. Use examples from the messages.**

Yuri	______	*cooking*	dinner.
I	______	______	a great time.
We	______	______	by the swimming pool.

B **Underline the correct alternative to complete the rule.**

RULES
Use the present continuous to talk about your life *every day/at this moment*.
Make the present continuous with subject + ______ + verb + -______.

C **Complete the questions with *'s* or *are*. Then listen and check.** (8.1)

1 What ______ you thinking about?
2 What ______ he doing?

D **Listen again and underline the stressed words. Then listen and repeat.**

▶ page 130 LANGUAGEBANK

soccer game — football match

4 A Match the pictures A–C with comments 1–3.

1 Great party! The kids *are dancing* in the yard and we ______ the beautiful spring day. I ______ with Laura's mom, and we ______ another piece of cake.

2 Don't come to Rome in summer! We ______ for the museum to open. My husband ______ pictures of the buildings and the crowd. I ______ very bored.

3 We ______ to Sarah and Jeff – they ______ a new CD at the studio. I <3 Sarah's voice! She ______ and Jeff ______ guitar, and they sound great!

B Complete the comments above with verbs from the box.

~~dance~~ chat eat enjoy feel listen make play sing take wait

C Work in pairs. Student A: Choose a person from one of the pictures. Student B: Ask yes/no questions in the present continuous and guess who it is.

A: It's a man.
B: OK. Is he standing in a line?
A: No, he isn't.

D Work in pairs and take turns. Write the names of three people you know. What are they doing now?

My friend Julia lives in Sydney. I think she's getting up now.

VOCABULARY

VERBS + PREPOSITIONS

5 A Complete the sentences. Check in the reading.

They also looked ______ the language.

Men often talk ______ sports.

B Underline the correct alternative.

1 think *about/on* a problem
2 listen *with/to* the radio
3 take a picture *of/about* a friend
4 wait *to/for* a train
5 read *on/about* a movie star
6 chat *with/from* a friend
7 talk *for/on* the phone
8 ask *about/to* pronunciation

S8.2

C WEAK FORMS: prepositions and articles Listen and check. Notice the weak sound of the prepositions and articles. Then listen and repeat.

D Work in pairs and take turns. Student A: Say a verb from Exercises 5A and 5B. Student B: Say the whole verb phrase. Then add other possible nouns.

A: think
B: think about a problem, think about a person

SPEAKING

6 Work in pairs. Student A: Look at page 144. Student B: Look at page 145.

WRITING

PRONOUNS

7 A Match this comment with one of the comments in Exercise 4A.

I saw them at a club last week. They were great – and her voice IS amazing!

B Read the comment above again. Write the people's names under the pronouns *them*, *they* and *her*.

C Read more comments below. Use pronouns to replace the underlined phrases.

Where did you take the picture of ~~Sarah and Jeff~~ *them*?

Sarah looks tired. That's not good for Sarah's voice!

I have Sarah and Jeff's last CD. Sarah and Jeff's last CD was great!

D Write a comment to go with a picture. Write two or three sentences and use pronouns.

E Swap your message with other students. Write a new comment about their pictures.

yard / line garden / queue

8.2 WHAT A DIFFERENCE!

G simple present and present continuous
P intonation in questions
V appereance

A Christian Bale, *American Hustle*

B Christian Bale, *Batman Begins*

LISTENING

1 A Look at the pictures. Do you know the actors or the movies? For which movies did they lose weight? For which movies did they put on weight?

B Listen to the conversation and number the pictures in the order the people talk about them.

C Work in pairs and discuss. What do the speakers say about these things?

D Listen again and check.

E Work in groups and discuss the questions.

1 Do you know other actors who changed their appearance for a movie?
2 What are good and bad things about losing and putting on weight for a job?
3 Would you like to do it?

> ***Blond/blonde*** **comes from French. Blonde refers to girls or women. Blond refers to everything else.**

VOCABULARY

APPEARANCE

2 A Work in pairs. Look at the pictures and answer the questions. Write the letter (A—E).

1 Who is:
a) very thin? *E*
b) slim?
c) a little overweight?
d) in his/her thirties?
e) wearing make-up?
f) wearing black?

2 Who has:
a) long blond hair?
b) short brown hair?
c) a beard?
d) a moustache?
e) glasses?

B Listen to a man describing two of the pictures. Which two is he talking about?

C Listen again and write the questions. Use the prompts to help.

1 Is / man / or / woman?
2 What / she / look like?

▶ page 140 PHOTOBANK

D INTONATION IN QUESTIONS Listen again. Which question goes down? Which question goes up then down?

E Work in pairs and take turns. Look at the jobs vocabulary on page 140. Student A: Choose one of the people and describe him or her. Student B: Ask questions and guess the person.

C Renée Zellweger, *Bridget Jone's Diary*

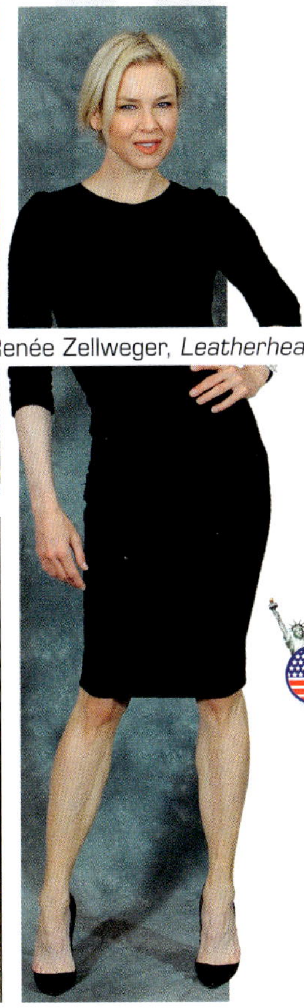

D Renée Zellweger, *Leatherheads*

E Christian Bale, *The Machinist*

GRAMMAR

SIMPLE PRESENT AND PRESENT CONTINUOUS

3 A Look at the sentences and underline the verbs. Which tenses are they?

1 She's wearing make-up.

2 He changes his appearance for every movie.

B Underline the correct alternative to complete the rules.

RULES

1 Use the *simple present/present continuous* for something we're doing now or around now.

2 Use the simple *present/present continuous* for something we do every day or usually.

C Complete the table with the verb *wear*.

What	______	you	usually ______	to work/ school?
What	______	you	______	now?

I	usually ______	a suit.
Now, I	______	jeans and a sweater.

4 A Look at the cartoons and discuss. What are the problems?

B Underline the correct alternatives below.

In an office, men usually [1]*wear/are wearing* dark suits, ties and shoes, but now Sam [2]*wears/'s wearing* jeans, a T-shirt and sneakers. He [3]*doesn't wear/isn't wearing* a tie. Another problem is that today he [4]*wears/'s wearing* sunglasses and most businessmen [5]*don't wear/aren't wearing* sunglasses at work.

C Complete the information about the second cartoon.

Walkers [1] ______ (not) usually [2] ______ a suit; they usually [3] ______ pants and walking jackets. Today, Jenny [4] ______ boots, but her boyfriend [5] ______ sandals – dangerous on a country walk. Another problem is that he [6] ______ (not) a backpack now, he [7] ______ a suitcase!

▶ page 130 LANGUAGEBANK

SPEAKING

5 Work in pairs. Sit back-to-back. Student A: Say six things you're wearing – four true and two false. Student B: Say which things are true and which are false.

A: I'm wearing a gray shirt.
B: True!

6 A Work in pairs and discuss. What clothes do you usually/never wear for:

- a walk in the country?
- dinner at a friend's house?
- a job interview?
- meeting friends in a bar or club?
- a party?
- an exercise class?

B Work with a new partner. Student A: Say the clothes you usually/never wear for the situations above. Student B: Guess the situation.

A: I usually wear jeans and a top. I never wear shorts.
B: A walk in the country?

pants trousers

8.3 WHAT DO YOU RECOMMEND?

F recommending
P word stress; linking
V types of movies

SPEAKING

1 A Complete the questionnaire below.

MOVIEWATCH

1 What was the last movie you saw?
2 What's your favorite movie?
3 Who is your favorite movie actor?
4 Who is your favorite movie actress?
5 Do you like watching movies:
 a) at home/at the movie theater?
 b) on TV/on your computer?
 c) on your own/with someone?
 d) only once/more than once?

B Work in pairs and compare your answers.

A

B

C

D

VOCABULARY

TYPES OF MOVIES

2 A Match the posters in pictures A–H with the types of movies in the box.

~~a romantic movie~~ *A*	a horror movie	a drama
a comedy	an animated movie	a musical
an action movie	a sci-fi movie	

B Complete the sentences with the types of movies.

1 People fall in love in *a romantic movie*.
2 There's a lot of singing and dancing in ____________.
3 I laugh a lot when I watch ____________.
4 ____________ is usually about space travel or aliens.
5 ____________ can be too scary for me.
6 There are usually a lot of guns and car chases in ____________.
7 I often cry when I watch ____________.
8 My four-year-old son's favorite movie is ____________.

C WORD STRESS Work in pairs. Find four types of movies in Exercise 2A with the stress pattern Oooo. What are the stress patterns of the other types of movies?

O o o o
horror movie

8.6 **D** Listen and check.

E Work in pairs and discuss. Do you like the same movies? Why/Why not? What kind of movies don't you like? Why?

A: What kind of movies do you like?
B: I like musicals.
A: Oh, really? Why?

E

F

movie 🇺🇸 🇬🇧 film

FUNCTION
RECOMMENDING

8.7

3 A Listen to two conversations. Which movies from the posters do the people talk about?

B Listen again. In which conversation does someone talk about these topics? Write 1 or 2.

1 action movies *1*
2 comedies
3 dramas
4 romantic movies
5 horror movies
6 sci-fi movies
7 the acting
8 the photography

4 A Put the words in the correct order.

1 you / can / movie / good / recommend / a?
2 like / of / kind / what / movies / you / do?
3 *Gravity* / about / how?
4 don't / sci-fi / I / like / really / movies.
5 know / you / *Happy-Go-Lucky* / do?
6 about / it / what's?
7 it / who's / in?
8 you'd / it / like / think / I.

8.8

B Listen and check. Then listen and repeat.

C Look at the sentences in Exercise 4A. Who is asking for a recommendation? Write A. Who is giving a recommendation? Write G.

▶ page 130 LANGUAGEBANK

5 Work in pairs and take turns. Look again at the movie posters A–H. Student A: Ask your partner to recommend a movie. Student B: Recommend a movie.

A: I have a long train journey this weekend. Can you recommend a good movie?
B: Let me think. What kind of movies do you like?

LEARN TO
LINK WORDS TO SPEAK FASTER

6 A Read the flowchart and complete 1–6 with two words in each space.

8.9

B Listen and check your answers.

Student A

Can [1]__________ a good action movie?

Student B

Let me think. [2]__________ *Unstoppable*? Do you [3]__________?

No, I don't think so. What's [4]__________?

Well it's about two guys on a train. And the train is traveling fast into a city, and it can't stop.

Sounds good. Who's [5]__________?

Denzel Washington and Chris Pine.

Oh, I like Denzel Washington.

I enjoyed it a lot. I think you'd [6]__________. It's very exciting.

American Speakout TIP
Word linking can help your speaking sound more natural. Remember you can link the consonant at the end of one word and the vowel at the beginning of the next word, e.g. *I enjoyed it a lot.*

C LINKING Look at sentences 1–6 in Exercise 6A and draw the links between words.

8.10

D Listen and repeat the sentences.

E Work in pairs and write ten key words to help you remember the conversation. Then close your books and practice the conversation.

7 A Work as a class and make a list of eight movies. Write the titles in English or in your language.

B Work in pairs. Student A: Choose one of the movies and answer Student B's questions. Student B: Ask questions from Exercise 6A. Guess the name of the movie.

SPEAKING

8 Work with a new partner. Recommend one of your favorite movies or a movie you saw recently.

A: One of my favorite movies is .../Last week, I saw ...
B: What's it about?

8.4 CHANGING TRENDS

DVD PREVIEW

1 **Underline the best alternative for you. Then work in pairs and discuss.**

1. I prefer shopping *in small shops/in big shopping malls/ online.*
2. The most important thing for me in shopping is *price/convenience/enjoyment.*
3. My shopping habits are *very/not very/a little* different from five to ten years ago.

2 **Read the program information and answer the questions.**

1. What different types of shopping does the program look at?
2. What kind of shop is the program mostly about?

Robert Peston Goes Shopping

It's hard to believe that once upon a time everyone did their shopping in small shops. The small shop was once an important part of our lifestyle, a place to meet and talk. But things are very different today compared to fifty years ago, and life for small shops has been difficult. In this program, we look at different trends in shopping over the years, from shopping malls to hypermarkets and of course online shopping. We find out how small shops are trying to stay alive.

DVD VIEW

3 **A** **Work in pairs. Write down one positive and one negative thing about (a) shopping in small shops and (b) shopping on the internet.**

B **Watch the program. Does it mention any of your ideas?**

C **Which words and phrases does the program use to talk about small shops and which about internet shopping? Write small shop (S) or internet (I) next to each one. Then watch the program again and check your answers.**

easy   cold
like car showrooms
not just a place to shop
the fashion   human

D **Underline the correct alternative. Then watch the program again and check.**

1. It was the place where people met to *talk/chat* and find out the latest *news/information*.
2. Internet shopping became the *fashion/trend*, the way everyone wanted to shop.
3. Big shops and small shops are now more like car showrooms. Shoppers go there to look at, *feel/touch* and try on products.
4. They have to *offer/give* something that people can't get anywhere *else/at all*.
5. A lot of people don't want to sit at home and shop. They want the *feeling/lifestylc* that small shops can give.

4 **Work in pairs and discuss. Does the program make you feel more positive or negative about shopping in small stores? Do you think it's important for shopping to have a "human side"?**

American Speakout a survey on trends

5 A Work in pairs and choose two topics from the list to discuss. What's different about these things now compared to 5–10 years ago? Which things are changing the most?

music | fashion | technology | TV programs/series | free-time activities | music/cultural festivals

S8.11 **B** Listen to a man answer questions about festivals. What does he say about changes in price, security, fashion and technology? Write notes.

C Read the key phrases below. Then listen again and check (✓) the ones you hear.

KEYPHRASES

Can I ask you a few questions?

What kind of [festivals] do you like?

[It's/They're] very popular at the moment.

How [are they/is it] different [now/from before/...]?

[Security/prices/...] is/are much [better/more expensive/cheaper/...] than before.

People like it because ...

It depends on [the festival].

Years ago, you couldn't always [get information on the internet].

6 A Work in pairs and choose one topic from Exercise 5A. Write 3–5 questions to ask other students about how this topic is different now from before.

B Talk to other students and ask your questions. Take notes on their answers.

C Tell the class three things that you found out in your survey.

writeback a summary of a survey

7 A Read this summary of the results of a class survey. Check (✓) the opinions which are the same as the man's. Put an ✗ by the ones that are different.

We asked everybody in our class about festival changes and trends. This is a summary of our results.

Everybody said they go to festivals. Most people go to rock music festivals, some go to folk music festivals, but only one of us goes to literature festivals.

We asked everyone about the changes in festivals. Here are the answers:

- Price – Everyone said festivals are more expensive than before.
- Security – Some people said there's no change. The rest of the group said there's much more security now than five years ago.
- Fashion – Some people didn't have an opinion about fashion at festivals. A few people said people wore more interesting and colorful clothes in the past.
- Technology – Two students said the biggest changes were in technology, but most of the group said there's no change. People found information and bought tickets on the internet five years ago, the same as now.

B Read the summary again. Underline phrases for talking about the whole group, and circle phrases for talking about part of the group.

C Write a summary of your survey results from Exercise 6B.

D Read other students' summaries. How is your opinion on a topic different from the whole group's?

Take notes | Make notes

8.5 ((LOOKBACK

G PRESENT CONTINUOUS

1 A Complete the sentences. Use the present continuous of the verbs in parentheses.

1 It ________. (rain)
2 A plane ________ over the building. (fly)
3 Someone ________ and reading. (sit)
4 Students ________. (talk)
5 Someone ________ on his/her computer. (work)
6 People ________ past the building. (drive)
7 Children ________. (play)
8 Someone ________ a phone call. (make)

B Work in pairs. Which of the things above are happening outside your classroom at the moment?

V VERBS + PREPOSITIONS

2 A Write the missing preposition.

1 look ________ a painting
2 talk ________ a TV program
3 take a picture ________ a friend
4 wait ________ a bus or train for a long time
5 think ________ food
6 read ________ a movie
7 chat ________ an old friend
8 listen ________ music
9 talk ________ the phone in English
10 ask ________ grammar

B Work in pairs and take turns. When did you last do these things?

A: When did you last look at a painting?
B: Last month. I went to the National Gallery and I looked at some paintings by Monet. What about you?
A: I never look at paintings!

V APPEARANCE

3 A Complete the appearance words.

1 br*o* *w* n, blo *n* *d*, bla__ __ or re__ hair
2 sh__ __ __ hair or lo__ __ hair
3 a mou__ __ __ __ __ __ __ or a bea__ __
4 gl__ __ __es
5 wearing ma__ __-up
6 brown or blue ey__ __
7 very th__ __ or a little ove__ __ __ __ __ __ __ __
8 in his or her twent__ __ __ or thirt__ __ __

B Work in pairs. Use the prompts below to make questions.

Is he or she ... ?

Does he or she have ... ?

C Work with other students and take turns. One student: Look at the pictures on pages 79 and 82. Choose one and close your book. Other students: Ask *yes/no* questions and guess which picture the student chose.

4 A What are the clothes? Add the vowels.

1 sn*e* *a* k *e* rs
2 j__ __ns
3 T-sh__rt
4 sh__ __s
5 p__nts
6 j__ck__t
7 s__cks
8 sk__rt
9 t__p

B Work in pairs. Student A: Say an item of clothing. Student B: Say the name of a person in the class who is wearing it.

G SIMPLE PRESENT AND PRESENT CONTINUOUS

5 A Write questions about students in your class. Use the simple present and present continuous.

1 wear glasses (*usually/today*)
Does Mia usually wear glasses? Is she wearing them today?
2 use an electronic dictionary (*usually/now*)
3 chew gum (*often/at the moment*)
4 speak English (*always in class/now*)
5 wear black (*often/today*)

B Work in pairs and take turns. Ask and answer the questions.

F RECOMMENDING

6 A Write the missing words to complete the conversation. One word is missing from each line.

A: I don't have anything to read. Can *you* recommend a good book?

B: How this book? *Doors of Stone*. It's sci-fi.

A: I don't really sci-fi.

B: What kind books do you like?

A: I travel books and romantic stories.

B: About *Life of Pi* by Yann Martel?

A: What it about?

B: It about a boy and a tiger on a boat.

A: That interesting.

B: I think you like it.

B Ask other students for book recommendations. Which of the books would you like to read?

9 transportation

SPEAKING
9.1 Talk about transportation in different cities
9.2 Talk about types of transportation
9.3 Apologize for being late
9.4 Deal with problems when flying

LISTENING
9.2 Listen to a man talk about traveling for free
9.3 Listen to a woman talk about her problems getting to work
9.4 Watch an extract from a documentary about a day at Heathrow airport

READING
9.1 Read an article about Mexico City's EcoBici

WRITING
9.3 Write a story using linkers
9.4 Write a website entry about your experience at an airport

How do you get to work?

INTERVIEWS

transportation	transport
Apologize	Apologise

9.1 CITYBIKES

G *can/can't, have to/don't have to*
P word stress; weak sound /ə/
V adjectives

SPEAKING

1 **Work in pairs and discuss.**

1 Is there a lot of traffic where you live?
2 When is the worst time to travel?
3 Do you prefer to travel around your town/city by car, by public transportation, by bike or on foot? Why?

VOCABULARY

ADJECTIVES

2 **A** **Circle three adjectives to complete the sentence:**

Cycling in the city is…

fast, unhealthy, safe, polluting, healthy, inconvenient, easy, dangerous, green, uncomfortable, convenient, difficult, comfortable, slow

B **Match each adjective with its opposite.**

fast – slow

9.1

C **Listen and check.**

D **WORD STRESS** **Listen again and underline the stressed syllable.**

American Speak out TIP

Look in your dictionary to find the pronunciation of new words. *Longman WordWise Dictionary* shows the word stress with a ˈ before the main stress, e.g. /ˈdɪfɪkəlt/ *difficult*. Find *dangerous* in your dictionary. How does it show stress?

E **Work in pairs. Student A: You like biking in the city. Student B: You like driving. Discuss which is better and why.**

A: Driving is faster.
B: It depends. In the mornings, biking is often faster because of the traffic jams!

biking cycling

MEXICO'S BIKE REVOLUTION

It's a quiet Sunday morning on the city's Avenida Reforma. On weekdays, there are tens of thousands of cars here, but today there's not one car. In 2007, Mexico City closed its main road to cars on Sundays. That was the first big step towards becoming a bike-friendly city, and three years later, in 2010, it started a new bike-sharing system, the "EcoBici".

Now, with over 4,000 bikes, 276 cycle stations, and 87,000 users, Mexico City has one of the most successful bike-share systems in the Americas. Cyclists can take a bike from one bike station and leave it at any other station in the city between the hours of 6:00a.m. and 12:30a.m. Users have to be over sixteen and pay 300 pesos by credit or debit card for a year's use. They don't have to pay anything for the first forty-five minutes of each journey.

Forty-nine-year-old businessman Mateo Reyes likes the scheme. "I only use my car when I'm too tired to cycle, but I go by bike when the traffic is bad. And the traffic is almost always bad." But he thinks it will take some time before cyclists and drivers learn to be happy sharing Mexico City's roads.

READING

3 **A** **Look at the photo of EcoBici, the bike share system in Mexico City. Write four questions with *how much*, *how many*, *who* and *where*.**

1 How much *does it cost*? 3 Who ___________?
2 How many ___________? 4 Where ___________?

B **Read the article. Did you find the answers to your four questions?**

C **Are the sentences true (T) or false (F)? Change the false sentences so that they are true.**

1 The Avenida Reforma has no cars on Sunday afternoons.
2 You always take and leave the bicycle in the same place.
3 You can't get an EcoBici bike at 2 a.m.
4 It costs nothing for one hour's biking.
5 Mateo Reyes always uses a bike.
6 Rafael thinks driving a taxi is more difficult now.

D **Work in pairs and discuss. Is this kind of bike system a good idea for your town/city? Why/Why not?**

Not everyone likes the EcoBicis. "There are more and more cyclists on the road, and that's not so good," says Rafael, a taxi driver. "We have to be extra-careful now. They ride in the middle of the traffic, they go too fast. It's dangerous for everyone."

GRAMMAR

CAN/CAN'T, HAVE TO/DON'T HAVE TO

4 A Underline the correct alternative. Then check your answers in the article.

1 You *can/can't* leave the bike at any bike station in the city.
2 A fifteen-year-old kid *can/can't* use the bikes.
3 Users *have to/don't have* to pay by debit or credit card.
4 Users *have to/don't have to* pay for the first forty-five minutes.

B Match sentences 1–4 above with meanings a)–d).

a) It's necessary. c) It's OK.
b) It's not necessary. d) It's not OK.

C Complete the table below.

Adults	*can*	use	the bikes.
Children	________	use	the bikes.
Users	*have* ________	give	their credit card details.
You	________ have to	________	for the first forty-five minutes.

9.2

D WEAK SOUND /ə/ Listen to sentences 1–4. Circle the correct pronunciation. When do we use the weak sound /ə/?

1 /kən/ /kæn/ 3 /hæftuː/ /hæftə/
2 /kənt/ /kænt/ 4 /dəʊnthæftuː/ /dəʊnthæftə/

E Listen again and check. Then listen and repeat.

5 A Complete the sentences with *can/can't, have to/don't have to*.

1 You __________ go by car, bus or taxi to get to the airport.
2 You __________ drive on the left in the U.K.
3 You __________ drive downtown, so come by bus. You __________ usually find a free seat on the bus.
4 You __________ be seventeen or over to drive in Spain.
5 You __________ use your cell phone when you drive. It's dangerous!
6 You __________ wear a seatbelt in your car – the driver and all the passengers.
7 You __________ wear a helmet on bikes, but it's safer if you wear one.
8 You __________ park here for free between eleven and three. Other times you __________ pay.

B Work in pairs. Which sentences are true for your town/city?

▶ page 132 LANGUAGEBANK

SPEAKING

6 A Work in groups. Student A: Look at page 146. Student B: Look at page 144. Student C: Look at page 143. Complete the table below with information about each city's tourist card.

	The Amsterdam card	The Madrid card	The Prague card
Price			
Transportation			
Entry to museums, etc.			
Other			

B Work in groups. Ask and answer questions to complete the information about the other cities. Which city has the best tourist card system?

I think Prague has the best system because it's the cheapest.

C Work in pairs. Talk about traveling in two or three towns/cities you know. Which one has the best transportation system?

A: How is the transportation system in your city?
B: Well, you can buy a travel card for the metro and buses, but sometimes it's faster to walk!
A: Why's that?

The term "downtown" is commonly used to denote a city center, and often it is where the historical, commercial, entertainment, shopping and political power are concentrated. In Canada, the term "city center" and "downtown" are used interchangeably. In Australia, the term "Central Business District" "CBD" is widely used to refer to the city center.

9.2)) FREE RIDE

G articles *a/an*; *the*, no article
P weak forms: *a, an, the*
V transportation collocations

VOCABULARY

TRANSPORTATION COLLOCATIONS

1 A Work in pairs. Cover the word webs below and look at the pictures. What types of transportation can you see?

B Write a list of eight more types of transportation. Then check in the Photo Bank.

▶ page 141 PHOTOBANK

2 A Look at the word webs below and cross out the type of transportation that does not go with the verb. Then add a correct type of transportation to each word web.

take: a train, a taxi, ~~a bike~~, *a bus*

get on/off: a car, a bike, a bus

get into/out of: a car, a taxi, a train

ride: a bike, a motorcycle, a car

go by: car, foot, train

B Work in pairs and take turns. Student A: Say a type of transportation. Student B: Say the verbs that can go with it.

A: bike
B: go by bike, get on a bike, ride a bike …

C Work in pairs and discuss.

1 How do you usually get to work/school?
2 What's your favorite type of transportation? Why?
3 Which types of transportation don't you like using? Why not?

D Choose one of the questions and ask other students. How many gave the same answer as you?

LISTENING

3 A Work in pairs and discuss.

1 How many different ways can you travel by road in your country?
2 Which is the most expensive, traveling by road, by rail or by water?
3 Is it possible to travel for free?

9.3

B Listen to the conversation and answer the questions.

1 Which types of transportation do the people talk about?
2 How did the man travel for free?

C Listen again. Write one good thing and one bad thing about each way of traveling for free.

D Work in pairs and discuss. Which of the two ways of traveling would you like to try? Why?

GRAMMAR

ARTICLES: *A/AN*, *THE*, NO ARTICLE

S9.4 **4 A Listen to an extract from the conversation and complete the text with *a/an*, *the*, - (no article).**

But they needed their car in [1]_____ Los Angeles. So they went by [2]_____ plane, and I drove their car to Los Angeles, to their hotel [3]_____ downtown. I had [4]_____ week to get there. I stopped in [5]_____ Grand Canyon on [6]_____ way. It was [7]_____ best journey ever – I love driving, and I love [8]_____ cars.

B Find examples for rules a)–g) from the text above.

RULES

a) Usually use *a/an* before countable singular nouns:
I have a car. *4*

b) Usually use no article before plural nouns:
I don't like buses. ____

c) Usually use no article before cities and countries:
Madrid is in Spain. ____

d) Use no article in some phrases:
by bus, on foot, at work, on vacation ____

e) Usually use *the* before nouns when there's only one:
the moon, the Eiffel Tower ____

f) Use *the* in some phrases:
in the morning, on the right, on the subway ____

g) Use *the* in superlatives:
the most beautiful, the worst ____

S9.5 **C WEAK FORMS: *a, an, the*** **We usually pronounce *a* /ə/, *an* /ən/ and *the* /ðə/ in phrases/sentences. Listen and write the four sentences you hear. Then listen again and repeat.**

1 ________________________________
2 ________________________________
3 ________________________________
4 ________________________________

5 A Work in pairs and complete the sentences. Use *a/an*, *the* or - (no article).

1 I like traveling by __-__ train, and I love going by _____ car.
2 Last year, I was on _____ vacation in _____ U.S.
3 There was _____ family in _____ New York.
4 I had _____ week, so I stopped in a few _____ places.
5 I have _____ friends there.
6 Is that _____ longest journey?
7 It's _____ city in _____ Kenya.
8 In _____ evenings, I loved watching _____ sun go down.

B Check your answers in audio script S9.3 on page 155.

In the U.S., the public transportation train system that go under a city are called *the subway*. In the U.K., it is called *the underground* or *the tube*. In many cities, the local subway system is known as *the Metro*.

6 A Look at questions 1–5. Choose one of the endings and write a short answer.

1 How do you get *to school/to work/home?*
By car.
2 What are three things *you like/you don't like/you liked when you were a child?*
3 What's a famous city in *India/China/Africa?*
4 When do you *check your emails/do your homework/relax?*
5 What's the name of *the President of the U.S.A./the student next to you/the teacher?*

B Work in pairs and take turns. Student A: read your answers to the questions above. Student B: close your book and guess the question.

A: By car.
B: How do you get to school?
A: No.
B: How do you get to work?
A: Yes!

American Speak out TIP
When you write a noun in your notebook, put it in a short phrase. This shows how to use the word with the articles *a/an*, *the* or no article. For example: *in the Grand Canyon, he's a doctor, I like cats.*

▶ page 132 LANGUAGEBANK

SPEAKING

7 A Read the information about transportation in different places. Circle the ones that are the same in your country. Check (✓) the ones you think are good ideas.

Believe it or not!

1 In Cuba, all government cars, vans and trucks have to pick up hitchhikers.
2 There is no speed limit on autobahns (highways) in Germany.
3 In Milan, Italy, you have to pay to drive downtown.
4 In Zermatt, Switzerland, you can't drive a gas car, only electric.
5 You can't sleep in your car in some cities in the U.S.
6 On some airlines, you can use your cell phone on the flight.
7 In Japan, there are women-only carriages on some trains.
8 In Bangladesh, passengers often travel on the outside of the trains.

B Work in groups and discuss your ideas.

A: This is interesting about Cuba. I think it's a good idea.
B: Yeah, some places don't have a cheap transportation system.
C: In my country you can't hitchhike. It's illegal.
B: Do you hitchhike?
A: Yes, but not very often. When I was eighteen, I …

trucks	lorries
highways / gas	motorways / petrol

9.3 SORRY I'M LATE

F apologizing
P intonation in apologies
V excuses

VOCABULARY
EXCUSES

1 A Work in pairs and discuss. Are you often late for work, school or meetings? Why/Why not?

B Work in pairs and match 1—5 with a)—e) below.

1 I lost	a) broke down.
2 I missed	b) the alarm clock.
3 My car	c) the train.
4 The traffic	d) my keys.
5 I didn't hear	e) was bad.

C Look at the collocations above and write five more excuses with the words in the box.

the bus   my ticket   was terrible   my phone   didn't start

FUNCTION
APOLOGIZING

2 A Look at these reasons for being late. Which one is the best reason? Which one is the worst?

Amazing excuses

We asked managers around the country what reasons their workers give for being late. Here are some of our favorites.

1 I'm very sorry I'm late. I thought today was Sunday, so I stayed in bed.
2 Sorry to be late. There was a long line at the coffee shop. I brought you one – here.
3 I'm terribly sorry I'm late. My train hit a cow.
4 I'm really sorry I'm late. My son took my car keys to school, so I took the bus to his school to get them.
5 I'm so sorry I missed the meeting. I feel awful about it. I drove to my old office by mistake.
6 I'm afraid I didn't hear my alarm clock because I had ear plugs in.

B Look at reasons 1—6 again. Underline seven expressions for saying sorry and how you feel.

9.6

C INTONATION IN APOLOGIES Listen and check. Does the voice sound high or low? Then listen and repeat.

D Look at the responses below. Is the manager happy (✓) or unhappy (✗) about the situation?

1 I don't believe you.
2 It's half past nine!
3 Don't worry about it.
4 That's OK. No problem.
5 Don't let it happen again.

▶ page 132 LANGUAGEBANK

3 A Work in pairs. Complete the conversation between a student and a teacher.

Student

Sorry / late. I'm afraid … (*say the reason*)

Teacher

That's …

And then … (*say what happened next*)

Really, don't …

I feel …

B Work in pairs and have another conversation. Apologize for being late and give a reason. Choose one of the pairs below.

a student – a teacher	a friend – a friend
a worker – a boss	a child – a parent
a husband – a wife	

C Listen to other students' conversations. Guess their roles.

LEARN TO

TELL A LONG STORY

4 A Look at the online diary extracts below. Why was the woman late each day?

Monday: ______________________

Tuesday: ______________________

Wednesday: ______________________

Monday
The train left fifteen minutes late. But that wasn't the problem – it simply didn't go very fast. We really knew there was a problem when a man on a bike went faster than us! I was an hour late for work. The boss wasn't happy … but she doesn't take the train.

Tuesday
OK, I didn't hear my alarm, so I woke up late and missed my train. I got the next one, but then the train stopped in the middle of nowhere … for twenty minutes! The guard said there was a signal problem, and then the air-conditioning stopped working! Imagine, no air-conditioning in the middle of summer! I was two and a half hours late for work and really hot and sweaty. My boss was very unhappy.

Wednesday
Service: 0 points. Originality: 10 points. We stopped again, for no reason, but then there was a reason – not the signals, not the engine, but a cow on the tracks! Poor thing, we didn't stop in time. This time, I was two hours late for work, and my boss didn't believe me …

9.7

B Listen to the woman talk to a colleague. Which two days does she talk about?

C Listen again. Which two things are different from the online diary above?

5 A Look at the linkers in the box and circle them in the listening extract below.

~~first of all~~ and but so finally because then after that

First of all, I got up late because I didn't hear my alarm, so I only woke up at eight thirty. I ran to the train station – usually I walk – but I missed the train by two minutes! Then I waited for the next train, the nine fifteen, and everything was fine until we just stopped – just *stopped* – in the middle of nowhere. The guard said that there was a signal problem. After that, the air-conditioning stopped working. It was like an oven – at least a thousand degrees! Finally, after forty minutes, we started moving … very, very slowly.

B Work in pairs and discuss.

1 Which linkers do you use for the beginning and end of the story?

2 Which two linkers mean next in the story?

SPEAKING

6 A EITHER: Imagine you are late for an important event, e.g. a wedding, a date with a boy/girlfriend, a job interview. OR: Think of a real situation when you were late. Take notes about five things that happened. Use these questions to help.

- When was it?
- Where were you?
- What happened?
- What did you do?
- What happened finally?

B Work in pairs and take turns. Student A: Tell your story. Student B: Show interest and ask follow-up questions.

A: This happened last year. I was on the way to Latvia, and my plane was late.

C Write your story using your notes from Exercise 6A. Remember to use linkers.

This happened last week. I was in …

9.4 AIRPORT

DVD PREVIEW

1 Work in pairs and discuss. What are the good and bad things about airports and flying?

2 A Put the actions below in the correct order.

a) check in *1*
b) the plane takes off
c) go through security
d) wait in the departure lounge
e) get on the plane
f) go to the departure gate
g) do some tax-free shopping
h) go through passport control

B 9.8 Listen and check. Then listen and repeat.

C Work in pairs and take turns. Student A: Say one of the actions in Exercise 2A. Student B: Say the next action.

A: You check in, and then you … ?
B: Go through security, and then you … ?

3 Read the program information and underline the correct alternative.

1 There's a *computer/weather* problem.
2 The program is about the activities of *airline workers/passengers*.

Airport

Airport is a TV series about day-to-day life at one of the busiest international airports in the world, London Heathrow. In tonight's program, there's a computer problem in air traffic control, and flights are delayed for hours or canceled. Hundreds of passengers have to wait in the crowded terminal, so the program looks at how people are feeling and how they spend their time waiting.

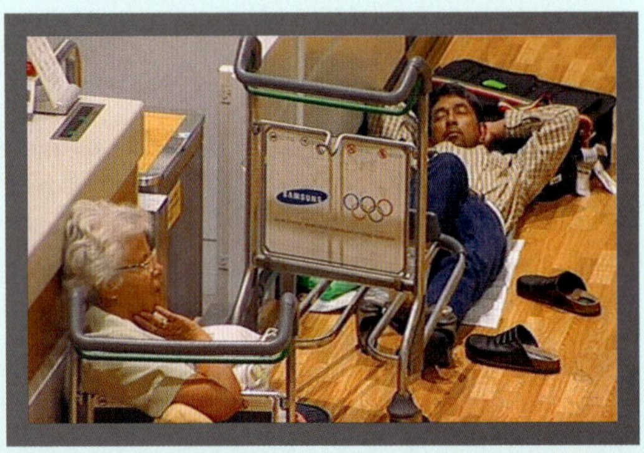

DVD VIEW

4 A Work in pairs and discuss. Which things 1–8 below do <u>you</u> do when you have to wait a long time at an airport? Which do you <u>never</u> do? What other things do you do?

1 stand in a line
2 make phone calls
3 watch a film
4 have a snack
5 go outside
6 argue with airline workers
7 play a board game
8 sleep on the floor

B Watch the DVD. Check (✓) the activities above you see.

C Watch again and match the person with the activity/activities.

Woman 1
Man 1
Woman 2
Man 2

is trying to get to Amsterdam.
wants to go to Berlin.
is there with her grandmother and parents.
can't find a place in a hotel.
thinks everything is very calm, very "Zen".

canceled (US) — cancelled (UK)

American Speakout deal with a problem

5 A Work in pairs. Read problems 1–6 below and discuss. What are two solutions for each problem?

At the airport:

1 Your luggage is too heavy, but you don't want to pay the $200 fee.
2 Your flight is delayed by twenty-four hours, and there's no place to sleep in the airport.
3 You arrive and go to get your luggage. Another passenger is walking out with your bag.

On the plane:

4 There's a screaming child in the seat behind you.
5 You ordered a vegetarian meal, but when your food arrives, it's chicken curry.
6 You can't sleep because a) you're cold and b) there's too much light.

S9.9

B Listen to the conversation. Which problem does the passenger have? What solution does the person give?

C Listen again and check (✓) the key phrases you hear.

KEYPHRASES

There's a small problem here.
But it's very important that [I arrive on time].
You don't understand.
I see/understand, but ...
Let me explain one more time.
It's your job to [bring me a meal].
Can I speak to the person in charge, please?

D Work in pairs. Choose a problem from 5A and role-play the situation. Use the key phrases to help.

writeback a website entry

6 A Read the website about problems when flying. Which thing do you dislike the most?

What do you hate about flying?

I hate it when ...

... kids run around and scream. Why don't their parents ______ them?

... I'm in the middle seat, and the people on my right and left have a conversation. Why don't they ______ together?

... people stand up before the plane stops at the gate. Why don't they ______ in their seats?

B Work in pairs and complete the questions in the text.

C Work in pairs and write three more things for the website list. Use these topics to help you with ideas.

noise
kids
food/drink
electronics
luggage
couples
music/movies
smells

38

D Add a question to each of your three ideas.

E Read the other students' lists and make a class list together.

9.5 ((LOOKBACK

V ADJECTIVES

1 A What are the adjectives? Add the vowels. Then match them with their opposites.

1 sl_w	comfortable
2 p_ll_t_ng	easy
3 d_ng_r_ _s	fast
4 d_ff_c_lt	green
5 _nh_ _lthy	healthy
6 c_nv_n_ _nt	inconvenient
7 _nc_mf_rt_bl_	safe

B Work in pairs. Which adjectives from Exercise 1A could you use to talk about 1–5?

1 A supermarket and a small local shop
2 Watching a movie at home or at a movie theater
3 A train and a car
4 Mineral water and tap water
5 Texting and phoning

C Work in pairs and discuss the topics above. Which of the two things do you like better?

A: I like going to small shops because they're more convenient.
B: Really? I think a supermarket is more convenient because …

G *CAN/CAN'T, HAVE TO/ DON'T HAVE TO*

2 A Complete the rules with the correct alternatives.

In a library …

1 you *can't/don't have to* talk on your cell phone.
2 you *can't/don't have to* pay for a book before you take it out.

On a plane …

3 you *can/have to* wear a seatbelt when the plane takes off.
4 you *can't/don't have to* smoke.

At home …

5 you *can/have to* relax.
6 you *can't/don't have to* pay to eat.

B Choose three of the places below and write two sentences for each place. Use *can/can't, have to/don't have to.*

a restaurant
____
____

a classroom
____
____

a beach
____
____

a movie theater
____
____

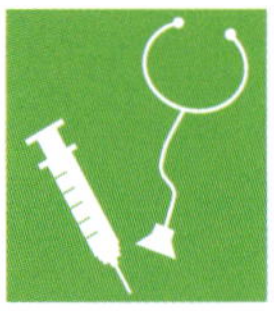
a hospital
____
____

a friend's house
____
____

C Work in pairs and take turns. Student A: Read out your sentences. Student B: Guess the place.

V TRANSPORTATION COLLOCATIONS

3 A Write three types of transportation that:

1 you can ride *a bike, …*
2 you can take
3 you can get on and off
4 you can get into and out of
5 you can go by

B Work in groups. One student: Write down a phrase from Exercise 3A that you did yesterday. Tell the other students where you traveled from and to. Other students: Ask questions and guess the type of transportation.

A: From my apartment to my office.
B: Did you get into a taxi?
C: Did you get off a train?

G ARTICLES: *A/AN, THE,* NO ARTICLE

4 A Complete the sentences with *a/an, the* or no article (-).

1 Most of us have to use _____ alarm clock to wake up in _____ morning.
2 Two of us didn't have _____ breakfast this morning.
3 Three of us live _____ downtown.
4 All of us think _____ bikes are better than _____ cars for traveling downtown.
5 One of us has _____ motorcycle.
6 Half of us took _____ taxi home last weekend.
7 None of us goes _____ home by train.

B Work in pairs. Write the questions and ask other students.

A: Do you have to use an alarm clock to wake up in the morning?
B: Yes, I do. I have to use two because I can't wake up!

C Was the information in Exercise 4A true or false?

F APOLOGIZING

5 A Write out the conversations.

Monday

A: I / sorry / I / late. I / not / hear / alarm clock.
B: That / OK. No problem.

Tuesday

A: I / terribly / sorry / late. I / miss / train / and / next train / be / late.
B: Not / worry / it.

Wednesday

A: I / so / sorry / late. I / lose / car keys / and then / car / not / start.
B: Not / let / happen / again!

B Work in pairs. Write two key words for each line of the conversations. Then close your book and practice the conversations.

10 plans

SPEAKING
10.1 Talk about your future plans/wishes
10.2 Make predictions about situations
10.3 Make and respond to suggestions for a day out
10.4 Describe unusual weather

LISTENING
10.1 Listen to a radio interview with lottery winners
10.4 Watch an extract from a documentary about the wettest place in Europe

READING
10.2 Read an article about nature's dangers

WRITING
10.2 Improve your use of linkers and write a short story
10.4 Write a message forum notice about your city

What are your plans for the future?

INTERVIEWS

10.1 LIFE'S A LOTTERY

G *be going to; would like to*
P weak forms: *going to, would*
V plans

LISTENING

1 A Work in pairs and discuss. Is there a lottery in your country? Do you think it's a good idea? Do you ever play the lottery?

B Look at the pictures below and read the newspaper extract. What's surprising about the story?

money grows on trees!

A gardener in Perth, Australia, thought he was the unluckiest person in town when he found a tree on top of his car after a storm. Then he saw a small colored piece of paper under some leaves. "I don't know why I picked it up."

But he's happy he did because today Martin and his wife are ten million dollars richer. The piece of paper was a winning Lotto ticket, and the couple found out yesterday they can keep the money. "We're thrilled, of course, but we're not going to change our life very much," said Martin's wife, Jean. "He enjoys his work as a gardener, and I love my job at the sandwich shop." "But we do have some plans," said Martin.

C Work in pairs and discuss. How do you think the couple plan to spend their money?

S10.1

D Listen to a radio interview and check your ideas. Check (✓) the couple's plans.

- stop working
- give money to someone
- have a party
- move home
- start a family
- go on vacation
- learn to fly
- buy a new computer
- buy a new car

E Discuss. What do you think of Martin and Jean's plans? Is winning the lottery always a good thing? Why/Why not?

GRAMMAR

BE GOING TO; WOULD LIKE TO

2 A Look at the sentences. Then underline the correct alternative to complete the rules below.

1 We're going to have a party.
2 I'd like to learn to fly.

RULES
1 Use *be going to* when you *have/don't have* a definite plan.
2 Use *would like to* when you want to do something or when you *have/don't have* a definite plan.

B Look at audio script S10.1 on page 149 and complete the table with the correct forms of *be going to* and *would like to*.

I' ______ We' ______ He' ______	going ______	stay look for buy	in my job. a house. a new car.

I' ______ We' ______	like ______	go to Greece. move.

What	______	you	going ______	do?
	______		like ______	

S10.2

C WEAK FORMS: *going to, would* Listen and check your answers.

D Circle the correct pronunciation of *going to* and *would*. Then listen again and repeat.

1 going to /tuː/ or /tə/?
2 would /wʊd/ or /wuːld/?

▶ page 134 LANGUAGEBANK

3 A Write the sentences in full. Use *be going to* for plans (P) or *would like to* when you want to do something (W).

1 I / move into a big apartment / downtown. (W)
I'd like to move into a big apartment downtown.
2 I / drive / sports car. (W)
3 I / take / a trip / in the Caribbean. (P)
4 I / not / give / any presents / my family and friends. (P)
5 I / move / to another country. (W)
6 I / buy / a boat. (P)
7 I / start / my own business. (W)
8 I / not keep / all the money for myself. (P)

B Imagine you won the lottery yesterday. What are your plans? Change the sentences so that they are true for you.

C Work in pairs and compare your answers. Find three things that are the same.

go on vacation — have a holiday

VOCABULARY

PLANS

4 A Complete the collocations with verbs from the box.

> have go for get move start do ~~go~~ learn stay take

1 *go* on vacation, a barbecue, a party
2 ______ married, some new jeans, a job
3 ______ some work, a course, something different
4 ______ shopping, clubbing, jogging
5 ______ in, with friends, in a hotel
6 ______ Spanish, to drive, to swim
7 ______ a walk, a meal, a drink
8 ______ a new job, a family, a new business
9 ______ to another country, home, into an apartment
10 ______ a break, time off, pictures

B Work in pairs. Student A: Say the verb. Student B: Say the phrases that go with the verb.

C Look at the collocations in Exercise 4A again. Add a new phrase to each verb.

American Speakout TIP
When you study, make lists of words that go together. Cover all the verbs and try to remember them. Then cover the other words and try to remember the full phrases.

SPEAKING

5 A Complete the table about what you are going to do/would like to do in the future.

	You	Student 1	Student 2	Student 3
this weekend	*shopping*			
next month				
next year				
in five years				

B Work in groups. Ask and answer questions about your plans/wishes for the future. Take notes in the table.

A: Rafael, what are you going to do this weekend?
B: Well, I'm going to watch the Real Madrid soccer game ...

C Tell the class about someone in your group. Can they guess who it is?

A: This weekend, he's going to watch a soccer game, and next month he's going to do a photography course. He'd like to go to the U.S. next year. In five years, he'd like to start a new business.
C: Is it Rafael?

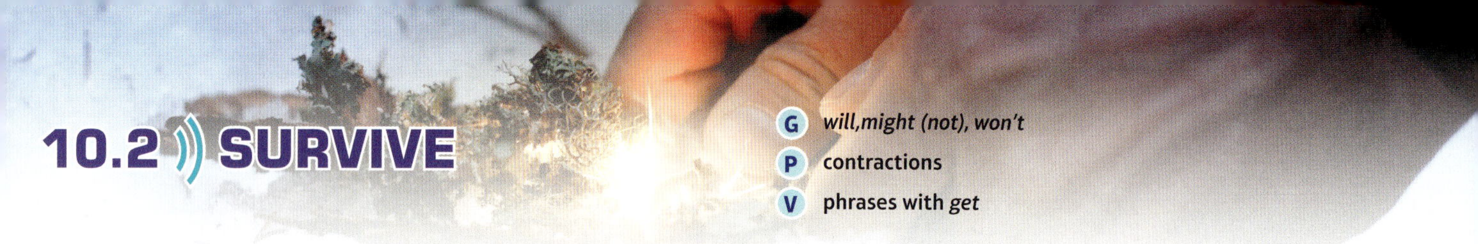

10.2 SURVIVE

G *will, might (not), won't*
P contractions
V phrases with *get*

VOCABULARY

PHRASES WITH *GET*

1 A Work in pairs and look at the pictures. How can each situation be dangerous or scary?

B Complete the phrases with get in the sentences with the words in the box.

~~hot~~ wet hungry thirsty lost sunburned warm stung tired cold

1 When I go to the gym in summer I get *hot*.
2 I didn't drink anything all day so I got ______.
3 I stayed up too late and I got really ______.
4 I forgot my umbrella yesterday and I got ______.
5 I'm really cold. Can I sit by the fire? I need to get ______.
6 I didn't eat breakfast so I'm getting ______.
7 I didn't have a map or my cell phone and I got ______.
8 I put my hand on a bee and I got ______.
9 There's no central heating and I often get ______.
10 I stayed out in the sun and I got ______.

C Write a situation using *so* and one of the *get* phrases.

I was out in Istanbul. I didn't have my satnav or a map so I got lost.

D Work in groups and take turns. Close your books. Student A: Read your sentence but stop after *so*. Other students: Guess the *get* phrase.

American Speak Out TIP
The verb *get* has different meanings in English. It can mean "become" (*get hungry*), "arrive" (*get home*), "obtain" or "buy" (*get a new car*). Which meaning does *get* have in these phrases: *get to work, get angry, get a new motorcycle, get sick, get some chocolate, get there?*

READING

2 A Work in pairs and discuss the questions in the text. Write two answers to each question.

Mother Nature's dark side

Nature is beautiful but it can also be dangerous. Are you ready for nature's little surprises? See how you do with these questions:

1 You are out walking, high up on a hill. There are a few trees and an open field below. Your car is five minutes away. Your cell phone is in your pocket. A storm starts, and there is lightning. What do you do?

2 You are at home, and there is an earthquake. What do you do? And what do you do if you're in a car?

3 You are in a garden, and you put your hand on a bee. You get stung on your arm. There are other bees nearby. What do you do?

4 You are out walking in a forest, and you get lost. It's getting dark, and there's no signal on your cell phone. What do you do?

B Work in pairs. Student A: Read the texts on page 145. Student B: Read the texts on page 143. Were your ideas correct?

C Close your books and tell your partner about your text. Who is the best survivor?

D Work in pairs and discuss. Which three things from the box are connected to each situation? Read your texts again and say what the connection is.

a car a credit card some wood a shelter a mirror a cell phone a pillow an ice pack an umbrella soap

sunburned — sunburnt

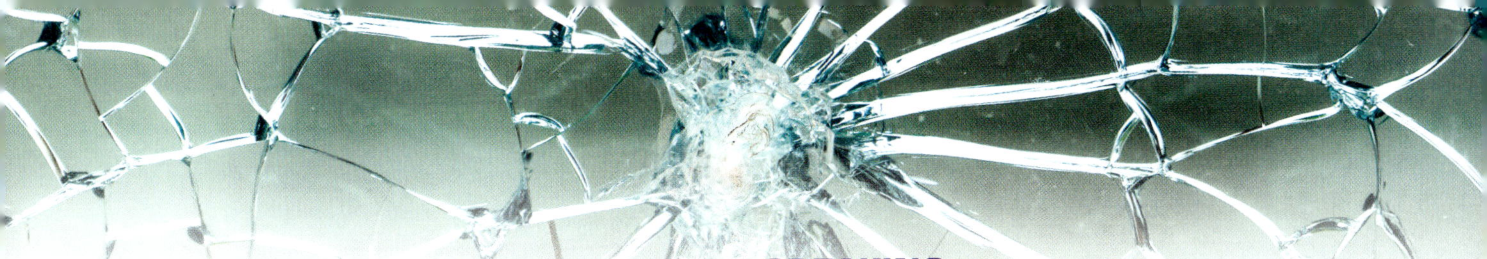

GRAMMAR

WILL, MIGHT (NOT), WON'T

3 A Read the sentences from the texts and put *might*, *will ('ll)* and *won't* in the correct place on the line. Then complete the rules.

1 You'll be safe inside your car.

2 A cell phone often won't work because there's no signal.

3 A building might fall on you.

a ______ b ______ c ______

I'm sure (negative) — Maybe — I'm sure

RULES

In speaking, *'ll* = ______, *won't* = ______.

After *will*, *might* and *won't* use ______.

5.10.3

B CONTRACTIONS Listen to sentences 1–3 above. Then listen again and repeat.

5.10.4

C Listen and number the pairs of sentences in the order you hear them. Then listen again and repeat.

1 a) You'll get too hot. ______

b) You get too hot. ______

2 a) We'll get cold. ______

b) We get cold. ______

3 a) They'll get tired. ______

b They get tired. ______

4 a) I'll get hungry. ______

b) I get hungry. ______

D Complete the sentences about the situations in the texts with *'ll*, *won't* or *might*. Then work in pairs and check your answers.

1 Don't stand under a tree because the lightning __*might*__ hit the tree, or you!

2 Don't touch anything metal in your car, and I'm sure the lightning ______ hurt you.

3 Get away from the bees because you ______ get stung again.

4 Don't pinch the bee-sting because the sting ______ get worse, that's for sure.

5 Don't leave your home in an earthquake. A building ______ fall on you outside.

6 Stay away from mirrors because they ______ break and cut you.

7 Build a fire so you ______ get cold.

8 Make a plan. You ______ feel better, that's sure.

▶ page 134 LANGUAGEBANK

SPEAKING

4 A Work in pairs. Look at the cartoon below and discuss. What are three problems the people might have?

B Work in pairs. Choose three objects from the box below that might help the people in the cartoon. Give reasons for your choice.

~~chocolate~~	a radio	a box of matches
a cell phone	sunscreen	a knife
a bottle of water	playing cards	

I think chocolate is useful because they might get hungry.

C Think of three other objects that might be useful.

D Work with another pair and compare your objects. Decide which five objects will help the people in the cartoon the most.

WRITING

TOO, ALSO, AS WELL

5 A Look at the sentences. What is the position of *too*, *also* and *as well* in these sentences?

1 Stay away from windows and mirrors, and bookshelves, **too**.

2 You can put an ice pack on your arm and **also** take some painkillers.

3 Build a simple shelter and make a fire so you can get warm and feel safer **as well**.

B Put *too*, *also* and *as well* into the story. Use each word/phrase once.

Lost in the jungle

We left the jeep and walked all morning, and we walked for five hours in the afternoon ^too^*. We had a short break for lunch. We stopped for a rest in the afternoon. In the evening, Sam taught us how to kill a snake and how to cook it. I didn't like the look of it, but I ate some, and Sam ate some.*

C Finish the story with your own ideas. Use *too*, *also* and *as well*. Write four or five sentences.

sunscreen or sunblock — sun cream

10.3 LET'S DO SOMETHING NEW

G making suggestions
P intonation: sounding positive
V art and culture

VOCABULARY
ART AND CULTURE

1 A Work in pairs and look at the items in the box. Which items can you see in the pictures?

a movie a painting a concert
a play *3* a drawing a photograph
a statue an exhibition
a dance performance

B Work in pairs and look at the items in the box above. Which …

1 always have music?
2 don't move?
3 always have movement?

C Look at the word webs below and cross out the word which does not go with the verb. Why? Complete the word webs with words from the box above.

watch: a movie, ~~a photograph~~, *a play*

look at: a dance performance, a drawing

go to: a concert, a statue

D Work in pairs. Cover the word webs and take turns answering the question "What can you …"
… watch?
… look at?
… go to?

E Work in pairs. Take turns asking and answering. Ask follow-up questions.

1 Do you like … ?
2 When did you last … ?

A: Do you like looking at photographs?
B: Yes, I do.
A: Really? What kind?
B: Oh, old black and white ones.
A: When did you last … ?

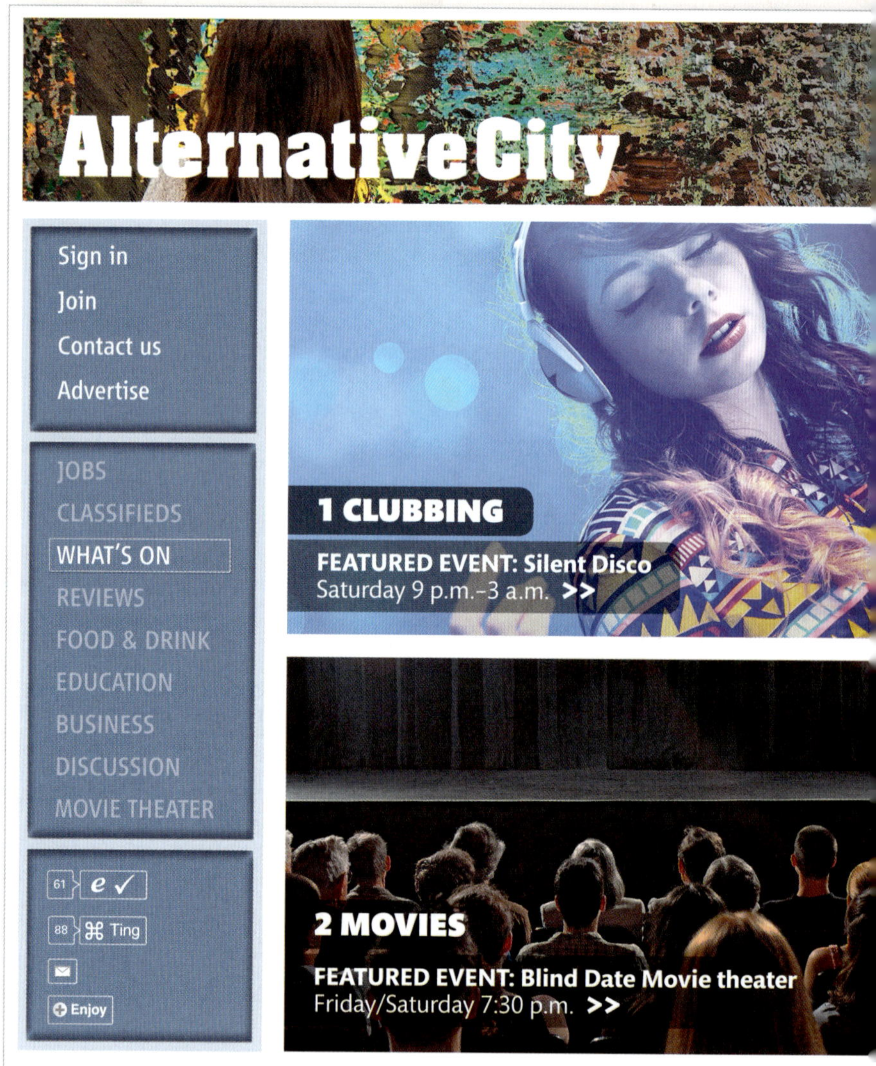

FUNCTION
MAKING SUGGESTIONS

2 A Work in pairs and look at the website. Why is it called AlternativeCity?

B Look at the website again and complete the table.

Event	What is it?	What do you think you do at the event?	Does it look interesting?
1			
2			
3			
4			

10.5

C Listen to the conversation. Which events do the people decide to go to?

D Work in pairs. Were your ideas in Exercise 2B correct? Check (✓) the correct ideas and change the incorrect ones. Then listen again and check.

E Work in pairs. Would you like to go to any of the events? Why/Why not?

For people who want to do something DIFFERENT

What do you want to do?

3 A Look at the sentences. Underline four phrases for making suggestions.

1 Let's do something different.
2 How about going to the theater?
3 Why don't we go to the museum?
4 Do you want to go to the theater in the evening?

B Complete the suggestions below. Then listen and check.

1 How ________ ________ to an exhibition?
2 Do ________ ________ to go to a concert?
3 Why ________ ________ ________ shopping?
4 ________ ________ to the park.

C INTONATION: sounding positive Listen to the sentences again. Does the speaker sound affirmative? Does his/her voice start high or low?

D Listen again and repeat.

E Work in pairs. Student A: Make a suggestion. Use ideas from Exercises 3A and B or your own ideas. Student B: Say *OK* if your partner sounds positive or *No, thanks* if he/she doesn't.

Do you want to …? / Great!

LEARN TO
RESPOND TO SUGGESTIONS

4 A Listen to the extracts from the conversation. Match 1–5 with the responses a)–g) below.

1 something new
2 silent disco
3 blind date movie theater
4 playback theater
5 museum meditation

a) Great!
b) I don't feel like doing that.
c) That's a good idea.
d) That sounds interesting.
e) It's not for me.
f) I'd like to go.
g) That doesn't sound very good.

B Look at phrases a)–g) above. Are they affirmative (+) or negative (-)?

C Work in pairs. Student A: Choose three weekend activities and make suggestions. Student B: Respond to the suggestions. When you respond negatively, give a reason.

A: Why don't we go for a walk in the park?
B: Mmm. I don't really feel like doing that. It's too cold!

▶ page 134 LANGUAGEBANK

SPEAKING

5 A Write a note of three activities you would like to do next week. Write a place and a time next to each activity.

B Work in pairs and take turns to suggest activities from Exercise 5A. Use the flowchart to help you. Add your partner's information to your notes.

Student A / **Student B**

- Student A: Call your friend.
- Student B: Answer the phone. Ask how he/she is.
- Student A: Answer. Then suggest an activity.
- Student B: You don't want to do this. Why not? Suggest another activity.
- Student A: Agree. Suggest a time to meet.
- Student B: Agree.
- Student A: Confirm plans and say goodbye.
- Student B: Finish the call.

C Call two more students and suggest activities. Add their information to your notes.

D Work in groups. Tell the other students about your plans. Who's got the most similar plans to yours?

I'm going to play tennis with Alfonso, and then I'm going to …

Shall we …? / Brilliant!

10.4 WILD WEATHER

DVD PREVIEW

1 A Match sentences 1–6 with pictures A–F.

1 It's stormy.
2 It's windy.
3 It's snowing.
4 It's sunny.
5 It's cloudy.
6 It's raining.

B Work in pairs and take turns. Student A: Point to a picture and ask about the weather. Student B: Reply.

A: What's the weather like?
B: It's raining.

2 A Look at the adjectives in the box and find three pairs of opposites.

~~hot~~	warm	wet	cool	cold	dry

B Complete the weather forecast with the words from the box.

In Houston today, it'll be [1] *hot* and sunny with temperatures up to seventy-seven degrees Fahrenheit. Tomorrow will be cloudy but [2]______, with a high of seventy. Things will change on Friday night: it'll be a [3]______ night with rain from midnight to early next morning. The temperature will fall to fifty, so it'll feel [4]______, but the rain will stop, so we'll have a [5]______ day all Saturday. Sunday will be windy and cloudy … and very [6]______, so make sure you wear your winter coat!

10.8

C Listen and check your answers.

Temperature is measured in Celsius for most of the world. These countries officially measure temperature in Fahrenheit: Bahamas, Belize, the Cayman Islands, Guam, Palau, Puerto Rico, the U.S. and the Virgin Islands.

DVD VIEW

3 A Read the program information. Which of these places do you think the presenter visits for each of the four programs: a) Florida, U.S., b) Greenland, c) Bergen, Norway, d) the jungle of Belize?

Wild Weather

In *Wild Weather* the intrepid adventurer, Donal MacIntyre, looks for the wildest weather in the world. He travels to different places and finds answers to the questions: Where does the weather come from? How does it work? There are four programs: Hot, Wet, Wind and Cold. Follow his journey as he finds and experiences dramatic moments of amazing weather.

B Watch the DVD and answer the questions.

1 Which program is it: *Hot*, *Wet*, *Wind* or *Cold*?
2 Would you like to live in Bergen?

C Watch the DVD again. Underline the correct alternative.

1 In Bergen it rains *one/two/three* out of three days.
2 There are *two/three/four* types of umbrellas.
3 They sell Bergen rain to tourists in *bottles/cups/cans*.
4 In one year, *105/125/225* tons of rain fall on a family house.
5 The longest period of rain in Bergen was in *1990/1992/1995*.
6 It rained for *73/83/93* days.

D Work in pairs and discuss the questions.

1 Do you like the weather in your town or city?
2 What weather do you like and dislike the most?
3 What's your favorite season? Why?

tons — tonnes

American Speakout a weather report

4 A Work alone. Think of a place and time when you experienced an interesting or unusual type of weather. Use the questions below to make notes about it.

1 When was it? What season/time of year?
2 Where were you?
3 Why were you there?
4 What was the weather like? Did it change?
5 How did you feel? How did other people feel?

5.10.9

B Listen to a woman talk about her time in Italy and her experience of the sirocco wind. Write her answers to the questions in Exercise 4A.

C Look at the key phrases below. Listen again and check (✓) the ones you hear.

KEYPHRASES

There's a small problem here.
But it's very important that [I arrive on time].
You don't understand.
I see/understand, but …
Let me explain one more time.
It's your job to [bring me a meal].
Can I speak to the person in charge, please?

5 A Work in pairs. Use your notes from Exercise 4A and the key phrases to describe your experiences. Check that your partner answers all the questions in Exercise 4A.

B Work with other students and take turns. Student A: Tell the other students about your experience. Other students: Listen and ask follow-up questions. Who had the most unusual experience?

writeback a message forum

6 A Read the message and part of a reply from a travel website. When are the best months to travel? Why?

Message forum 02-Feb-16 12:26 p.m.

Posted by: Maria, Spain:
My friend and I are going to visit Scotland next year for two weeks. We want to rent a car and drive around. When is the best time to go? What about clothes? Can you recommend any good places to visit? We like cities but also we'd like to see the countryside.

Message forum 03-Feb-16

Posted by: Doug, Scotland:
The best time to visit is May or September because the weather is usually OK – but in Scotland, the weather changes all the time. Be prepared for everything from hot sunshine to really bad rain. Also, the traffic is quieter in May and September, and it's easier to get hotels and B&Bs. Bring a warm sweater and a raincoat and a hat as well because there's an old saying: "If you can't see the mountains, it's raining. If you can see them, it's going to rain in five minutes." And places to visit? Well, you have to visit Edinburgh and …

B Write a reply to the same question about your city. Use some of these phrases to help you. Use 80–120 words.

Be prepared for …

The best time to visit is … because …

Bring … because …

Also …

You have to visit …

rent / around — hire / round

G BE GOING TO; WOULD LIKE TO

1 A Look at the list. Write sentences using *be going to* and *would like to*.

1 *I'd like to have dinner with Gemma, but I can't – she's busy.*
2 *I'm going to Oklahoma. I have my bus ticket.*

Weekend wish list
1 dinner with Gemma ✗ she's busy!
2 go to Oklahoma ✓ (got bus ticket)
3 go to the U2 concert ✗ not got tickets!
4 meet Andy for drinks ✓ (he said OK)
5 Watch Gone with the Wind on DVD ✓ (borrowed it from Cindy)
6 sleep all day ✗ not have time!

B Make your own "Weekend wish list". Then look at the list and check (✓) the things that are possible. Write reasons for the things that aren't possible.

C Work in pairs. Tell your partner about your plans for the weekend.

V PLANS

2 A Complete the questions with the correct verbs.

1 On your next vacation, do you want to:
- go to the beach or d__ something different?
- st__ __ in a hotel or with friends?

2 You have a free Saturday. Do you want to:
- g__ shopping or g__ __ __ __ a walk?
- in the evening, st__ __ in and do nothing, or h__ __ __ a party and then g__ clubbing?

3 Time for some big changes. Do you want to:
- g__ __ married or go traveling?
- m__ __ __ to an English-speaking country or stay in your country?
- st__ __ __ a business or t__ __ __ a long break from work?

B Work in pairs and take turns. Ask and answer the questions.

V PHRASES WITH *GET*

3 A Put the letters in order to find the words that go with *get*. The first letter of each word is underlined.

1 dclo	6 irtde
2 udbrunens	7 otls
3 gutns	8 rmwa
4 hrityts	9 tew
5 hto	10 ughrny

B A man was lost at sea for five days. Read the information and make sentences with *get*.

1 He ate all the food on the first day.
He got hungry.
2 He didn't sleep very much.
3 He sat in the bottom of the raft.
4 He didn't have a jacket or a hat.
5 He drank seawater.
6 He went swimming.

C Work in pairs and discuss. What were his three worst mistakes and problems?

I think number one was his worst mistake. I think he got very hungry.

G *WILL, MIGHT, WON'T*

4 A You and ten friends are going to spend the weekend in a hotel on a high mountain. Read the information.

- It's a beautiful, quiet place.
- It always rains at this time of year.
- Walking in the mountains is beautiful, but very dangerous.
- There are ten beds.
- The hotel has a very good kitchen. Their restaurant can serve meals for twenty-five people maximum.
- Not all the students like "mountain life"!

B Complete the sentences with *might, might not, 'll* or *won't*.

1 It ________ rain.
2 We ________ get bored.
3 It ________ be very peaceful.
4 Someone ________ get hurt.
5 The food ________ be very good.
6 There ________ be enough food.
7 Some people ________ like it, but I'm sure I ________ like it.
8 There ________ be enough beds for all of us.

C Work in pairs and compare your answers.

D Discuss. Would you like to go on this kind of weekend break? Why/Why not?

F MAKING SUGGESTIONS

5 A Correct the sentences.

1 Why we don't have a party in the school garden?
2 Let's to have 90s music.
3 How about start at seven o'clock?
4 That sound good.
5 Do you want make some pizza?
6 I don't feel like do that.
7 That's good idea.
8 I like to bring some drinks.

B Work in groups. Make suggestions for a class party. Think about the place, food, music, etc.

C Tell the other groups about your party. Which one would you like to go to?

We're going to have a barbecue in the park. We're going to bring some chicken and ...

11 health

SPEAKING
11.1 Talk about what to do when you don't feel well
11.2 Talk about ways of reducing stress
11.3 Offer to help someone
11.4 Talk about diets

LISTENING
11.1 Listen to a radio show about colds and flu
11.3 Listen to situations where people offer to help
11.4 Watch a clip from a documentary about fat and sugar

READING
11.2 Read an article about multi-tasking

WRITING
11.2 Make your stories more interesting with adverbs
11.4 Write some advice for a health forum

Do you have a healthy lifestyle?

INTERVIEWS

11.1 I DON'T FEEL WELL

G *should/shouldn't*
P weak form: *should*
V the body; health

VOCABULARY

THE BODY; HEALTH

1 A Look at the pictures A—E. How many parts of the body can you see and name? List any other words you know.

▶ page 140 PHOTOBANK

B Work in pairs and take turns. Student A: Say a part of the body. Student B: Point to it the pictures A—E.

2 A Which health problems can you see in the pictures A—E?

1 I have a headache.
2 I have stomachache.
3 My leg hurts.
4 I have a cold.
5 I have a temperature.
6 I have a cough.
7 I have a sore throat.
8 I have a runny nose.

B SENTENCE STRESS Listen and mark the stressed syllables (1 or 2) in each sentence. Then listen again and repeat.

American Speakout TIP

Many words in English have a very different pronunciation from their spelling. You can underline problem letters and write the sound underneath,
e.g. cou<u>gh</u> /f/ head<u>ache</u> /k/
In your notebook, do the same for *thumb* and *stomachache*.

C Work in pairs and complete the sentences using the words in the box. You can use each word only once.

arm back tired ear finger better

1 I have a/an _____ache/_____ache.
2 My _____/_____ hurts.
3 I feel _____/_____.

D Work in pairs and take turns. Student A: Choose a problem from Exercise 2A or 2C and mime it. Student B: Guess what's wrong.

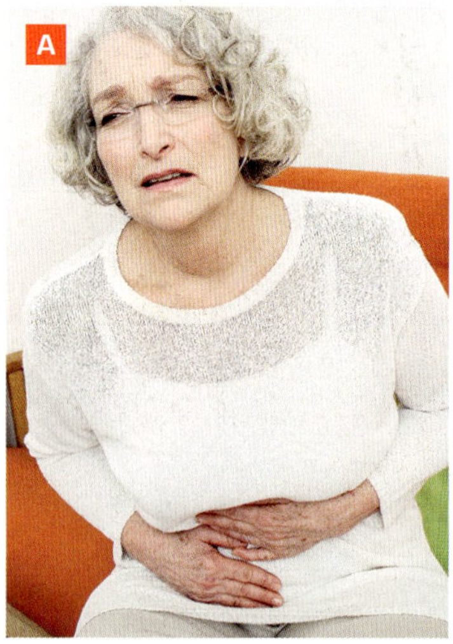

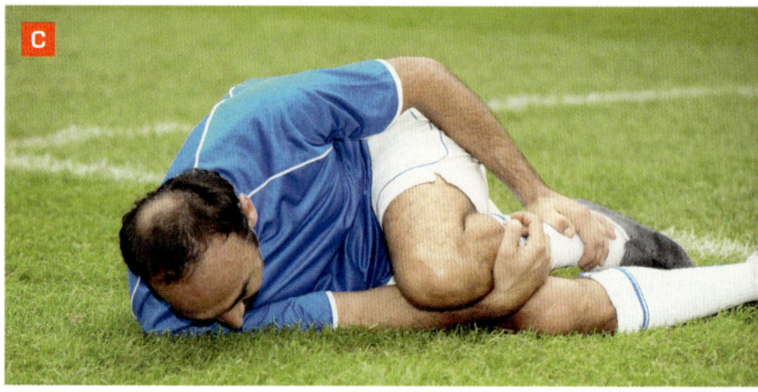

LISTENING

3 A Work in pairs and discuss.

1 What do you do when you have a cold? Do you go to work or school? Do you stay at home and rest, or do you go to the doctor and take medicine?
2 What's the difference between a cold and flu?

B Look at the health problems in Exercises 2A and 2C and write them in the correct place in the table.

Flu	A cold	Both
a headache		

C Listen to a radio show and check your answers.

D Work in pairs. What did the doctor say? Underline the correct alternative. Then listen again and check.

1 Flu starts *suddenly/slowly*. You *can/can't* work.
2 A cold starts *suddenly/slowly*. You *can/can't* work.
3 After a cold you feel better after *two or three days/a week*.
4 After the flu you often feel *fine/tired* after three weeks.

E Work in pairs and discuss. How often do you get a cold or flu? What information in the radio show was new for you?

GRAMMAR

SHOULD/SHOULDN'T

4 A Look at the sentences and underline the correct alternative to complete the rules.

1 You should drink lots of water.

2 You shouldn't take antibiotics.

RULES

1 Use should for something that is *necessary/a good idea*.

2 Use *shouldn't* for something that is *not necessary/a bad idea*.

B Complete the table.

You	should	___________	to bed.
	___________	go back to work	too soon.

5.13

C Listen and check.

D WEAK FORM: *should* Work in pairs and answer the questions. Then listen again and repeat.

1 Is the pronunciation of *should* /ʃʊd/ or /ʃu:ld/?

2 Is *should* usually stressed or not stressed?

▶ page 136 LANGUAGEBANK

5 A Look at problems 1–4 and advice a)–h). For each problem, write two pieces of advice, one with *should* and one with *shouldn't*.

1 I'm tired.

You should get more sleep.
You shouldn't go to bed so late.

2 I'm hungry.

3 It's raining, and I have to go.

4 I feel ill.

a) be here in class
b) eat something
c) ~~get more sleep~~
d) go home
e) go out now
f) go to bed so late
g) take an umbrella
h) skip breakfast

B Work in pairs and take turns. Cover the advice a)–h) above. Student A: Say one of the problems. Student B: Give advice with *should/shouldn't*.

SPEAKING

6 A Work in pairs and answer the questions.

1 In situations a)–f), do you usually go to a pharmacy, a doctor, a dentist or a hospital?

a) You ate some fish last night. This morning you have a terrible stomachache.
b) You broke a glass and cut your thumb badly.
c) You woke up this morning with an earache.
d) Your eyes are really red and tired.
e) You have a terrible toothache.
f) You stayed out in the sun too long this morning, and you got very sunburned.

2 Discuss. Can you remember a time when you had any of these problems? Where were you? What did you do?

B Look at the phrases below. In a pharmacy, which phrases does the customer say and which ones does the pharmacist say? Write C or P.

Take these tablets three times a day. P
I have (a) terrible …
Put this cream on your …
Put these drops in your …
Could I have some bandages?
Do you have anything for …
You should …
You shouldn't …
Can you recommend anything?
When did it start?

C Work in pairs. You are on vacation in another country. Choose a problem from Exercise 6A and role-play the situation.

D Work in groups and take turns. One pair: Role-play your conversation. Other students: Do you agree with the advice?

skip breakfast / bandages — miss breakfast / plasters

11.2)) ONE THING AT A TIME

G adverbs of manner
P sentence stress: adverbs
V communication

Are you a multi-tasker?

I had lunch with a friend yesterday. In one hour, she answered three text messages, had two short phone conversations, checked her email, ordered her food, ate it and paid for it. And in that one hour, she and I didn't stop talking for more than a few seconds.

My friend is a typical multi-tasker, and maybe you are, too. Multi-tasking – doing two or more tasks at the same time – is normal for many people. But it's not good for you.

READING

1 A **Work in pairs. Look at the picture and answer the questions.**

1 What does a multi-tasker do?
2 Are you a multi-tasker?
3 How many different tasks can you do at one time?

B **Read the introduction to the article. How many different tasks did the writer's friend do?**

C **Work in pairs. Write three ways that multi-tasking is bad for you. Then read part two of the text. How many of your ideas are the same?**

What happens when you multi-task?

1 You think you work quickly, but in fact you work slowly. Multi-taskers do less work in an eight-hour day than non-multi-taskers.

2 Your memory gets worse. You forget names and numbers. You can't remember normal things easily, for example your bank PIN number.

3 You eat very fast, and you eat too much. You don't think about your food when you're eating.

4 You have problems with friends and loved ones. You don't listen to them carefully, and they feel this.

5 You do some tasks badly. You make mistakes because you are doing two things at the same time.

6 Finally – and this is the big one – your stress levels go up, and that's the biggest problem.

D **Read the last part of the text. Work in pairs and discuss. Do you think the writer's plan is a good idea?**

What can you do about it?

It's very easy: Do one thing at a time. When you eat, eat. When you read, read. And when you talk to a friend, only talk – and listen.

Remember my friend? Next week we're going to meet in the park, turn off our phones, have no food or drink, and just talk and listen. That's my plan – SHE doesn't know it yet. I'll let you know what happens.

VOCABULARY

COMMUNICATION

2 A **Look at the word webs below and cross out the verb which does not go with the noun. Then look in the text and find one more word for each word web.**

a text message: get, ~~order~~, send, ______

your phone: answer, turn on, turn off, ______

a conversation: talk, start, finish, ______

names and numbers: exchange, answer, remember, ______

B **Work in pairs and cover the word webs. Student A: Say a phrase from Exercise 2A. Student B: Say another phrase with the same noun.**

A: send a text message
B: get a text message
A: answer a text message

C **Work alone. Choose a verb from Exercise 2A to complete the questions.**

1 How often do you ________ texts?
2 Do you always ________ a text right away?
3 Do you ________ your phone at night?
4 Is it easy for you to _______ a conversation in English?
5 Do you ever ________ someone's name?
6 Is it difficult for you to ________ phone numbers?

D **Work in pairs and take turns. Ask and answer the questions.**

right away | straightaway

GRAMMAR

ADVERBS

3 A Look at the sentence and the rule. Underline the correct alternatives to complete them.

You think you work *quick/quickly*, but in fact you work *slow/slowly*.

RULES

1 Use adverbs of manner to say *how/when* we do something.

2 Adverbs usually come *before/after* a verb phrase.

B Complete the table. Use the reading text in Exercise 1C to help.

Adjective	Adverb
slow	*slowly*
quick	
fast	
bad	
careful	
easy	

C Work in pairs. How do you make a regular adverb? Which adverb is irregular?

S11.4

D SENTENCE STRESS: adverbs Listen to the sentence in Exercise 3A. Notice how the stress is on the adverbs. Listen and repeat.

▶ page 136 LANGUAGEBANK

4 A Complete the sentences and make them true for you. Use the correct form (adjective or adverb) of one of the words in parentheses.

1 I like it when the teacher speaks *slowly*. (*quick/slow*)
2 It's _________ for me to remember new words in English. (*easy/hard*)
3 I think I speak English _________. (*good/bad*)
4 I have a _________ memory. (*good/bad*)
5 When I have lunch or dinner, I usually eat _________. (*fast/slow*)
6 I think I usually eat _________. (*healthy/unhealthy*)
7 I can't study when it's _________. (*quiet/noisy*)
8 I usually get to work/school _________. (*late/early*)

B Work in pairs and compare your sentences. How many are the same?

SPEAKING

5 Work in pairs. Student A: Look at page 146. Student B: Look at page 143.

WRITING

ADVERBS IN STORIES

6 A Look at pictures A–D. What do you think happened? Put them in the correct order. Use the prompts 1–4 to help.

1 Saturday / Ken / get up / eat breakfast / get on / bike.
2 he / ride / down the road / not / look / ahead. / cat / run / in front / him.
3 he / fall off / bike / break /arm.
4 evening / he / sit / home / with / broken arm.

B Use the prompts to write the story. Remember to use linkers.

1 On Saturday, Ken got up, ate breakfast and …

C Change the adjectives in the box below into adverbs. Then add three of them to your story in Exercise 6A.

quick careful careless dangerous early fast late sad slow

On Saturday, Ken got up late, ate breakfast quickly …

D Write the next part of the story with three more adverbs. Start with "Six weeks later, on Saturday morning, Ken got up … ".

E Work in pairs and exchange your stories.

11.3)) HELP!

F offering to help
P intonation in offers
V verbs of movement

VOCABULARY
VERBS OF MOVEMENT

1 A Look at the situations below. Which problems can you see in the pictures?

1 You're sitting on a bus. You're feeling very tired, and you have a long journey. You see a woman. She's **standing,** and she's **carrying** a baby.

2 You are walking along a road. You see a young man. He's **pushing** his car.

3 You're in a busy city. You're in a hurry because you have an important meeting, and you're late. A person in front of you **drops** his pen.

4 You see a woman who's around twenty. She's carrying a heavy suitcase down some steps, and she's in trouble because she can't **lift** it.

5 You see a person with a bad leg. He drops some magazines and papers and can't **pick** them **up** easily.

6 You see a man by the road. He is **lying** on the ground, and he isn't moving.

7 You see a blind person. He's trying to **cross** the road, but the traffic is busy.

B Work in pairs and discuss. In each situation, do you help? What can you say and do?

FUNCTION
OFFERING TO HELP

2 Read the article and guess the missing city name.

The most helpful city

When someone sees a person in trouble, do they stop and help or just "walk on by"? Researchers from the U.S. decided to answer the question "Which is the most helpful city in the world?" They went to twenty-three capital cities and did three experiments to find out:

a) A person is walking along the street and drops his/her pen.
b) A person with a broken leg drops some papers.
c) A blind person is trying to cross the road.

They found that people in Spanish-speaking cities were usually the most helpful. Madrid, San Salvador and Mexico City each scored highly. People in these cities gave help with a smile and seemed happy to give their time. People in New York came near the bottom: they were often too busy or were in a hurry. They also said they sometimes didn't offer help because it was dangerous or because people got angry with them. And the most helpful city in the world? ____________, in Brazil.

S11.5

3 A Listen and match conversations 1–3 with situations a)–c) in the text.

B Listen again and complete sentences 1–4 below.

1 ______ me help.		3 ______ I help you?	
2 ______ do it.		4 ______ carry your bag?	

S11.6

C Listen to two speakers. Check (✓) the offer that sounds more polite.

1 A ______ B ______ 3 A ______ B ______
2 A ______ B ______ 4 A ______ B ______

S11.7

D INTONATION IN OFFERS Listen to the offers and repeat. Notice that they all start high.

who's around → of about

D

E

4 A Match problems 1—5 with offers a)—e).

1 I can't open the window.
2 I'm hungry.
3 I can't reach the dictionary.
4 I can't lift this bag.
5 It's cold in here.

a) I'll get it for you.
b) Let me carry it.
c) I'll make you a sandwich.
d) Do you want me to close the window?
e) Let me try … Ooh, it's stuck.

B Work in pairs and take turns. Student A: Say a problem. Student B: Cover Exercise 4A. Listen to the problem and offer to help.

A: I can't open the window.
B: Let me try … Ooh, it's stuck.

S11.8

C Listen to the situations. What's happening?

D Work in pairs. Listen again and offer to help.

1 (glass breaking) Here, let me help. What a mess!

▶ page 136 LANGUAGEBANK

Do you want me to…? Shall I…?

LEARN TO

THANK SOMEONE

5 A Look at audio script S11.5 on page 149 and complete the sentences.

Conversation 1

M: Here, let me help. What a mess!
W: Thank [1] _______. It's my leg. It's difficult …
M: Oh, don't move. I'll do it.
W: Thanks [2] _______.
M: No [3] _______.

Conversation 2

W: Uh … Excuse me?
M: Yeah.
W: You dropped this.
M: Oh. Thanks [4] _______.
W: That's [5] _______ .

Conversation 3

W: Do you want me to carry your bag?
M: No, no, it's fine, thanks.
W: Here you are.
M: Thanks [6] _______. That's [7] _______.
W: You're [8] _______.

B Underline five ways of thanking someone. Circle three ways to reply when someone thanks you.

6 A Look at the flowchart and put the conversation below it in the correct order.

Ask about the problem. → Say the problem. → Offer to help. → Accept the offer. → Reply.

1 A: That's OK.
2 B: Thanks a lot.
3 A: Sit down. I'll get you some water.
4 A: Are you OK?
5 B: No, I don't feel well.

B Use the flowchart and role-play the conversation. Student A: Look at page 145. Student B: Look at page 144.

SPEAKING

7 Work in pairs. Choose a situation from Exercise 1A or your own idea. Act out the situation and have a conversation of at least thirty seconds.

8 Work with other students. Can you remember a time when you helped someone or when someone else helped you? What happened? How did you feel?

11.4 FAT OR SUGAR?

DVD PREVIEW

1 Work in pairs and discuss.

1 Which types of food in the pictures do you eat a lot of? Which types of food do you rarely eat?

2 Look at the pictures A–F. Which are high in fat (F), and which are high in sugar/carbohydrates (S)?

2 Read the program information and answer the questions.

1 Which types of food in the pictures above can Chris eat? Which can Xand eat?

2 Who do you think wins the bike race?

3 Do the "doughnut test". Which doughnut do you think most people choose?

Horizon: Sugar Versus Fat

It's one of the big questions of our time: Which is worse for you, fat or sugar? Twin brothers (and doctors) Chris and Xand Van Tulleken go on a special diet to try to answer the question. For one month, Chris eats only high-sugar food and no fat, and Xand eats only high-fat foods and no sugar. They do a number of experiments. For example, in a bike race up a hill, which one of them is the fastest? Finally, the twins do the "doughnut test". They ask people in New York and London to choose their favorite type of doughnut.

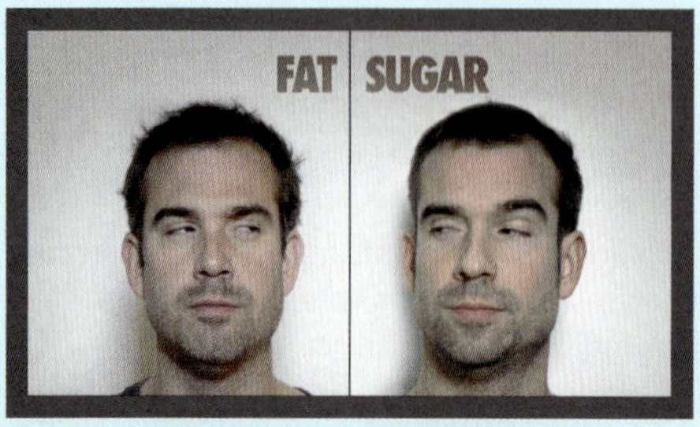

DVD VIEW

3 A Watch the DVD and check your answers to the questions in Exercise 2.

B Work in pairs and match these sentence halves from the video.

1 Which is worse for us: _d_

2 Is sugar really public enemy number one, ___

3 … you can have mayonnaise, ___

4 I want you to remember the doughnut you chose, ___

5 And it's thick, it's luxurious, it's rich, it's creamy, ___

6 And there's something really special about this doughnut: ___

7 It's the same 50–50 mix

a) and it's really boring.

b) and we're going to see if the people in New York will choose the same one as you.

c) but you're not allowed any fruit …

d) fat or sugar?

e) it has an exactly 50–50 mixture of fat and sugar.

f) that we find in so many processed foods.

g) or is it fat?

C Watch the video again and check.

D Work in pairs and discuss. Does the program change how you feel about food? How might you change the way you eat?

The doughnut test: Which would you choose?

American Speakout a panel discussion

4 A Work in pairs. Write 6–8 questions to ask the twin brothers Chris (sugar) and Xand (fat), Hilary (a healthy eating expert) and a doctor. Use the words and phrases below to help.

About the diet	About the future
dangerous?	eat more/less X?
problems?	change your diet?
worst thing/best thing?	do more exercise?
miss the most?	**stop eating X?**
cheat?	**recommend?**

What was the worst thing about the diet?
Are you going to … ? Should we … ?

11.9 **B** Listen to the discussion. How many questions were the same as yours?

C Listen again and check (✓) the key phrases you hear.

KEYPHRASES

I have a question for Chris/Xand/Hilary/the doctor.
What do you mean?
Do you agree with him/her?
Can you tell us more about that?
Could you give an example?
I don't understand. Could you explain?
Can I ask you about [your diet/the future/…] ?

D Work as a class. Four students are on a panel and are Chris, Xand, Hilary and the doctor. Other students: Ask the panel members your questions.

writeback a website message

5 Work in pairs. Read the three questions from a forum posting. Choose one and complete Message 4 to give some advice. Use the key phrases to help.

Message 1 posted yesterday

Hi. I have a real problem with chocolate. I can't stop eating it – after meals and in my coffee break and in the middle of the afternoon. I always have some in my bag or in my desk. How can I stop?

Posted by: Teresa, Spain
Reply | Previous Message | Next Message

Message 2 posted yesterday

Help! I started working from home three weeks ago. Now I have a terrible backache, and my eyes hurt. I'm on the computer for about eight hours every day. Any advice?

Posted by: YuchenChi, China
Reply | Previous Message | Next Message

Message 3 posted yesterday

I stopped smoking a year ago, and now I'm overweight. I often feel stressed and unhappy. I think I might start smoking again, but I don't want to. What can I do?

Posted by: Great Amigo, Mexico
Reply | Previous Message | Next Message

Message 4 posted yesterday

Hi, ______. Don't worry! The same thing happened to ______, and I understand completely. Here are three pieces of advice I can give you:

- The best thing is ______.
- You should ______.
- And finally, ______.

I hope that helps!

All the best, ______.

Reply | Previous Message | Next Message

11.5 LOOKBACK

V THE BODY; HEALTH

1 A Complete the dialogues.

Dialogue 1

A: What's wrong?
What's wrong with you?

B: I have a terrible co_ _ _ _ ,
A runny n_ _ _ _ , a bad s_r_
thr_ _ _ _.

A: I can't stay here. I'm off!

Dialogue 2

A: My a_ _ _ _ hurt, my l_ _ _ _ hurt, I think I have a bad flu.

B: Do you have a t_mp_r_t_ _ _ _?

A: Yes, what can I do?

Dialogue 3

A: I have an awful h_ _ d_ _ _ _ _.

B: My f_ng_ _ _ _ hurt a lot.

A: My e_e_ are t_r_d.

B: My b_ck_ _ _ _ _ 's bad.

A & B: We don't know what we have!

B Work in pairs. Read the dialogues.

G *SHOULD/SHOULDN'T*

2 A Read the situations and make a note of what the person *should/shouldn't do*.

a) My arm hurts, so I can't use my computer. I have to finish a report by tomorrow.

b) I have a terrible backache. I'm going on vacation tomorrow, and I have two heavy bags to carry.

c) I have a headache and a bad sore throat. I have an important interview for a new job tomorrow.

d) My leg hurts, so I can't walk very far. I'm going out tomorrow night, and I want to dance.

B Work in pairs and take turns. Role-play the four situations above using your ideas.

V COMMUNICATION

3 Work in pairs. Match phrases 1–6 with a)–f). Then ask and answer the questions.

1 How many text messages *c*
2 Do you ever get
3 Can you have
4 What do you do when you forget
5 Do you remember
6 Do you ever turn off

a) a conversation and watch TV at the same time?
b) your phone? When?
c) ~~do you send a day?~~
d everyone's name in the class?
e) someone's name and they remember yours?
f) text messages in English?

G ADVERBS OF MANNER

4 A Write the opposite adverbs.

1 early – *late*
2 loudly
3 slowly
4 well
5 carelessly

B Complete the sentences with a verb from the box below and an adverb of your choice.

speak(s)	eat(s)	talk(s)
drive(s)	walk(s)	go(es)
to bed		

1 I _______ too _______.
2 Everyone _______ too _______ on their cell phones.
3 My closest friend _______ too _______.
4 Everyone _______ too _______.

C Work in groups and take turns. One student: Say one of your sentences. Other students: Give advice or say your opinion using *should/shouldn't*.

A: Everyone talks too loudly on their cell phones.
B: Yes, they should speak quietly.

F OFFERING TO HELP

5 Work in pairs. What can you say in each situation?

1 You're at a friend's house, and she breaks some glasses.
2 You're walking down the street, and someone falls off his bicycle.
3 You're on a train, and a woman next to you becomes ill.
4 You're at home, and you pour hot coffee on a friend's shirt.
5 Your friend is cutting vegetables and cuts his finger badly.
6 Your friend wants a coffee, but she doesn't have enough money to buy one.

6 A Complete the conversation with the words in the box.

'll	me	a	're
you	~~help~~		

A: Good morning. Can I *help* you?

B: Yes, the shower in my room doesn't work.

A: I send someone to look at it.

B: Thank. And when does the City Museum open?

A: Let look on the computer … It opens at ten today.

B: Thanks. And can you get me a taxi to go to the museum?

A: No problem. I call for one now?

B: In about an hour, please.

A: Certainly.

B: Thanks lot.

A: You welcome.

B Work in pairs. Practice the conversation.

What's wrong? What's the matter?

12 experiences

SPEAKING
12.1 Ask and answer questions about life experiences
12.2 Describe how you feel about different situations
12.3 Make telephone calls and say telephone numbers
12.4 Talk about an exciting or frightening experience

LISTENING
12.1 Listen to people talking about their experiences
12.3 Listen to phone conversations
12.4 Watch a clip from a documentary about sharks

READING
12.2 Read about a dangerous job

WRITING
12.1 Write an email using linkers
12.4 Write a story about an exciting or frightening experience

What's the most exciting thing you've done?

INTERVIEWS

12.1)) GREAT EXPERIENCES

G present perfect
P sentence stress: present perfect
V experiences

VOCABULARY

EXPERIENCES

1 A Complete the phrases below with the words in the box. Use the pictures to help you.

~~be~~ ride do sleep climb meet go watch

1 _be_ in a play/in a movie
2 ________ a bungee jump/a parachute jump
3 ________ someone famous/a great new friend on a train or plane journey
4 ________ an elephant/a motorcycle
5 ________ to a live athletic event/to a karaoke bar
6 ________ outside/in an unusual place
7 ________ a mountain/a volcano
8 ________ the sun rise/your favorite band or singer live in concert

B Work in pairs. Look at pictures A–E and discuss the questions.

1 Which activities above can you see in the pictures?
2 Which activities would you like to do? Why?
3 Which activities would you not like to do? Why not?

LISTENING

S12.1

2 A Listen to a survey about great experiences. Check (✓) the things the speakers have done or seen.

	1	2	3
karaoke			
an elephant ride			
the sun rise			
a volcano			
a bungee jump			
being in a movie			

B Look at these sentences. Which speaker might say each one? Write 1, 2 or 3.

1 "It's my favorite song!"
2 "I did it on vacation in Italy."
3 "I'd like to try it. It looks fun but scary!"
4 "I wasn't very good, but lots of people watched it on YouTube."
5 "Everyone in Japan does it."
6 "I enjoyed it more than my husband did."

C Listen again. Which sentences do the speakers actually say?

D Work in pairs. What does it mean in each sentence in Exercise 2B?

E Work in pairs and discuss. Which experience would you most like to have?

A

B

C

D

E

athletic | sporting

GRAMMAR

PRESENT PERFECT

3 A Look at the sentences and underline the verbs. Then choose the correct alternatives to complete the rules.

I've watched the sun rise. He's been in a movie.

RULES

1 Use the present perfect to talk about a *present/past* action.

2 Use the present perfect to talk about general experiences in your life when you *say/don't say* an exact time.

S12.2

B SENTENCE STRESS: present perfect Listen and complete the table. Then listen again and repeat.

I	______	climbed	a volcano.
	______ never	watched	the sun rise.
	haven't	______	outside.

______	you ever	ridden	an elephant?
No,	I	______.	

C Work in pairs and complete the information.

1 Make the present perfect with ______ /______ and the past participle of the verb.

2 The past participle of regular verbs (*watch*, *climb*) is the same as the ______ of the verb.

▶ page 138 LANGUAGEBANK

4 A Complete the table with the correct past participles. Check in your dictionary or the irregular verbs list on page 127.

Regular Verbs	Past participle	Irregular Verbs	Past participle
1 watch	*watched*	7 do	*done*
2 climb	______	8 be	______
3 stay	______	9 have	______
4 try	______	10 meet	______
5 travel	______	11 go	______
6 use	______	12 see	______

B Use four of the past participles above to write sentences about you. Two sentences should be false.

I've had lunch with the President.

C Work in pairs and take turns. Student A: Say your four sentences. Student B: Guess which two are false.

American Speak out TIP

Look for patterns to help you remember. In your notebook, write the past participles:
meet – met, sleep … ride – ridden, write … grow – grown, know … swim – swum, drink … drive – driven, give …

SPEAKING

5 A Complete the questions with your own ideas.

1 Have you ever been to ______?
2 Have you ever slept in a ______?
3 Have you ever had ______?
4 Have you ever met ______?
5 Have you ever ______?

B Work in groups. Ask and answer the questions above. Who has done most things in your group?

A: Have you ever been to the Sahara Desert?
B: Yes, I have.
C: No, I haven't, but I'd like to.

WRITING

LINKERS REVIEW

6 A Read the email below. Which country are the people visiting?

Dear Helena

This country is very different from what I expected. It's very hot in the day, [1] *but* it's nice and cool at night, [2]______ I always carry a sweater in my bag. We sleep in tents, [3]______ sometimes on the boats, and every day we get up at six. We've seen the temples in Kom Ombo and Edfu, and [4]______ the ones at Abu Simbel. They were amazing! We haven't seen the Pyramids [5]______ we'll only get to Cairo on Saturday.

We have two days in Cairo. On Saturday, [6]______ we're going to the museum, [7]______ we're going to visit a famous mosque and an old church, [8]______. In the afternoon, we're going to Khan Al-Khalili Market. We want to buy a lamp for Lily and one for us [9]______. Then [10]______ we're going to have dinner on a boat on the river. It's going to be a long day!

Best!

Ollie and Kriszti

B Complete the email with the linkers in the box.

~~but~~ also finally as well because then or so too first

C Write an email to another student about one of these topics: An amazing trip, a live concert or an interesting experience. Write 80–100 words and include at least five different linkers.

D Work in pairs. Exchange your emails. Ask your partner questions about their experience.

12.2)) AFRAID OF NOTHING

G present perfect and simple past
P irregular past participles
V prepositions

Eunice Huthart has accidents all the time. She's jumped off ships and fallen off buildings. She's driven cars very fast and crashed them, and she's loved every moment. Eunice is a stunt double in movies and does things that most of us think are crazy.

Waking up with aches and pains is all part of the job.

Crashing a car at high speed, walking away, and then waking up the next morning with a few aches and pains is all part of the job for a stunt double.

Eunice has done stunts in Harry Potter and James Bond movies. She's been Angelina Jolie's stunt double in many movies, from the *Lara Croft: Tomb Raider* series to *Maleficent*.

Eunice has broken some bones, and perhaps her worst accident was during *Titanic* when she jumped off the ship onto some boxes and broke her cheek bone. Eunice worked on *Titanic* in her first year as a stuntwoman, in 1996.

Broken bones and other injuries are normal for stunt doubles. So why do they do it? Most talk about the excitement, the challenge and the big money.

Eunice now works more as a stunt director, directing other stunt performers. Altogether she has worked on over fifty movies.

Eunice loves her job, but in the end she's a family person. When asked about the most memorable moment in her life, she talked about the birth of her daughter and Liverpool winning the European Cup.

Broken bones and other injuries are normal.

READING

1 A Read the definition of *stunt* below. Can you think of any famous stunts?

> **S** **stunt 1** /stʌnt/ *noun* a dangerous thing that someone does to entertain people, especially in a movie: *There's a great stunt in which his car has to jump across a fifteen-meter gap.*

From Longman Wordwise Dictionary.

B Read the article. How many stunts does it mention? How many of the movies in the article do you know?

C Read the article again. Are sentences 1–6 true (T) or false (F)?

1 She likes doing car stunts.
2 She started doing stunt work over fifteen years ago.
3 She gets angry when she hurts herself in her job.
4 She often works as a stuntwoman these days.
5 Stunt doubles get a lot of money for their work.
6 Her work is more important than her family.

D Circle four movement verbs in the first paragraph of the text. Write the verb, simple past and past participle. Use your dictionary or the irregular verbs list on page 127 to help.

jumped – jump jumped jumped

E Work with other students. What are three good things and three bad things about being a stunt performer? Would you like to have the job?

meter metre

GRAMMAR

PRESENT PERFECT AND SIMPLE PAST

2 A Look at the sentences. Underline the correct tense of the verbs.

1 She has done stunts in Harry Potter movies. *(simple past/present perfect)*

2 Eunice worked on *Titanic* in 1996. *(simple past/present perfect)*

B Underline the correct alternatives.

RULES

1 With the present perfect, you *say/don't say* the exact time in the past.

2 With the simple past, you *say/don't say* the exact time in the past.

▶ page 138 LANGUAGEBANK

3 A Write the questions in full. Use the present perfect and *ever*.

1 see / *Titanic*?

2 break / your arm?

3 eat / anything unusual?

4 swim / in a river?

5 make / anything to wear?

6 go / to a really hot or cold country?

B Look at the conversation. Which verb forms are used? Why?

A: Have you ever seen Titanic?
B: No, I haven't. Have you?
A: Yes, I have. I saw it online last year.
B: What did you think of it?

C Work in pairs and take turns. Ask and answer the questions in Exercise 3A. Remember to ask follow-up questions.

D Ask other students two questions about things you haven't done. How many students have done these things?

A: Have you ever seen a live soccer game?

4 A IRREGULAR PAST PARTICIPLES Work in pairs. Write the past participles of the verbs in the box under the correct sound below.

~~sleep~~ ~~sing~~ ~~speak~~ ~~drive~~ ~~buy~~ read write
think fly win meet do give choose bring

/e/	/ʌ/	/əʊ/	/ɪ/	/ɔː/
slept	*sung*	*spoken*	*driven*	*bought*

B Listen and check. Then listen and repeat.

VOCABULARY

PREPOSITIONS

5 A Look at the pictures. What is the man doing?

B Match the prepositions in the box with the pictures A–J.

down through up out of under towards
away from across over into

C Some of the prepositions have opposites. Look at the pictures again and find the opposites of these prepositions: *down, over, away from, out of.*

D Complete the situations with a preposition of movement. More than one might be possible.

1 driving *through* a very long tunnel

2 going _________ in a glass elevator

3 walking _________ a big dog

4 walking _________ a big park alone

5 going _________ a bridge when a train is going _________ the bridge

6 riding a bike fast _________ a big hill

7 walking _________ a rope bridge

8 walking _________ a room full of new people

SPEAKING

6 A How do you feel about the situations in Exercise 5D? Write one of the phrases in the box below next to each one.

I love it. It's not a problem. I really don't like it.
I'm afraid of it. I've never done it.

B Work with other students and discuss your ideas.

A: How do you feel about driving through a very long tunnel?
B: I really don't like it. In fact I really hate it. I feel sick.
C: Why? Have you had a bad experience?
B: Not really, I just don't like it.

12.3)) HELLO, I'VE GOT A PROLBEM

F calling
P sentence stress
V calling expressions

SPEAKING

1 A Work in pairs and take turns. Ask and answer questions 1–5. For each "yes", ask your partner what happened.

1 Have you ever lost your …
keys? cell phone? credit card?

2 Have you ever locked yourself out of your …
house? car? office?

3 Have you ever missed a …
train? bus? plane?

4 Have you ever been very late for …
a meeting? an appointment? a concert?

5 Have you ever gotten lost in …
a city? a building? the countryside?

B Who had the most interesting experience? Tell the class about it.

C In which of the situations did you use your phone to help with the problem?

VOCABULARY

CALLING EXPRESSIONS

2 A Complete the sentences with words/phrases from the box.

~~take a message~~ leave a message call answer call (someone) back

1 You answer the phone. It's a call for your colleague Patricia, but she's not in the office today, so you *take a message* for her.

2 You phone your friend Mark, but he's not at home, so you ________ on his answering machine.

3 You want Mark to ________ you ________ this evening.

4 It's the evening. You ________ Mark, but he's taking a shower.

5 Ten minutes later the phone rings and you ________ it. It's Mark.

B Work in pairs and compare your answers. Which two verbs mean to call?

FUNCTION

PHONE CONVERSATIONS

3 A Listen to three conversation extracts. Which situations from Exercise 1A are they?

B Cross out the incorrect alternative. Then listen and check.

Extract 1

B: Hi, Sean. [1]*It's/I'm* Debbie.
A: Hi, Debbie. What's up?
B: [2]Is Kevin *there/here*?
A: No, he's not. He went out about ten minutes ago.

Extract 2

B: [3]Could I *leave/have* a message for him?
A: Of course.
B: [4]Just *ask/say* him to *cell phone/call* me.

Extract 3

B: Hello. [5]Could I *speak/chat* to customer services, please?
A: [6]Just a *hold/moment*.
C: Customer services.
B: Hello. [7]*I am/This is* Alan Simpson. I've got a problem.

Extract 4

B: [8]Could you *call/answer* me back?
C: Of course. Could you give me the number there?
B: Just a moment … It's 34 for Spain, 91 for Madrid, then 308 5238.
C: [9]Let me *check/buzz* that. 34 91 308 5238.
B: That's right.
C: Fine. Hang up and [10]I'll call you *up/back* right away.

C Match the conversation extracts 1–4 with descriptions a)–d) below.

a) Asking someone to call back *4*
b) Starting a call to a business
c) Starting a call to a friend
d) Leaving a message

D Underline the key stressed words in calling phrases 1–10 in Exercise 3B.

E SENTENCE STRESS Listen and check. Then listen and repeat.

▶ page 138 LANGUAGEBANK

answering machine / call
call (someone) back / taking a shower

answerphone / ring
ring (someone) back / having a shower

4 A Work in pairs. Look at the flowchart and write the conversation in full.

Hello?

Hi, Sam / Jill
Hi, Sam. It's Jill.

Hi, Jill. How / you?
_________?

OK, thanks. / Gerry there? _________?

No. / not here ______.

message / him? ______?

OK.

ask / call me? ______?

What / number?
________?

339-924-1823

Let / check / ________
339-924-1833?

No, / 339-924-1823

1823. OK.

Thanks, Sam.

Bye.

Bye.

B Work in pairs. Read out your conversation.

LEARN TO

SAY TELEPHONE NUMBERS

5.12.7

5 A Complete the phone number. Then listen and check.

312-540-3911 = ______ one ______ five four ______ three nine ______ ______

B Listen again. Draw a line between the words where you hear a short break.

American Speak out TIP

In telephone numbers:

- say *"oh"* for the number zero.
- when there are two of the same number, e.g. 77, say *"seven seven"* or *"double seven"*.
- add a one to the beginning of the number when calling long distance, e.g. say 1-658-923-4479.
- group the numbers according to the dashes, for example, the number 212-783-6565: 212 (pause) 783 (pause) 6565. How do you pronounce numbers in your country?

C Work in pairs. Draw a line between the numbers where you think a pause is good. Practice saying the numbers.

1 310-203-4012
2 755-920-6332
3 81013005492
4 52-5526-2794

D Work in pairs and take turns. Student A: Look at page 145. Student B: Look at page 146.

SPEAKING

6 Work in pairs. Student A: Look at page 143. Student B: Look at page 146. Role-play the situations.

12.4 SHARK THERAPY

DVD PREVIEW

1 Work in pairs. Look at the pictures and discuss the questions. Are you afraid of any of these animals? Which ones? Why?

2 A Complete the sentences with words from the box.

~~frightened~~ nervous excited upset proud afraid

1 Some people are *frightened* or ________ of the dark.

2 When you are positive and happy before your birthday or a party, you feel ________.

3 When you are happy about something you've done, often something difficult, you feel ________.

4 Before an exam or going to the dentist, you feel ________.

5 When you fail an exam, you feel ________.

B Complete sentences 1–6.

1 I'm afraid of ________.

2 I get very excited before ________.

3 I'm not frightened of ________.

4 I felt very proud when I ________.

5 I get nervous when I have to ________.

6 I last felt upset when ________.

C Work in pairs and compare ideas. Are any the same?

DVD VIEW

3 A Read the program information. Why does Tanya go to the Bahamas?

Shark Therapy

Tanya Streeter is a world-famous diver, but she has one big problem. She's afraid of sharks! To overcome her fear, she needs help or "therapy" and travels to the Bahamas to get it. Here, she learns how to swim with them … and comes face-to-face with a dangerous tiger shark.

B Watch the DVD. When do you think Tanya feels the most afraid?

C Underline the correct alternatives. Then watch again and check.

1 It's safer to wear a *black/green/shiny* wetsuit.

2 Tanya uses a *knife/stick/gun* to protect herself from the sharks.

3 *No/One/Two* shark(s) *try/tries* to bite Tanya.

D Look at the program extracts below. Watch the DVD again and correct the mistakes.

1 "At first, it isn't ~~difficult~~." *easy*

2 "I didn't think that they were going to be … very … friendly."

3 "I noticed the mask, and I think we should change the mask completely."

4 "Jim throws meat into the water to attract the sharks."

5 "Tanya, look behind you over on your right."

6 "That was frightening! Tanya did great."

7 "I've started to overcome my very real feeling."

E Work in pairs and answer the questions.

1 At the end of the program do you think Tanya was:

a) frightened?

b) excited?

c) proud?

2 Would you like to try therapy with sharks or with any animals from Exercise 1? Why/Why not?

American Speakout a frightening experience

4 A Think about an exciting or frightening experience you've had. Look at the questions below and take notes:

- How old were you?
- Where was it?
- What happened? (write the verb phrases)
- How did you feel?
- What happened in the end?
- How did you feel in the end?

B Listen to a man talk about an experience. Was it exciting or frightening? What happened?

C Listen again and check (✓) the key phrases you hear.

KEYPHRASES

This happened in [time/place] when I was [age].

One day, … Then, … After that, …

I felt [excited/nervous/frightened/…]

I got [hot/hungry/tired/…]

In the end, …

It was [one of] the most [exciting/amazing/frightening/…] experiences I've ever had.

D Work in groups and take turns. One student: Talk about your experience. Use the key phrases and your notes to help. Other students: Listen and ask two follow-up questions about each event.

writeback a short story

5 A Before he talked about his experience, the man took some notes. Look at the notes below and number the events in the correct order.

went for a walk 1
one dog bit my arm
didn't move, didn't look at the dogs
remembered advice
dogs ran toward me
heard some dogs
realized I was in a new place
dogs jumped and barked

B Work in pairs and compare your answers.

C Use your notes from Exercise 4A and write about your experience in 80–100 words. Remember to use some of the key phrases to help.

realized / realised

12.5 LOOKBACK

V EXPERIENCES

1 A What are the activities? Add the vowels.

1 w__tch the s__n r__s__
2 sl__ __p __ __ts__d__
3 r__d__ an __l__ph__nt
4 m__ __t someone f__m__ __s
5 g__ to an __thl__t__c __v__nt
6 d__ a p__r__ch__t__ j__mp
7 cl__mb a m__ __nt__ __n
8 b__ in a m__v__ __

B Work in pairs and discuss.

1 Which activities above can you do in your country? Where can you do them?
2 Which activities above do you think are special/boring/exciting?
3 Which activities above would you like to do/try? Why?

G PRESENT PERFECT

2 A Write the sentences in full.

1 I / never / eat / fish eyes.
2 I / never / go / to an art gallery.
3 I / never / see / the sun rise.
4 I / never / drive / a Mercedes.
5 I / never / drink / tea with milk for breakfast.
6 I / never / play / golf.
7 I / never / cook / dinner for my parents.
8 I / never / speak / English on the phone.
9 I / never / go / to an outdoor festival.
10 I / never / hear / Katy Perry live.

B Change the last part of each sentence so that it is true for you.

I've never eaten cabbage.

I've never been to an art gallery, but I'd like to.

C Work in pairs and compare your answers.

G PRESENT PERFECT AND SIMPLE PAST

3 A Complete the questions. Use the correct form of the verbs in parentheses.

Have you ever …

1 *ridden* a horse? (ride)
2 ________ in a small plane? (fly)
3 ________ in a lake? (swim)
4 ________ a long distance? (cycle)
5 ________ on a train? (sleep)
6 ________ a mountain? (climb)

B Work in pairs and take turns. Ask and answer the questions in Exercise 3A and ask follow-up questions.

A: Have you ever … ?
B: Yes, I have.
A: Oh, when was that?

V PREPOSITIONS

4 A Look at the word webs and cross out the place/thing which does not go with the preposition of movement.

through: a country, a city, a wood, ~~a road~~

down: a country, a river, some stairs, a road

over: a country, a bridge, a bathroom, a mountain

into: a room, a river, a country, some stairs

across: a city, a person, a bridge, a room

B Work in pairs. Student A: Choose one of the prepositions. Say three things that can come after it. Student B: Guess the preposition.

A: A country, a mountain, a bridge
B: Over?

F CALLING

5 A Complete the telephone conversation. Write two words in each gap.

A: Hello, the Learn English Center.
B: Hello, [1] ________ Sofia Mitsotakis. [2] ________ speak to my teacher, Rachel, please?
A: [3] ________ moment. [4] ________ check … I'm afraid she's in class at the moment.
B: I see. Could [5] ________ a message for her?
A: Sure. Go ahead.
B: Could you [6] ________ to call me this afternoon?
A: Yes, could you [7] ________ your number?
B: It's 535-8230.
A: OK. She'll [8] ________ back.
B: Thank you.

B Work in pairs. Student A: Call the school to speak to your English teacher. Student B: You are the receptionist. The teacher can't come to the phone. Continue the conversation with your ideas.

IRREGULAR VERBS

Verb	Past simple	Past participle
be	was/were	been
become	became	become
begin	began	begun
bite	bit	bitten
blow	blew	blown
break	broke	broken
bring	brought	brought
build	built	built
buy	bought	bought
catch	caught	caught
choose	chose	chosen
come	came	come
cost	cost	cost
cut	cut	cut
do	did	done
draw	drew	drawn
drink	drank	drunk
drive	drove	driven
eat	ate	eaten
fall	fell	fallen
feel	felt	felt
find	found	found
fly	flew	flown
forget	forgot	forgotten
freeze	froze	frozen
get	got	got/gotten
give	gave	given
go	went	gone
grow	grew	grown
have	had	had
hear	heard	heard
hide	hid	hidden
hit	hit	hit
hold	held	held
hurt	hurt	hurt
keep	kept	kept
know	knew	known
learn	learned/learnt	learned/learnt
leave	left	left

Verb	Past simple	Past participle
lend	lent	lent
let	let	let
lie	lay	lain
lose	lost	lost
make	made	made
mean	meant	meant
meet	met	met
pay	paid	paid
put	put	put
read	read	read
ride	rode	ridden
ring	rang	rung
run	ran	run
say	said	said
see	saw	seen
sell	sold	sold
send	sent	sent
shine	shone	shone
show	showed	shown
shut	shut	shut
sing	sang	sung
sit	sat	sat
sleep	slept	slept
smell	smelled/smelt	smelled/smelt
speak	spoke	spoken
spend	spent	spent
spill	spilled/spilt	spilled/spilt
stand	stood	stood
swim	swam	swum
take	took	taken
teach	taught	taught
tell	told	told
think	thought	thought
throw	threw	thrown
understand	understood	understood
wake	woke	woken
wear	wore	worn
win	won	won
write	wrote	written

7 LANGUAGE BANK

GRAMMAR

7.1 Comparatives

Adjective		Comparative	Rule
one-syllable adjectives some two-syllable adjectives adjectives: ending in *-e* ending in *-y* ending in a consonant + vowel + consonant	cold quiet large noisy hot	colder quieter larger noisier hotter	adjective + *-er* adjective + *-r* adjective ~~-y~~ + *-ier* double the final consonant of the adjective + *-er*
many two-syllable adjectives all longer adjectives	boring expensive	more boring more expensive	*more* + adjective
irregular adjectives	good bad far	better worse further/farther	

Use comparatives (+ *than*) to compare things and people.
My sister's ***taller than*** *me.* *A restaurant is* ***quieter than*** *a club.*

7.2 Superlatives

Adjective	Superlative	Rule
cold nice friendly big	the coldest the nicest the friendliest the biggest	*the* + adjective + *-est* *the* + adjective + *-st* *the* + adjective ~~-y~~ + *-iest* double the final consonant of the adjective + *-est*
boring interesting	the most boring the most interesting	the *most* + adjective
good bad far	the best the worst the furthest/farthest	

Use superlatives to talk about the number one thing in a group.
Maria's spelling is ***the best*** *in the class.*
Note: The spelling rules for superlatives are the same as for comparatives.

7.3 Giving Directions

Asking for directions		
Excuse me,	can you tell me the way to could you tell me the way to how can I get to	the station, please? Main Street, please?
	is there an	athletics store near here?

Giving Directions		
Go It's	straight/ahead.	
	past	the bank.
Turn	left/right	at the intersections. onto Lake Road.
It's	on	the left/right. the corner of ...

Use imperatives (e.g. Turn, Go, Stop) or You + infinitive to give directions.
Go *straight at the traffic lights.*
You turn *right at the post office.*

When speaking, check information by repeating what you hear.
The ***third*** *right?*
So, I take the next ***left****?*

Correct information by stressing the correction.
No, the ***first*** *right.*
No, the next ***right****.*

PRACTICE

7.1

A Write the comparative of the adjectives.

1 fast *faster*
2 close ______
3 big ______
4 beautiful ______
5 easy ______
6 cheap ______
7 important ______
8 happy ______
9 intelligent ______
10 late ______

B Complete the sentences with comparatives. Use the adjectives in parentheses.

1 A café is _______ _______ a nightclub. (quiet)
2 It's _______ in south India _______ in north India. (hot)
3 My brother is _______ _______ you. (funny)
4 Your job is _______ _______ _______ mine. (interesting)
5 The people here are _______ _______ the people in my town. (kind)
6 Winter this year was _______ _______ winter last year. (bad)
7 When I was young I was _______ _______ _______ I am now. (serious)
8 These earphones are _______ _______ those ones. (good)
9 The beach is _______ _______ the swimming pool. (far)
10 The museum's _______ _______ the art gallery. (closer)

7.2

A Write the superlative of the adjectives.

1 great *the greatest*
2 quiet ______
3 comfortable ______
4 close ______
5 noisy ______
6 cheap ______
7 interesting ______
8 hot ______
9 fast ______
10 crowded ______

B Complete the sentences. Use the superlative of the adjectives in the box.

~~long~~ busy big high good old deep popular

1 *The longest* bridge in the world is the Pearl Bridge in Japan. It's 6,532 feet.
2 ______________ tourist destination in Europe is Disneyland Paris. Over twelve million people visit it in a year.
3 ______________ and ______________ lake in the world is Lake Baikal, in southern Siberia, Russia. It's 5,249 feet deep and over twenty-five million years old.
4 ______________ rainforest in the world is the Amazon. It's 13,123,000 feet.
5 ______________ mountain in the U.S.A. is Mount McKinley. It's 6,194 meter. ______________ view is at the top.
6 ______________ train station in the world is Shinjuku Station in Tokyo. Over three million people use it every day, and it has over 200 stops.

7.3

A Read the conversation. Add six more missing words.

A: Excuse *me*. Can you tell me way to the beach?

B: Yes, you turn right the movie theater. Then straight for about fifteen minutes.

A: Fifty minutes?

B: No, fifteen minutes. Then turn left Menier Avenue. Go the café your right. You can see the beach straight ahead. You can't miss it.

A: Thank you very much.

GRAMMAR

8.1 Present Continuous

+	I	'm	having	a great time.
	He/She/It	's	sitting	on the balcony.
	You/We/They	're	waiting	for a train.
–	I	'm not	enjoying	this food.
	He/She/It	isn't	working	at the moment.
	You/We/They	aren't	doing	anything.

?	Am	I	leaving?	Yes,	I	am.
					you/we/they	are.
	Are	you/we/they		No,	I	'm not.
					you/we/they	aren't.
	Is	he/she/it	working?	Yes,	he/she/it	is.
				No,		isn't.

Use the present continuous to speak about something happening now/at this moment.
In speaking or in emails and letters to friends, usually use the contracted form: *I am reading.* = *I'**m** reading.*
In the negative, it is also possible to use contractions:
*He'**s not** working.* *They'**re not doing** anything.*
Don't use contractions in positive short answers: *Yes, **we are**.* NOT ~~*Yes, we're.*~~

Spelling the *-ing* Form

Most verbs + *-ing*	wait do	waiting doing
Verbs ending in *-e*, *e* + *-ing*	write take	writing taking
Most verbs ending in a consonant–vowel–consonant, double the final consonant *-ing*	swim run	swimming running

8.2 Simple Present and Present Continuous

Mario usually	wears	a jacket and tie.
Now he	's wearing	jeans and a T-shirt.

What	do	you	do?	I'm a police officer.
	are		doing?	I'm writing down your number!

Use the simple present to talk about habits or routines.
***We often watch** DVDs on Friday evenings.*

Also use it to talk about things which are always true or true for a long time.
***Eva works** downtown.*

Use the present continuous to speak about something happening at this moment.
*Sorry, I can't chat now. **I'm cooking** dinner.*

8.3 Asking For a Recommendation

Can you recommend	a good an interesting	movie? book?
I don't really like I really like I love/hate		romantic movies. sci-fi books.
What's it about? Who's in it? (for a movie)		

Giving a Recommendation

What kind of	movies books	do you like?
I think	you'd like	*Gold River.* it.
How about What about Do you know	*X-Men?* *A Tale of Two Cities?*	
It's about …		

PRACTICE

8.1

A Write the *-ing* form of the verbs.

1 live ____________
2 go ____________
3 come ____________
4 put ____________
5 feel ____________
6 make ____________
7 get ____________
8 stand ____________
9 drive ____________
10 meet ____________

B Write a phone conversation using the prompts below.

Bruno: Hi, Gerald. It's me. you / sleep? *Are you sleeping?*
Gerald: No, I'm at work. I / read.
Bruno: What / you / read?
Gerald: I / read some reports. What / you / do?
Bruno: Karl and I / play cards and listen / to music.
Gerald: So / you / not / work / today.
Bruno: Well / we / take a break.
Gerald: Uh-oh. I / talk / on the speaker phone. My boss / listen.
Bruno: you / joke?
Boss: No, he / not / joke!

8.2

A Complete the sentences with the verbs in the box in the correct form.

listen to (x2) write have (x2) call stay (x2) watch (x2) ~~wear~~ (x2)

1 I ___*wear*___ glasses, but I _*'m not wearing*_ them now.
2 I don't normally ____________ TV, but I ____________ it now.
3 We usually ____________ salad for lunch, but today we ____________ sandwiches.
4 I ____________ an email to my mother at the moment — usually I ____________ her.
5 We often ____________ classical music in the office, but today we ____________ pop.
6 He usually ____________ in a five-star hotel, but now he ____________ in a self-catering apartment.

B Complete the questions with the verbs in parentheses. Use the simple present or the present continuous.

1 ___*Do*___ you ___*study*___ English every day? (study)
2 _______ you ____________ English now? (study)
3 _______ your friend ____________ every day? (work)
4 _______ your best friend ____________ at the moment? (work)
5 _______ your teacher ____________ blue today? (wear)
6 _______ your teacher often ____________ blue? (wear)
7 _______ you usually ____________ grammar exercises alone? (do)
8 _______ you ____________ this exercise alone? (do)
9 _______ you ____________ to music a lot? (listen to)
10 _______ you ____________ to music at the moment? (listen to)

8.3

A Read the conversation and correct six mistakes.

Ines: Do you recommend a good movie?
Jim: What kind of movies you like?
Ines: Action movies, mostly, and I really like comedies.
Jim: Do you know it *Rush Hour*?
Ines: No, I don't. Who's on it?
Jim: Jackie Chan and Chris Tucker.
Ines: What it's about?
Jim: Jackie Chan is a detective, and he comes to New York to help a friend.
Ines: It sounds interesting.
Jim: I think you like it.

GRAMMAR

9.1 *Can/Can't, Have To/Don't Have To*

I/You/He/She/We/They	can	use	the bikes for free.
	can't	park	downtown
I/You/We/They	have to	pay	ten dollars.
He/She/It	has to		
I/You/We/They	don't have to	pay	anything – it's free.
He/She/It	doesn't have to		

Use *can* when something is OK/permitted.
Use *can't* when something is not OK/not permitted.
Use *have to* when something is necessary/obligatory.
Use *don't have to* when something is not necessary/obligatory.

Compare:
*You **can't** come to the party.* (You didn't get an invitation.)
*You **don't have to** come to the party.* (You got an invitation, but it's OK to stay at home.)
Make the question with *Do you have to* + infinitive, *Does he/she have to* + infinitive.

9.2 Articles

No Article		
usually use no article	before plural nouns when we speak in general	I like cats, but I don't like dogs. Sodas are bad for you.
	before cities and most countries	Shanghai is in China. I went to Russia last year.
	in some phrases	go by car/train/bus/taxi go on foot go/get home/to work/ to school be at home/work/school have breakfast/dinner/lunch

A/An		
usually use *a/an*	before singular countable nouns	It's a new car. I've got a younger brother. There's an apple in the fridge.
	before jobs	My sister's a teacher.

The		
usually use *the*	before nouns when there's only one	The President visited us last year. Could you close the door, please?
	in some phrases	in the morning/afternoon/evening on the weekend in the city/ on the right/left

9.3 Apologizing

Apologizing				**Responding**	
I'm	very really terribly so	sorry	I'm late. I missed the meeting. to be late.	+	That's OK. No problem. Don't worry about it. No, really. It's fine.
Sorry					
I'm afraid			(+ reason) I missed the bus. I didn't hear my alarm clock. I lost my keys.	–	I don't believe you. Don't let it happen again.

When you apologize, say how you feel: *feel* + adjective.
*I **feel** really **bad** about it.*

When someone apologizes too much, use *No, really. It's fine.*
A: *I'm so sorry I'm late.*
B: *Don't worry about it.*
A: *But I feel terrible …*
B: No, really. It's fine.

Use *Don't let it happen again.* only when you're really angry.

PRACTICE

9.1

A Look at signs A–F. What do they mean? Underline the correct alternative.

1 Motorcycles *don't have to/can't go* here. They *have to/don't have to* go on another road.

2 You *can/have to* park here for free. You *can't/don't have to* pay for fifteen minutes' parking.

3 Bikes *have to/can* keep left. People on foot *don't have to/can't* walk on the left.

4 You *can/can't* catch the bus here. You *have to/don't have to* wait more than ten minutes.

5 You *can't/don't have to* ride your bike. You *can/have to* get off and walk.

6 You *can/can't* take a taxi here. You *can/can't* park here.

A

B

C

D

E

F

B Complete the conversations. Use the correct form of *can/can't*, *have to/don't have to* and the verbs in parentheses.

Conversation 1

A: You [1] __have to wear__ (wear) a jacket and tie to this dinner. It's a very formal party.

B: But it's so hot!

A: Well, you [2] ________________ (wear) your light jacket.

Conversation 2

A: You [3] ________________ (come) to the meeting. It's not very important.

B: That's good because I [4] ________________ (come) – I'm too busy.

Conversation 3

A: I [5] ________________ (get) a birthday present for Sandra. I completely forgot yesterday.

B: It's OK. You [6] ________________ (get) anything. I bought her a present from both of us.

A: Thanks! What did you buy?

9.2

A Complete the text with *a/an*, *the* or no article (-).

Lucio is from [1] __-__ Italy, and he's [2] ______ doctor. He was born and grew up in [3] ______ Venice, but now he lives just outside [4] ______ small town in the south. Every day, early in [5] ______ morning, he leaves [6] ______ home and drives to his clinic downtown. He usually has [7] ______ lunch with [8] ______ colleagues and sometimes teaches in [9] ______ afternoon. On [10] ______ weekend, he often visits his brother's family. They live in the countryside, about two hours away by [11] ______ car.

B Complete the sentences with *a/an*, *the* or no article (-).

1 I think __-__ cars are safer than motorcycles.

2 I'd like ______ scooter for my birthday.

3 It's the best airline in ______ world.

4 I rode ______ bike to school when I was younger.

5 I hate ______ boats. I'm always sick!

6 I live in a small village and walk to ______ train station every day.

C Read the conversation. Find and correct six mistakes with *the*. (Two are correct.)

Pedro: Mrs. Thorpe, where can I buy the dictionary?

Mrs. T: There's the bookstore on South Street. I think they sell the dictionaries. What kind do you want?

Pedro: I need the English–Spanish dictionary for my English class. The teacher said we have to get one. The only problem is that books are very expensive here.

Mrs. T: Maybe you can borrow one. Does your school have the library?

Pedro: Yes, it does. That's the good idea. I can ask there.

9.3

A Read the conversation and correct the six mistakes.

Teacher: Can I have your homework?

Student: Oh, I really sorry. I think of left it at home.

Teacher: Don't worry it. Did you do it?

Student: Yes, of course.

Teacher: Which part did you think was difficult?

Student: I don't remember.

Teacher: Did you *really* do it?

Student: Uh … I afraid I forgot to do it. I'm feel bad about it.

Teacher: Don't left it happen again!

GRAMMAR

10.1 *Be Going To*

+	I	'm	going to	be there start leave	soon. tonight. tomorrow.
	He/She/It	's			
	You/We/They	're			
–	I	'm not			
	He/She/It	isn't			
	You/We/They	aren't			

Use *be going to* + infinitive to talk about plans and intentions.
I'm going to do my homework tonight.
With *be going to* + *go*, you don't need to repeat *go*.
She's going ~~(to go)~~ to the post office.
Use *be going to* with future time phrases, e.g. tomorrow, *soon, this weekend, next week, in two years.*
In two weeks' (time) I'm going to be on vacation!

?	Am Is Are	I he/she/it you/we/they	going to	finish today?	+	Yes,	I	am.
							he/she/it	is.
							we/you/they	are.
					–	No,	I	'm not.
							he/she/it	isn't.
							we/you/they	aren't.

Would Like To

+	I/You/ He/She/It/ We/They	would 'd	like to	go. eat.
–		wouldn't		

Use *I'd like to* + infinitive to talk about what you want to do.
It's hot. I'd like to go for a swim.
You can also use *want to* + infinitive for the same idea.
I want to go to the gym.
Note: *I'd like to* is more polite than *I want*.

?	Would	I/you/he/she/it/we/they	like to	drink some tea?	+	Yes,	I/you/he/she/it/we/they	would.
					–	No,		wouldn't.

10.2 *Will/Might (Not)/Won't*

+	I/You/ He/She/It/ We/They	'll (will)	be cold. come.
		might	
–		might not	
		won't (will not)	

Use *will* + infinitive and *won't* + infinitive to predict the future when you are sure about something.
Your book will be here tomorrow. *I'm sure he won't come.*
Use *might* + infinitive to predict the future if you are not sure.
I might see Yuki tonight. (= it's possible, but I'm not sure)
It is also possible to use *will, might, might not* and *won't* with *there*.
I think there will be a lot of people at the party.

?	Will	I/you/he/she/it/we/they	win?	+	Yes,	I/you/he/she/it/we/they	will.
				–	No,		won't.

10.3 Making Suggestions

How about	going	to a concert?
Why don't you/we Should we	watch	a movie?
Let's	cook	something.

Use *How/What* about + infinitive + *-ing* in questions. *What about having lunch now?*
Use *Why don't* + subject + infinitive in questions. *Why don't we watch a movie?*
Use *Should we* + infinitive in questions. *Should we watch a movie?*
Use *Let's* + infinitive in positive sentences. *Let's go to the beach.*

Responding To Suggestions

+	Cool/Great! (That) sounds interesting/good. I'd like to go. (That's a) good idea.
–	I don't (really) feel like doing that/going. That/It doesn't sound very good. No thanks.

PRACTICE

10.1

A Complete the sentences with the correct form of *be going to*. Use the verbs in parentheses.

1 I ________________ the movie theater tonight. (go)
2 We ________________ an apartment next week. (look at)
3 ________________ ready in time? (you / be)
4 We ________________. (not wait)
5 They ________________ a new car. (buy)
6 When ________________ to Rome? (Steve / go)

B Underline the correct alternative.

1 I *'d like to go/'m going* to the theater, but there are no more tickets.
2 I *'d like to go/'m going* to a concert tonight. I have the tickets here.
3 We *'d like to/'re going* to buy a bigger apartment, but we don't have enough money.
4 I *'d like to/'m going* to take a trip to Zurich tomorrow. My train leaves at 7 a.m.

C Complete the sentences with the words in the box.

like (x2)   don't   'd (x2)   would (x2)   want

A: Would you [1]_______ to go to the party?
B: Yes, I [2]_______, but I have too much work.
A: Would you [3]_______ to dance?
B: No, thanks. I [4]_______ like to sit down for a minute!
A: What [5]_______ you like to do on your birthday tomorrow?
B: I don't know, I [6]_______ want to think about it. I feel quite old!
A: Do you [7]_______ to have dinner with me tonight?
B I [8]_______ love to!

10.2

A Complete the conversation with *'ll, will, won't* or *might*.

A: Oh, no. The dog ran away again!
B: Don't worry — he [1]_______ come back.
A: Are you sure he [2]_______?
B: OK, he [3]_______ not come back today — that's possible. But I'm sure he [4]_______ come back tomorrow.
A I don't believe you! He [5]_______ come back. We [6]_______ never see him again — I'm sure.
B: Oh, look … Here he is now!

B Circle the two correct alternatives.

1 He *will / won't / might* eat it – I'm sure!
2 It *might / 'll / won't* rain, so bring an umbrella.
3 There *might not / won't / might* be enough time to watch all of the movie, so let's not start.
4 I *might not / 'll / won't* go by train. It's quicker by car.
5 She *might / won't / 'll* call tomorrow, so please take a message.
6 We *might / 'll / won't* be late, so don't wait for us.

10.3

A Put the words from the box in the correct places in the conversation.

~~about~~   good   idea   sound   don't   like   have   we

Sam: I'm tired. How *about* taking a break now?

Jim: I don't feel stopping.

Sam: Oh, come on! Let's a coffee.

Jim: Why you make some coffee? I'll go on working.

Sam: That's a good. Should have a sandwich?

Jim: No, thanks, I want to finish this.

Sam: OK. You work, I'll have lunch.

Jim: That doesn't good.

Sam: Really? Sounds to me.

GRAMMAR

11.1 *Should/Shouldn't*

+	I/you/he/she/it/we/they	should	sleep.
			drink lots of water.
–		shouldn't	take antibiotics.
			eat late at night.

?	Should	I/you/he/she/it/we/they	stay	inside?	Yes,	I/you/he/she/it/we/they	should.
					No,		shouldn't.

Use *should* + infinitive to give advice.
*You **should** take an aspirin.*
Use *should* to recommend something.
*You **should** see that movie.*
Use *have to* not *should* when something is necessary.
*You **have to** drive on the right.* NOT ~~*You should drive on the right.*~~
Note: *You **should try** this soup.* NOT ~~*You should to try this soup.*~~

11.2 Adverbs

	Adjective	**Adverb**
Most adjectives, add *-ly*	bad loud careful	badly loudly carefully
Adjectives ending in *-y*, ~~*-y*~~ + *-ily*	easy angry	easily angrily
Adjectives ending in *-le*, change to *-ly*	terrible	terribly
Irregular adverbs	good fast hard (= difficult) early late	well fast NOT ~~fastly~~ hard NOT ~~hardly~~ early late

Use adverbs of manner to say how you do something. *I can swim **well**. She spoke **quietly**.*
Use adverbs of time to say when you did something. *I went to bed **early**. She had lunch **late**.*
Use adverbs with verbs. *He **drives badly**.*
Use adjectives with nouns. *He's a **bad driver**.*
With *be* and *feel*, use adjectives. *The film **was terrible**. I **feel terrible**.*
Adverbs usually go after the verb. *I **arrived** early.*
OR after the verb phrase. *I **started work** early. She **drove her car** quickly.*
OR at the end of a sentence or phrase. *I **arrived at work** early. She **drove to the stores** quickly.*

11.3 Offering To Help

Problems	**Offers**		**Thanking**	**Responses**
I can't lift this case. It's hot in here.	I'll Let me	do it. try.	Thank you very much. Thanks a lot. Thanks so/very much. That's kind of you.	You're welcome. No problem. That's OK.
	Should I	do it? try?		

Use *I'll* (NOT ~~*I will*~~), *Let me* and *Should I* + infinitive to offer help.

PRACTICE

11.1

A Complete questions 1–6. Then match them with replies a)–f).

1 I don't have much time. ___*Should I*___ send Kirsten an email? *d)*

2 Ben doesn't like the color of his cell phone. __________ get a new one?

3 Look at my hair – it's a mess! __________ get a haircut?

4 Some students never say anything in class. __________ speak more?

5 My daughter wants to travel in South America. __________ learn Spanish?

6 There are so many words we don't know. __________ buy an electronic dictionary?

a) Yes, you should. It's too long.

b) Yes, they should. It's important to practice.

c) No, he shouldn't. The old one is fine.

d) No, you shouldn't. Call her – it's quicker.

e) Yes, she should if she has enough time.

f) Yes, you should get an English–English one.

B Complete the sentences with *should* or *shouldn't* and a verb from the box.

get go take stay try wear change

1 My camera's very old. I ___*should get*___ a new one.

2 You __________ this drink. It's delicious!

3 Do you think I __________ my money here or at the airport?

4 You __________ black. I think it doesn't look good on you – sorry!

5 They __________ by taxi. It's too expensive.

6 She looks tired. She __________ a vacation.

7 We __________ out in the sun too long. We'll get sunburned.

11.2

A Complete the sentences. Use the adjective or adverb form of the words in parentheses.

1 The teacher was very __________. She spoke to the students __________. (angry)

2 She dances __________. She's such a __________ dancer. (beautiful)

3 I passed the exam __________. It was __________. (easy)

4 Shhh – be __________. The baby's sleeping. We have to talk __________. (quiet)

5 She's a __________ teacher. She teaches __________. (good)

6 I sing __________. I'm a __________ singer. (terrible)

B Complete the story. Use the adverb forms of the adjectives in the box.

~~early~~ late easy quick angry slow

The other morning, I woke up [1]___*early*___ because the neighbors were shouting [2]__________. I didn't want to stay at home, so I made some breakfast [3]__________ and ran out of the door to work. I forgot to take an umbrella, and it started raining, so I got very wet. I got to the station at 7:50 and caught the eight o'clock train [4]__________. I was surprised when I looked around because the train was empty. Because of the rain, the train went very [5]__________, so I arrived at the office [6]__________. There was no one there. Then I realized that it was Sunday, and I didn't have to work!

11.3

A Complete the six conversations below. Use the verbs in parentheses to help.

Conversation 1

A: I can't find the information anywhere.

B: I' _______ _______ on the computer. (check)

Conversation 2

A: I don't understand this homework.

B: _______ me _______ a look. (have)

Conversation 3

A: My hands are full. I can't carry all these things.

B: _______ I _______ something for you? (carry)

Conversation 4

A: The radio is too loud.

B: _______ I _______ it down? (turn)

Conversation 5

A: The top on this bottle is too tight.

B: _______ me try to _______ it. (open)

Conversation 6

A: I haven't got any change for the parking machine.

B: No problem. I _______ _______. (pay)

GRAMMAR

12.1 Present Perfect

+	I/You/We/They	've	climbed watched tried slept	Mount Everest. the sun rise. milk in tea. outside.
	He/She/It	's		
–	I/You/We/They	haven't		
	He/She/It	hasn't		

Make the present perfect with *have/has* + past participle.
Use the present perfect to talk about past experiences in your life.
Usually you don't know or say when exactly these things happened.
For regular verbs, the past participles are the same as the simple past:
verb + *-ed*, *-d* or ~~*y*~~ *-ied*.
*miss – **missed** – **missed**, move – **moved** – **moved**, study – **studied** – **studied***
For irregular verbs, look at the list on page 127.

?	Have	I/you/we/they	(ever) swum	in a river?	Yes, No,	I/you/we/they	have. haven't.
	Has	he/she/it			Yes, No,	he/she/it	has. hasn't.

ever = "in your life". We often use it for more unusual experiences.
*Have you **ever** met a famous person?* (Compare to *Have you met my husband?*)
In the negative you can use *never*. *I've **never** played golf.*

Go has two past participles: *been* and *gone*:

*She **went to** India.* = *She went there and she's there now.*

*She's **been** to India.* = *She went there in the past and she came back.*

12.2 Present Perfect and Simple Past

Use the present perfect to talk about past experiences in your life. You don't say exactly *when*.
*I've **been** to Egypt. I've **seen** the Great Pyramid.*
Use the simple past if you say when something happened.
*I **went** to Egypt three years ago. I **saw** the Great Pyramid when I **was** there.*
When speaking, it is possible to start a conversation by asking a question in the present perfect and then asking about more details in the simple past.
***A: Have** you **ever been** to Egypt?*
***B:** Yes, I have. I **went** there three years ago.*
***A: Did** you **like** it?*
***B:** Yes, it **was** great!*

*I've **seen** the Great Pyramid.*

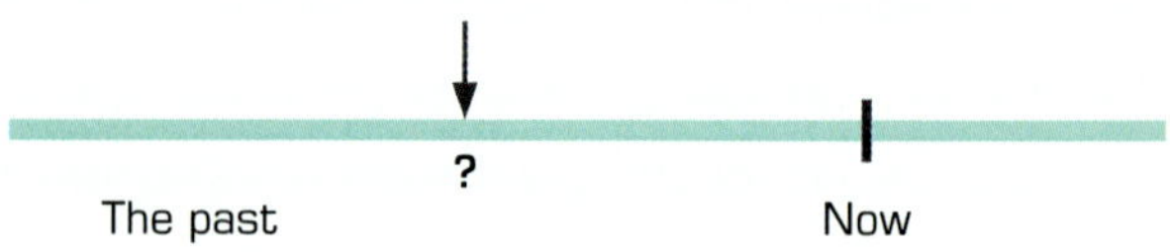

*I **went** to Egypt in May 2014.*

12.3 Calling

Calling a friend	Hi, Philippe. It's Debbie. Is Lise there?
Calling a business	Hello. This is Carla Rimini. Could I speak to Harry Jones, please?
Calling back	Could you call/ring (me) back? Just ask him/her to call/ring me. I'll call you back.
Leaving/taking a message	Could I leave a message for him/her? Just a moment. Let me get a pen. Let me check that.

Use *It's* + name (informal) or *This is* + name (formal) NOT ~~*I am*~~.
*Hello, **this is** Ali Hassan.*

PRACTICE

12.1

A Write sentences in the present perfect.

1 you / ever / eat / Japanese food?
2 I / eat / Thai food two or three times
3 We / never / sleep / in a four-star hotel before
4 They / drive / across Europe many times
5 he / ever / go / to the U.K.?
6 Lise / have / three husbands
7 I / never / lose / my cell phone
8 She / learn / Arabic, Spanish and Chinese
9 you / ever / climb / a volcano?
10 My parents / never / use / a tablet

B Correct ten mistakes in the conversation.

A: You have ever been to Australia?
B: No, I have. And you?
A: Yes, I've.
B: And have you gone to China, too?
A: No, but I been to Korea.
B: You've travel to many countries in your life …
A: Yes, I has. I've meeted a lot of people, and I've try a lot of interesting food.
B: But you haven't learn to speak English perfectly!
A: Not yet …

12.2

A Read the email and underline the correct alternatives.

To

Hi Renata,

Thanks for the email. Lucky you … going to Italy next month! You asked me about Venice. Yes, [1] I *'ve been/went* there. [2] I *'ve been/went* there for a long weekend last year. [3] It *has been/was* beautiful. [4] I *'ve loved/loved* all the bridges and old squares. [5] I *'ve also visited/also visited* Rome. [6] We *have been/were* there in 2006. It's busier than Venice, but I know you like old buildings and churches, so maybe you'd like Rome better. [7] I *'ve never traveled/never traveled* in the Italian countryside, but my friend Emily [8] *has driven/drove* around the south, and she says it's lovely but very hot at that time of year. Anyway, I'm sure you'll have a great time! Send me some photos.

Simone

B Complete the sentences using the prompts in parentheses.

1 ___Have you seen___ *Gravity*? (you / see)
Yes, I ___saw___ it a few months ago.

2 ____________ Sarah? (you / meet)
Yes, we _______ last year.

3 ____________ to Spain? (Lea / go)
Yes, she _______ there last month, and she's going to stay for a year.

4 ____________ an accident on his motorcycle? (Paolo / ever have)
Yes, he _______ a small accident a month ago.

5 ____________ Anna Karenina? (you / read)
Yes, I _______ it in college.

6 ____________ school? (your children / finish)
Yes, they _______ a long time ago.

12.3

A Complete Judy's sentences.

Judy	Dan
1 Hi, Dan. _______ Judy.	b
2 Is Megan _______?	
3 Could I leave a _______ for her?	
4 Dan, it's important!	
5 Could you ask her to _______ me?	
6 No. It's 335-579-3939.	

B Complete the conversation with the correct response from Dan.

a) A message … ? Oh, I can't find a pen. Could you call me back?
b) Oh, hi Judy.
c) Does she have your number?
d) Let me just look … OK, I've got one.
e) OK, got it. I'll tell her.

PHOTO BANK

Lesson 8.2 JOBS

1 **A** Match the jobs with the pictures.

B Complete the gaps with *a* or *an*.

1 lawyer
2 teacher
3 accountant
4 police officer
5 engineer
6 politician
7 hairdresser
8 sales clerk
9 chef
10 doctor
11 receptionist
12 nurse
13 personal assistant (PA)
14 waiter/waitress
15 athlete
16 actor/actress
17 businessman/ businesswoman

A

B

C

D

E

F

G

H

I

Lesson 8.5 APPEARANCE

A Oprah Winfrey

B Taylor Swift

C Quentin Tarantino

D Michelle Yeoh

E Benedict Cumberbatch

F Lionel Messi

Lesson 8.2 APPEARANCE AND CLOTHES

1 A Look at the photos and find an example for each word or phrase in the box.

tall short slim* overweight**
bald straight hair curly hair long hair
short hair medium build

*also use *thin*, but *slim* is more positive
***fat* is also possible, but is very negative

B Match the names of the clothes with the letters A—N.

1 socks
2 jeans
3 suit
4 jacket
5 pants
6 shirt
7 tie
8 top
9 skirt
10 sweater
11 shorts
12 dress
13 T-shirt
14 coat

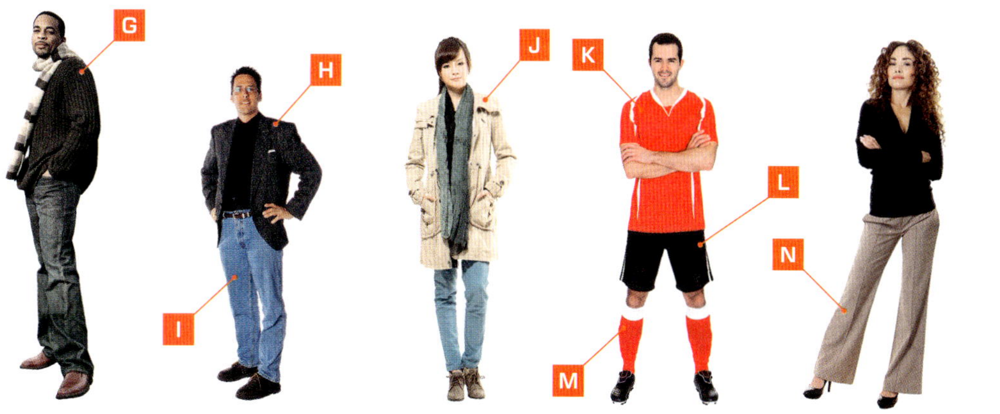

2 Write which words are adjectives (adj), uncountable nouns (U), countable singular nouns (C sing), countable plural nouns (C pl).

Lesson 11.1 BODY PARTS

1 Match the names of the body parts with the photos.

1 arm
2 back
3 ear
4 eye
5 face
6 finger
7 foot
8 hand
9 head
10 knee
11 leg
12 elbow
13 neck
14 nose
15 shoulder
16 mouth
17 thumb
18 toe

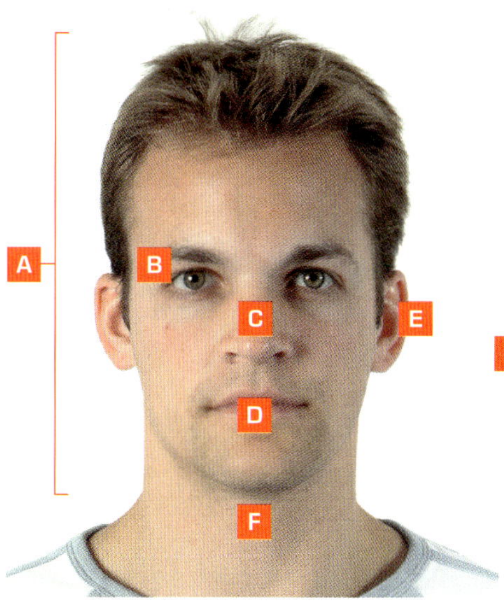

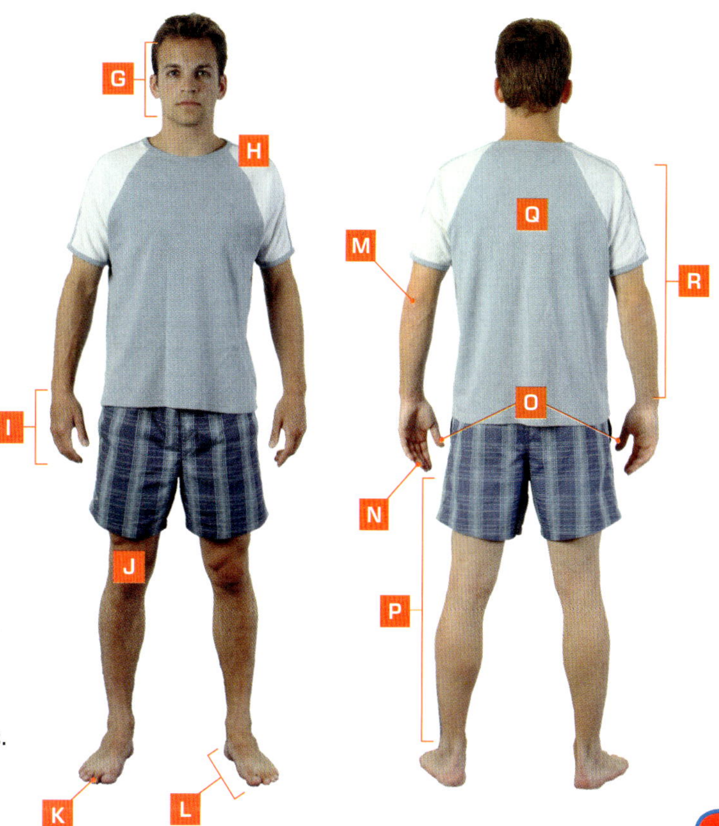

2 What do you have one, two, eight and ten of? Make a list.
1 = head, face, nose …

Lesson 9.2 TRANSPORTATION

1 Match the types of the transportation with the pictures.

1 a bike
2 a boat
3 a bus
4 a car
5 a ferry
6 a horse
7 a truck
8 a motorcycle
9 a plane
10 a scooter
11 a ship
12 a taxi
13 a train
14 a tram
15 a subway train
16 a van

2 Put the words into the transportation groups.

a bike

land

sea

air

Lesson 10.2

2 B Student B

How to be safe in an earthquake

Stay inside. Get under a strong table or desk and hold onto the furniture. Stay away from windows and mirrors because they might break. Stay away from bookshelves, too. They might fall on you. If you are in bed, stay there and put a pillow over your head. Do not run outside. A building might fall on you. If you're in a car, drive away from buildings, bridges and trees and stay in your car. Wait until the end of the earthquake before you leave your car.

What to do if you get lost in a forest

First, stay calm, stay in one place and make a plan. A plan will help you to feel better. Build a simple shelter and make a fire so you can get warm and feel safer as well. Also remember that water is the most important thing, so look for water, but don't move far away from your starting place or you might get more lost. And don't be surprised about your cell phone – in a forest a cell phone often won't work because there's no signal.

Lesson 11.2

5 Student B

A **Read this list of ways of reducing stress. Put a check (✓) for good ideas and an X for bad ideas.**

Have a technology-free hour every day. No computers, tablets or phones.

Don't sleep with your phone.

Do a five-minute meditation every day.

Take a short nap after lunch – twenty minutes a day.

Eat meat only once day a week.

Spend more time with friends.

Do exercise or play sports for one hour a day.

Watch comedy movies.

B **Work with other Student Bs and compare your ideas. Choose the top three good ideas.**

A: Which ideas do you think are good?

C **Work with a Student A and tell each other your top three ideas. Choose the best three ideas.**

A: What are your top ideas?
B: Well, first I think you should/shouldn't …

D **Work with all the other students and choose the best three ideas.**

Lesson 9.1

6 A Student C

Lesson 7.3

5 D Student A: Check this information. Read it to Student B.

1 Kris lives on Madison Drive.

2 His house is five minutes from here.

3 It's on the left.

Now listen to Student B. Use the information below to correct any mistakes.

1 The Castle's on Seventh Street.

2 It's on the right.

3 Take the number nine bus.

Lesson 12.3

6 A Student A: Situation 1. You work in customer services for the credit card company. When the customer calls, ask three questions (e.g. "Where did you lose it?"). Finally, tell them to call a different number (It's ____________).

B Situation 2. Your friend calls and has missed the last train. You can't go and pick him/her up. Suggest alternatives: taxi, bus, walking.

Lesson 9.1

6 A Student B

Lesson 7.3

5 D Student B: Listen to Student A. Use the information below to correct any mistakes.

1 Kris lives on Pennsylvania Avenue.

2 His house is ten minutes from here.

3 It's on the right.

Now check this information. Read it to Student A.

1 The African Art's on Independence Avenue.

2 It's on the left.

3 Take the number five bus.

Lesson 7.3

4 Student B: You want to go to the Washington Monument and you want to find the White House. Ask Student A for directions.

Write directions for the American Indian Museum, a famous historical museum (U on the map) and Smithsonian Metro Station (M on the map). Then cover the directions and answer Student A's question.

Lesson 11.3

6 B Student B

Problem 1

I'm really tired.

Problem 2

I can't see the whiteboard.
It's too dark in here.

Problem 3

I'm really thirsty, but I don't have any money for a coffee.

Lesson 8.1

6 Student A: Ask and answer questions to compare your picture with Student B's. Don't look at Student B's picture. Find eight differences in the pictures.

What's Mike doing? What's he wearing?

Lesson 8.1

6 Student B: Ask and answer questions to compare your picture with Student A's. Don't look at Student A's picture. Find eight differences in the pictures.

What's Mike doing? What's he wearing?

Lesson 10.2

2 B Student A

How to stay safe near lightning

First, get down the hill — high places are dangerous. Don't stand under trees because lightning often hits trees. In the open field, don't lie down on the ground. Put your feet together, then crouch down. Don't put your hands on the ground. Stay away from metal – never use a cell phone or an umbrella when there is lightning near you. You'll be safe inside your car, if you can get to it — lightning goes around cars. But don't touch anything metal in the car.

What to do if you get stung by a bee

First, move away from the other bees — they might sting you, too. When a bee stings you, don't pinch the stinger with your fingers or it will get worse. Use a credit card and push the stinger out. Then wash your arm with soap and water and raise it above your heart for a short time. You can put an ice pack on your arm and also take some painkillers. If you still have problems, go see your doctor.

Lesson 8.1

2 D

The first writer is probably a woman in her thirties.

The second writer is probably a man in his twenties.

Lesson 11.3

6 B Student A

Problem 1

It's cold in here.

Problem 2

This computer doesn't work.

Problem 3

It's too noisy. The music's too loud, and I can't concentrate.

Lesson 12.3

5 D Student A: Work with other Student As. Draw a line between the numbers where you think a pause is good. Practice saying the numbers.

Sam	
Ahmed	582303166
Nina	
Chen	366214927
Simon	
Fatima	0445567823901
Yuko	
Penny	01285955427

E Work in pairs. Student A: Ask Student B for the telephone numbers. Answer Student B's questions.

A: What's Sam's phone number?
B: It's … What's Ahmed's phone number?
A: It's …

Lesson 7.3

4 Student A: Write directions for the Canadian Embassy. (G on the map) and to the Smithsonian Museum (on the map). Then cover your directions and answer Student B's question.

You want to go to the American Indian Museum and you want to find the National Gallery of Art. Ask Student B for directions.

Lesson 11.2

5 Student A

A Read this list of ways of reducing stress. Put a check (✓) for good ideas and an X for bad ideas.

Turn off your phone for one hour a day.

Sleep nine hours a night.

Take a karate class.

Take a five-minute break from work every hour.

Don't drink coffee.

Do something you enjoy, e.g. singing, twice a week.

Play video games.

Paint your walls green – it's a relaxing color.

B Work with other Student As and compare your ideas. Choose the top three good ideas.

A: Which ideas do you think are good?

C Work in pairs with a Student B and tell each other your top three ideas. Choose the best three ideas.

A: What are your top ideas?
B: Well, first I think you should/shouldn't …

D Work with all the other students and choose the best three ideas.

Lesson 12.3

5 D Student B: Work with other Student Bs. Draw a line between the numbers where you think a pause is good. Practice saying the numbers.

Sam	92404711
Ahmed	
Nina	788630154
Chen	
Simon	044633739912
Fatima	
Yuko	00442816933
Penny	

E Work in pairs. Student B: Answer Student A's questions. Ask Student A for the telephone numbers.

A: What's Sam's phone number?
B: It's … What's Ahmed's phone number?
A: It's …

Lesson 12.3

6 A Student B: Situation 1. You've lost your credit card. Call the credit card company and report the lost card.

B Situation 2. You missed the last train. You lost your cell phone and almost all your money, so you call your friend from a phone booth. First, ask him/her to call you back and give the phone number (It's ____________). When he/she calls back, ask him/her to come and get you.

Lesson 9.1

6 A Student A

Unit 7 Recording S7.2

M = Man W = Woman

M: So, on vacation, how do you like to travel? By plane, train or car?
W: Well, I don't like airports, so put train. I hate traveling by car.
M: Me, too. I put "plane" because, well, planes are faster than trains.
W: Not always! OK, number two. It says "I like staying in a) a hotel, b) a self-catering apartment or c) a tent".
M: Forget the tent! Uh. In an apartment. And you?
W: In a hotel.
M: Really? A hotel's more expensive than an apartment!
W: Yeah, but it's more comfortable. Hmm … next question. Do you prefer relaxing on a beach, doing something athletic or going sightseeing?
M: What does it mean … something athletic?
W: Uh … playing tennis or maybe golf.
M: No, thank you! Not on vacation. But I hate staying on the beach all day. Boring!
W: OK – there's one we answered the same. So we agree about that.
M: Yeah, sightseeing's definitely more interesting than the beach!
W: Right. When do you like going on vacation: In the spring, summer or winter?
M: In spring – I never go on vacation in winter, but I don't really like very hot weather. Tourist places are more crowded in summer.
W: True. But the weather's better. Summer's hotter than spring. I love hot weather.
M: Well, we don't agree there. Anyway, next question. What do you like eating: Local dishes, the food you usually eat, or fast food?
W: Local dishes, I think. You?
M: Definitely!
W: Hmm, interesting. Next … At night I like going for a walk, going to a restaurant or going to a club.
M: Uh, going to a restaurant.
W: Oh, good. Me, too. I don't like noisy places.
M: Yes, I agree. Restaurants are quieter … more relaxing. But I like going for a walk too, sometimes, so I'm not sure. OK, let's say "going to a restaurant".
W: And the last question … how long is your ideal vacation?
M: Three months.
W: You can't have three months! The answer is a weekend, a week or a month.
M: OK, a month then.
W: Me, too!
M: Maybe we can travel together …

Unit 7 Recording S7.5

I = Interviewer J = Jeff

I: So Jeff, a few questions about the trip. What was the coldest place you visited?
J: The coldest place was in the mountains in Kyrgyzstan. There was lots of snow, too.
I: Really? And what was the hottest place?
J: Well, it was Turpan, China. I think it was over one hundred and twenty-two degrees Fahrenheit.
I: Oh, was it? And what was the friendliest place?
J: That's an impossible question. I can't say. We met so many fantastic people. I think Iran; the people there were so kind. Perhaps that was my biggest surprise.
I: OK. What was the longest you traveled in one day?
J: One day we traveled about ninety-three miles in Western China. That was a long day!
I: Very! So, what was the most beautiful building you saw?
J: There were some great ones in all of the countries, but my favorite building was the Bibi-Khanym Mosque in Uzbekistan. I think it's the most beautiful building in the world.
I: Wow. So, what was the most amazing experience of the journey?
J: Arriving in Istanbul after seven thousand five hundred miles. A-ma-a-a-zing!

Unit 7 Recording S7.7

W = Woman M = Man

Conversation 1

W: Excuse me.
M: Yes.
W: Can you tell me how to get to the Air and Space Museum?
M: Yeah. You go straight on this pedestrian street. And, can you see those sculptures?
W: Yes.
M: Well turn right at the corner after the Sculpture Garden.
W: Turn right?
M: Yes. Then you go past some grass, that's the middle of The National Mall, and you'll arrive at the intersection of 7th street and Jefferson Drive. On your right, you'll see a large cylindrical building. That's the Hirshhorm Museum. You can't miss it.
W: OK.
M: There are always a lot of walking tours there. Turn left on Jefferson Drive, and it will be on your right side with a large pointed silver sculpture on top.
W: Thanks. So, it's at the corner after the Sculpture Garden and then past some grass, and then it's on the left, on Jeff … ?
M: Jefferson Drive.
W: Jefferson Drive. Right, thanks.
M: No problem.

Conversation 2

W: Excuse me. Is The Capitol near here?
M: Uh. Let me think. Yes, the Capitol is at one end of The National Mall. But it's not very close.
W: Can you tell me how to get there?
M: I think the easiest way is … uh … OK, go straight here for three blocks. Then turn left. The name of the street is 3rd Street.
W: 3rd Street.
M: Yes, and keep walking. Go past the East Building of the National Gallery of Art on the left. The next street is a diagonal. Go left at the corner. I think it's Pennsylvania Avenue.
W: Pennsylvania Avenue. OK.
M: Go straight for a short block. Then turn left on 1st Street. The Capitol is on the right. You can't miss it. It's really big.
W: Can I just check the first part? So straight here for three blocks, then turn right after the East Building of the National Gallery of Art.
M: No, turn left.
W: Turn left and after a short block go left onto 1st.
M: Yes.
W: Uh … can you repeat the last part?
M: OK, at the East Building of the National Gallery of Art go left.
W: OK, and then the Capitol is on the right.
M: Yes.
W: How far away is it?
M: Oh, about twenty minutes from here.
W: Thanks very much.
M: You're welcome.

Unit 7 Recording S7.11

OK, so this place is in Massachusetts. Boston is in the east of Massachusetts and most tourists don't know about it. It's called *The Cradle of Liberty*, which derives from its role in the American Revolution. There are lots of boats and historical and interesting places. There are lots of good restaurants and cafés next to the water. I like it because I can sit there, have a coffee and watch people on the boats or by the water. Boston is a lovely place in the daytime or at night. And it's one of the best places to take pictures. You can take a picture of the sailboats, the water or the people. Some of the people are very interesting. I think the best time to take a picture is in the early morning or in the early evening because it's really quiet and the light is beautiful.

Unit 8 Recording S8.3

Conversation 1

W = Woman M = Man

W: Amazing.
M: What are you reading?
W: Look at this.
M: Who are they? Oh, that's Christian Bale, yeah?
W: Yup, in one of the Batman films. And this?
M: I don't know.
W: It's the same actor. Christian Bale. All three of these.
M: Wow, that is amazing. He's so … different. He's a lot bigger here, and he has glasses.
W: Yeah, and longer hair.
M: Which movie is that from?
W: *American Hustle*.
M: Oh yeah, I remember now. And this one?
W: That's him too, in *The Machinist*. He lost almost sixty-four pounds for that movie.
M: Unbelievable. How did he do it?
W: Um, let me see. Uh. He just had one apple and a cup of coffee every day. And water. And he ran a lot.
M: That's not very healthy …
W: Then he put on one hundred and ten pounds for the next Batman film.
M: Crazy.
W: I think he's great, though. He always changes his appearance for each film.
M: A lot of actors do that.
W: Yeah, that's what this article is about. Look at these.
M: That's uh, don't tell me, don't tell me … uh … I saw the movie … ah, *Bridget Jones's Diary*. I liked it. Oh … what's her name?
W: Renée Zellweger.
M: That's right. That's an old movie, and how old is she now?
W: In her forties, I think. But she was in her early thirties when she was in Bridget Jones.
M: I think she looks nice.
W: Yeah, and look. This is her, too.
M: Wow!
W: This is her in *Leatherheads*. It came out in 2008.
M: How did she do that?
W: Uh … it says she put on twenty-two pounds for Bridget Jones. Pizza, chocolate, doughnuts. And then she lost it. But she doesn't look so different.
M: No, just thinner, really. And she's wearing black in this picture, so she looks thinner. Her face is the same. I actually think she looks better like this, in Bridget Jones.
W: I know what you mean. Oh, this is interesting.
M: What?
W: Zellweger ate doughnuts to put on weight. And what's the first thing Christian Bale ate when he wanted to put on weight?
M: Doughnuts?
W: Yup. Now I'm hungry.

Unit 8 Recording S8.4

W = Woman M = Man

Conversation 1

W: Is it a man or a woman?
M: A woman.
W: What does she look like?
M: I think she's in her thirties. She has straight blond hair. She's a little overweight. She's reading something.
W: Oh, it's Renée Zellweger in …

Conversation 2

W: Is it a man or a woman?
M: A man.
W: What does he look like?
M: He has short brown hair. He's very thin.
W: Oh, I know … it's Christian Bale in …

Unit 8 Recording S8.7

Conversation 1

P = Phil H = Harry

H: … and we had a great time. Hey, Phil.
P: Yeah?
H: I have a long train journey next week. I'm off to Edinburgh. Can you recommend a good movie? For the journey?
P: Uh … let me think. What kind of movies do you like?
H: Well, action movies and uh … dramas, that kind of thing.
P: Uh … How about *Gravity*?
H: Oh, that movie with uh … oh, who's in it?
P: Sandra Bullock and George Clooney. It's very good.
H: Mmm. I don't really like sci-fi movies.
P: I don't either, but this one is good … it has a lot of drama, and the acting is great. Sandra Bullock is amazing.
H: What's it about? It's two astronauts, right?
P: Yes, it's about two astronauts, and they have an accident in space, and they try to get back home. That's all. But it's fantastic. The photography is great. I think you'd like it.
H: OK. Sounds good. Thanks.
P: No problem.

Conversation 2

C = Clara R = Rachel

R: Hey, Clara. Can you recommend a good movie?
C: At home or at the movie theater?
R: At home.
C: What kind of movies do you like?
R: Uh, different kinds, uh, comedies, dramas, romantic movies …
C: Do you want a new movie?
R: No, it can be new or old.
C: What about *Let the Right One In*? It's a kind of love story.
R: Mmm. I saw that on TV last year. It's more of a horror movie. I don't really like horror movies.
C: Let me think … Do you know *Happy-Go-Lucky*?
R: No, I don't think so.
C: Well, it's a comedy but also a drama. I really liked it. And I laughed a lot.
R: What's it about?
C: Uh, it's about a teacher in London. Her name's Poppy; she's really kind to everyone, and she's always happy. It's about her life. Uh … she takes driving lessons, and there are problems at her school, and … anyway, I think you'd like it.
R: Sounds good. Who's in it?
C: I don't know their names. But the actress playing Poppy is fantastic.
R: OK. Thanks. I'll try it.

Unit 8 Recording S8.11

W = Woman M = Man

W: Can I ask you a few questions?
M: Sure.
W: Do you often go to music festivals?
M: Oh, yes. I love festivals, not just music, but all types. I started going to music festivals when I was very young.
W: Really? What kind of festivals do you like?
M: I like all kinds.
W: For example?
M: Rock festivals, folk festivals, theater, literature …
W: Oh, so you really do like all kinds of festivals. Do you think festivals are very different now?
M: Compared to years ago? Oh, yes.
W: How are they different?
M: Well, lots of ways.
W: OK, I'll say something about festivals, you tell me how it's different now.
M: OK.
W: Price?
M: More expensive. Much more expensive.
W: OK. What about, uh, security?
M: Well, security is much better now. Sometimes it's too good! They check your bag when you go in, and it takes a long time.
W: Mmm.
M: And there are more security people around. But it feels safer at these big festivals now.
W: That's interesting. Uh … how about what people wear? You know, fashion at festivals.
M: Oh, I don't know. It depends on the festival.
W: That's OK. One more thing: Technology.
M: Oh, that's a big change. Years ago you couldn't always get information on the internet. Or buy tickets.
W: Wow. I can't imagine that.
M: And a simple thing like cell phones. Not everybody had one. So, when you wanted to find your friend at a big festival, it was really difficult.
W: That's really interesting. Thanks for your time.
M: No problem!

Unit 9 Recording S9.3

W = Woman M = Man

W: We never travel long distance. It's too expensive. And I hate traveling by plane.
M: Really? What about trains or cars?
W: Well, I like traveling by train, and I love going by car because you can stop anywhere. But they're all too expensive now.
M: Mmmm … not really. You can travel for free.
W: Sure, if you go by bike or on foot.
M: No. Last year, I was on vacation in the U.S., and I drove across the country for free.
W: How?
M: I had a Driveaway car.
W: A driveway?
M: No, drive-A-way. Driveaway. It's a company.
W: How does it work?
M: Well, there was a family in New York, and they wanted to go to Los Angeles, but they didn't want to drive there. It's more than three thousand miles. But they needed their car in Los Angeles. So they went by plane, and I drove their car to Los Angeles, to their hotel downtown. I had a week to get there. I stopped in the Grand Canyon on the way. It was the best journey ever – I love driving, and I love cars.
W: That's amazing. And it's free?
M: Yeah, I just paid for gas.
W: And did you have time to stop?
M: I had a week, so I stopped in a few places. St. Louis – I have friends there – the Grand Canyon.
W: That sounds great.
M: It was wonderful. Not good for everybody. You can't choose the date or the place you want to go. But good for me.
W: Yeah … and is that the longest journey? The longest you traveled for free?
M: Uh, let me think. I once traveled about eight thousand seven hundred miles for free … by ship. I was in Mombasa.
W: Where's that?
M: It's a city in Kenya.
W: And?
M: Well, it has a lot of big container ships. I found a ship that went to Indonesia.
W: For free?
M: Well, I worked on the ship.
W: Oh, that sounds hard.
M: Not really. Well, long days, yes. But I learned a lot. And I loved the slow life. At night, I loved watching the sun go down.
W: Was it difficult to find a ship?
M: It wasn't easy. But if you have time, it's possible.
W: That's the problem, isn't it? When I was younger, I had more time.
M: Do you want to travel with me next summer?
W: Where to?
M: Around India.
W: Mmmm. Maybe not.

Unit 9 Recording S9.7

K = Kama V = Val

K: Hey, Val. Did you stay in bed too long this morning?
V: Ha-ha! It's these trains – they're terrible!
K: Why? What happened this time?
V: Well, first of all, the train was late leaving the station, but only about fifteen minutes or so. After that, it just went at walking speed – all the way to Chicago. Really! There was a guy on a bicycle on the road next to us … I think he got to Chicago before we did!
K: Well, you're two hours late … and the boss wants to see you.

K: Hey, Val. The boss wants to see you. Whoa! What happened to you? You're all wet!
V: Believe me, it's a long story. First of all, I got up late because I didn't hear my alarm, so I only woke up at eight thirty. I ran to the train station – usually I walk – but I missed the train by two minutes! Then I waited for the next train, the nine fifteen, and everything was fine until we just stopped – just stopped – in the middle of nowhere. The guard said that there was a signal problem. After that, the air-conditioning stopped working. It was like an oven – at least a thousand degrees! Finally, after forty minutes, we started moving … very, very slowly. What could I do? Uh-oh, there's the boss.
K: Yeah. She's not happy. Two and a half hours late, Val … Good luck!

Unit 9 Recording S9.9

A = Attendant P = Passenger

A: Your meal, Sir.
P: Thank you. Uh, excuse me.
A: Yes, can I help you?
P: Hope so! I'm sorry, but there's a small problem here ... I ordered a vegetarian meal – but this is meat.
A: Oh, just a moment ... I checked, and we don't have a record of your order.
P: What?! But I always order vegetarian. I'm a frequent flyer.
A: I understand, sir, but we don't have any more vegetarian meals.
P: I don't believe it! You always have extra meals in business class.
A: Yes, but this is economy class.
P: You don't understand. Let me explain one more time. I don't eat meat. I ordered vegetarian. I can't fly to Tokyo without dinner. It's your job to bring me a meal. A business class vegetarian meal is fine.
A: Just a moment. Here you are, Sir. A vegetarian meal.
P: Thank you ... but this is already open. And it's cold. Uh, can I speak to the person in charge, please?

Unit 10 Recording S10.1

I = Interviewer J = Jean M = Martin

I: Jean and Martin, the luckiest couple in Australia today ... welcome.
J/M: Thank you.
I: So Jean, when did you find out?
J: Martin called me at work. I didn't believe him at first.
M: She said, "You're lying!" I said I didn't believe it myself.
J: Yeah.
I: And is it true that you're not going to stop working?
J: That's right. We enjoy our jobs.
M: Yes. People think gardening work is hard and boring ... but it isn't. I work outdoors, and I enjoy it. So yes, I'm going to stay at my job.
I: So what are you going to do with the money?
M: First thing, we plan to give some money to Jean's parents in America.
J: They're retired, and they need a little help.
I: Oh, that's nice. And how about for yourselves? Any plans?
M: Well, we got married last year, but we didn't have a big party. So we're going to have a party and invite all our friends and family.
I: Nice.
J: And we'd like to move. At the moment we're living in a small apartment. So we're going to look for a house near the beach.
M: Yes, maybe near the beach, or ...
I: And are you going to take a break? Travel around the world?
J: Not a big break, just a short trip ... to Thailand.
M: I'm not sure about Thailand.
I: Oh, what would you like to do, Martin?
M: I'd like to go to Greece.
I: Fabulous. And do you want to buy anything else? Maybe a new computer ... or ... ?
M: Well, I want to buy a plane. Just a small one, a small plane.
I: Oh. Do you fly?
M: No, I ...
J: He doesn't fly. The plane is a kind of dream.
M: Well, I'd like to learn to fly.
I: Sounds wonderful. Thanks very much for talking to us today. Oh, just one last question ... You get the money tomorrow, right? What's the first thing you're going to do?
J: He's going to buy a new car, of course! The old car didn't survive that tree.

Unit 10 Recording S10.5

W = Woman M = Man

W: Hey, let's do something new this weekend.
M: That's a good idea. Uh ... What do you mean ... new?
W: I mean something we don't usually do. Something ... different. OK ... AlternativeCity. Hey, look at this.
M: Silent disco? What's that? Dancing with no music?
W: No, it's ... You get headphones, wireless headphones, and you can hear the music, and you dance.
M: I don't understand. Why?
W: Well, there's different music and you can choose. So you dance to your favorite music, with headphones. Do you want to try it?
M: No. I don't feel like doing that. What's this one?
W: Blind date movie. That's ... Oh, we book a movie ticket, but ... they don't tell us the movie.
M: That doesn't sound very good. Cool if it's a good movie, but if it's a bad movie?
W: No, it's OK. If we don't like the movie, at the end they give us our money back.
M: Mmm. No. That doesn't sound interesting to me.
W: OK, so how about going to the theater?
M: That's not new.
W: No, playback theater. It's a very small theater. And people in the audience tell stories about their lives. The actors act out the stories.
M: Oh. Do I have to tell a story?
W: No, you can just watch. It says it can be very funny or more serious.
M: OK. That sounds interesting.
W: I'd like to go. Let's do that.
M: Cool!
W: OK, that's tomorrow evening at seven. And why don't we go to the museum in the afternoon?
M: For ... museum meditation? What's that?
W: Listen to this. You go with a small group into one of the rooms and meditate for an hour.
M: Meditate. Do you look at the paintings or statues?
W: I don't know. Maybe you close your eyes.
M: Oh, then you look at the paintings.
W: Mmmm, yes, and then talk about them.
M: Great! So ... do you want to go to the theater at night and the museum in the afternoon?
W: Sounds great. And for dinner?
M: Let me see. Oh, dinner in the dark?

Unit 10 Recording S10.8

In Houston today, it'll be hot and sunny with temperatures up to seventy-seven degrees Fahrenheit. Tomorrow will be cloudy, but warm, with a high of seventy. Things will change on Friday night: it'll be a wet night with rain from midnight to early next morning. The temperature will fall to fifty, so it'll feel cool, but the rain will stop, so we'll have a dry day all Saturday. Sunday will be windy and cloudy ... and very cold, so make sure you wear your winter coat!

Unit 10 Recording S10.9

I can remember the sirocco very well. I was in Pisa, in Italy, about five years ago. I worked there as a teacher for two years. I love hot, sunny weather, and the summers were wonderful. I remember my first summer. It was very hot, but then one day the weather changed. It got hotter. I woke up one morning, and everywhere was white. There was white sand over all the cars and the streets. And everything was dry, your eyes, your mouth. Everything. The car was like an oven ... the metal of the car door was really hot. It was difficult to breathe. People told me it was the sirocco. The sirocco is a strong wind from Africa, from the desert. At work, everyone got very tired. Me, too. I was glad when it was over.

Unit 11 Recording S11.2

P = Presenter Dr H = Elizabeth Harper

P: And this week in *Health Matters*, we're talking about colds and flu. What's the difference, and more importantly, what should you do when you have a cold or flu? With me in the studio is Dr. Elizabeth Harper.
Dr. H: Hello.
P: Dr. Harper ... First, can you tell us ... how is the flu different from a cold?
Dr. H: Well, one big difference is how they start. Flu starts very suddenly. One minute you're fine, you're OK, the next minute you feel terrible. You have a headache – often a very bad headache – and sometimes a cough. You have a sore throat and your arms and legs hurt. You feel awful.
P: OK. And do you usually have a temperature?
Dr. H: Yes, you get very hot. Usually you have a temperature of over one hundred degrees Fahrenheit, and you're too sick to do anything. You can't work. You just want to go home and go to bed.
P: So it's serious?
Dr. H: Yes. Don't try to work. You should go to bed. Get lots of sleep. Sometimes you have to stay in bed for a week or more. You shouldn't go back to work too soon.
P: Anything else?
Dr. H: Yes, you should drink lots of water.
P: Right. And what about a cold? How is a cold different from the flu?
Dr. H: Well, a cold starts slowly. It might take two or three days to start. It's a cold when you have a bad throat ... or a cough and a runny nose and you don't feel very well. But – and here's the big difference – if you can get up and go to work, then you've probably got a cold, not the flu.
P: So should you go to work with a cold?
Dr. H: Uh, it depends. You don't want to give your cold to other people at work, so some people take two or three days off work or work from home. But, yes, you can usually work, and after a week you usually feel better.
P: And after the flu?
Dr. H: After the flu, you often feel very tired for a very long time, maybe three or four weeks.
P: Should you rest a lot?
Dr. H: Well, it depends, but be careful. For example, don't do too many activities or exercise intensely until you feel better.
P: Another question about colds and flu. What do you think about antibiotics?
Dr. H: Well, you shouldn't take antibiotics with a cold and ...

Unit 11 Recording S11.5

W = Woman M = Man

Conversation 1

W: Oh, no.
M: Here, let me help. What a mess!
W: Thank you very much. It's my leg. It's difficult ...
M: ... Oh, don't move. I'll do it.
W: Thanks a lot.
M: No problem.

Conversation 2

W: Uh ... Excuse me?
M: Yeah.
W: You dropped this.
M: Oh. Thanks so much.
W: That's OK.

Conversation 3

W: Can I help you?
M: Oh, thanks.
W: The traffic's really bad here.
M: Yes.
W: Do you want me to carry your bag?
M: No, no, it's fine, thanks.
W: Here you are.
M: Thanks very much. That's kind of you.
W: You're welcome.

Unit 11 Recording S11.9

S1, 2, 3 = Students D = Doctor H = Hilary

S1: I have a question for the doctor.
D: Yes? What's your question?
S1: Do you think these diets are dangerous?
D: What do you mean?
S1: Well, is it dangerous to eat only sugar or only fat?
D: Yes, well, this was an experiment. You shouldn't go on a sugar or fat diet for a long time.
S2: Hilary, do you agree with him?
H: Yes, of course. These are not healthy diets.
S2: So what do you recommend for people to eat and not eat?
H: That's a very good question. The answer is complicated.
S2: Well, should we stop eating anything?
H: Well, some foods are bad for you.
S2: Could you give an example?
H: Well, we know that processed foods are bad for you. So try to eat less processed food.
S3: How do we know what's processed?
H: In the supermarket, look at the label. And of course, we should eat lots of fresh food, fruit and vegetables.
S3: I see. Uh, I have a question for Chris. Can I ask you about your diet? What was the worst thing about it?

Unit 12 Recording S12.1

I = Interviewer M = Man

Conversation 1

I: Excuse me. Do you have a second? We're asking people about great experiences, unforgettable experiences …
M: Oh … Uh, yes, if it's quick.
I: Great! Could you look at this list? Have you done any of these things?
M: Hmm … Yes, yes, I have. I've been to a karaoke bar, in Japan. I sometimes go to Tokyo on business.
I: How was it?
M: Scary! I like singing, but I'm not a very good singer. Or my wife tells me I'm not a good singer. But at a karaoke bar in Japan, you have to get up and sing. Everyone does …
I: And you did, too?
M: Yes. And it was amazing. Unforgettable. *My Way*. It's my favorite song. You know. Do you want me to sing it?
I: Uh, no, no. That's okay. Have you done anything else on the list?
M: No, no, I don't think so. Sorry, I have to run …

Conversation 2

I = Interviewer W = Woman

I: Excuse me …
W: What?
I: Have you ever ridden an elephant?
W: What? Why? Uh, no. No, I haven't …
I: We're doing a survey on unforgettable experiences. Can I show you this list? Have you done any of these activities?
W: Oh, OK. OK. Let's see … Uh … No, no, no, no. Oh, I've watched the sun rise. Over Istanbul … so that's one thing. I never get up early, but I was with my husband on vacation and he was sick, so we were awake all night. So we saw the sun rise.
I: Sounds great!
W: Well, I enjoyed it more than my husband did. It was amazing, really. Unforgettable.
I: And anything else on the list?
W: Well I've seen a volcano in Indonesia. And yes, I've climbed a volcano. In Italy, on vacation. I got very tired, but it was awesome!
I: Really? Where was that?
W: Well, it was …

Conversation 3

I = Interviewer W = Woman

I: Excuse me. We're doing a survey … about unforgettable experiences.
W: Right …
I: Two minutes. Could you just look at this list? Have you done any of these things?
W: OK. Well … I'm not really an outdoor person, so … I haven't slept outside. Or climbed a volcano. And I've never watched the sun rise. Mmm … I've never done a bungee jump. I'd like to try it. It looks fun but scary! But I've never done that.
I: And the other things?
W: Hmm … oh yes, I've been in a movie. I'm not a very good actor. In fact, I'm a terrible actor.
I: Is it a famous movie?
W: Well, no, it was a short video, a little drama. My friend makes short videos, and once she asked me to act in one. It's on YouTube. It got over ten thousand hits. That was amazing!
I: Wow! That's interesting. What was it about?
W: Well, I played this woman, and she was …

Unit 12 Recording S12.4

Conversation 1

S = Sean D = Debbie

S: Hello.
D: Hi, Sean. It's Debbie.
S: Hi, Debbie. What's up?
D: Is Kevin there?
S: No, he's not. He went out about ten minutes ago.
D: Oh …
S: What's up?
D: Well, I locked the keys in the car. Kevin has the spare key.
S: Oh, that's sad!
D: Could I leave a message for him?
S: Of course.
D: Just ask him to call me.
S: On your cell phone?
D: No, that's in the car … I'll give you a number.
S: Hold on … OK, go ahead.
D: OK, let's see … It's 322, 6-3-2-8.
S: Got it. I'll tell him.
D: Thanks, bye.
S: Bye.

Conversation 2

C = Customer O = Operator CS = Customer services

O: Berkley Bank.
C: Hello. Could I speak to customer services, please?
O: Just a moment.

CS: Customer services.
C: Hello. This is Alan Simpson. I've got a problem. I think I've lost my credit card.
CS: I see. I'm sorry, this line is very bad. Where are you calling from?
C: I'm in Madrid, actually. In fact, I'm calling from a pay phone, and I only have one minute on this card. Could you call me back?
CS: Of course. Could you give me the number there?
C: Just a moment … It's 34 for Spain, 91 for Madrid, then 308 5238.
CS: Let me check that. 34 91 308 5238.
C: That's right.
CS: Fine. Now hang up – I'll call you back right away.
C: Thank you.

Conversation 3

W = Woman M = Man

W: Hello?
M: Oh, thank goodness. Hello, uh … Who's this?
W: My name's Marianne.
M: Thanks for picking up.
W: Well, the phone rang, so I picked it up.
M: Yes, well, that's my cell phone. And you found it.
W: Oh, OK … It's yours. Do you want to get it back?
M: Yes, thanks. Where are you?
W: Central Park, by the fountain. It was here in the grass.
M: Ah, yes … I thought it might be.
W: So where are you?
M: Not far away. I can be there in ten minutes.
W: OK, I'll wait here.
M: Great. Thanks a lot!

Unit 12 Recording S12.8

This happened in Australia … when I was about twenty-five. I spent a few days at a hotel in Alice Springs and went to Ayers Rock and … well, anyway, one day, I went out for a walk … in the outback. It was a lovely day, so I walked and walked … and then I realized I didn't really know where I was. I was a bit stupid, really… because I decided to go further … I guess I thought I'd find the way back. Um … anyway, after that I heard some dogs. First I heard them barking, and then I saw them … there was a group – maybe five or six dogs, wild dogs, coming toward me. I felt really frightened, but I remembered some advice I, uh …, I read in my guidebook: Don't move, and don't look at the dogs. So I froze, like a statue … I didn't move … and I looked at a tree, not at the dogs, and didn't move my eyes. The dogs were all around me, jumping and barking … I thought they were going to bite me. Then one dog did bite my arm, just a little, but still I didn't move. In the end, after about twenty minutes, the dogs went away. I stayed there for a few more minutes and then luckily found my way back to the hotel. It was the most frightening experience I've ever had!

American SPEAK OUT

Elementary Workbook

Frances Eales • Steve Oakes • Louis Harrison

Pearson

VOCABULARY

TRAVEL ADJECTIVES

1 A Rewrite the sentences using the words in the box. There are two extra words.

~~empty~~ noisy cheap boring uncomfortable slow expensive quiet fast comfortable crowded interesting

1 There were no visitors in the museum.
The museum was _empty_.
2 This bed's very hard – I can't relax on it.
This bed's ______.
3 The train travels at 102 miles an hour.
The train is very ______.
4 There were a lot of people on the beach.
The beach was ______.
5 The book's good and has a lot of useful information.
The book's ______.
6 The hotel is perfect – no cars outside, no children around, so I can sleep all day.
The hotel is ______.
7 The car was $35,000, so he didn't buy it.
The car was too ______ for him.
8 I didn't like the movie. I slept for most of it.
The movie was ______.
9 These jeans didn't cost a lot.
These jeans were pretty ______.
10 I can't sleep because of the party in the apartment below.
The party is very ______.

W7.1

B Listen and repeat the adjectives from Exercise 1A.

C Listen again and write the adjectives in the correct column for each stress pattern.

1 O	2 Oo
cheap	_empty_
3 Ooo	**4 oOo**
5 oOoo	

GRAMMAR

COMPARATIVES

2 Find and correct the mistakes in the sentences.

1 Hondas are popular than Suzukis.
Hondas are more popular than Suzukis.
2 South Africa's hoter than Italy.
______
3 I'm more old than my brother.
______
4 Indian food is spicyer than English food.
______
5 Lena's intelligenter than me.
______
6 Cola is sweetter than lemonade.
______
7 Chinese is more difficult that English.
______
8 Chips are badder for you than fries.
______

3 Complete the article with the comparative form of the adjectives in parentheses.

EITHER ... OR ...?

We ask singer and actress Sonia Haig to choose. Which is better?

Q: Singing or acting?
A: Singing. Singing is [1] _easier_ (easy) for me than acting.

Q: Healthy food or junk food?
A: Junk food. I know healthy food is [2] ______ (good) for me, but after a concert, all I want is a pizza or a hamburger and chocolate!

Q: Relaxing on a beach or visiting an art gallery?
A: Oh, visiting an art gallery because it's [3] ______ (interesting). Sitting on a beach is boring.

Q: Dinner at a restaurant or dinner at home?
A: That's a difficult question. I like cooking, but I like having dinner at a restaurant because it's [4] ______ (romantic) than eating at home.

Q: Family or friends?
A: Family. I'm [5] ______ (close) to my sister than to my friends, and I call my parents every day.

Q: Summer or winter?
A: Well, I love looking at snow, but winter is [6] ______ (cold), and I prefer being hot. OK, summer.

Q: New York or Paris?
A: I love Paris, but I love New York more because it's [7] ______ (big) than Paris, and I like all the stores. I have an apartment near Central Park.

Q: Cats or dogs?
A: Dogs. They're [8] ______ (friendly) than cats!

Chips Crisps

READING

4 A Read the emails. Are Tim and Mike good travel partners?

Hi Dan,

Mike and I arrived in Barcelona on Saturday. The first night we were in a self-catering apartment near the beach. I didn't sleep well because it was too noisy, so yesterday I moved to a hotel downtown. Mike stayed at the apartment because it's pretty cheap. My hotel's very comfortable and quiet, and it has Spanish TV, so I can practice my Spanish in the evenings.

Yesterday, Mike came with me to the Picasso Museum. I thought it was fantastic, but he wanted to leave after an hour. He said it was boring, so we went to the beach and met some local people, and he talked to them for almost three hours – that was boring! Of course, he spoke in English because he doesn't know much Spanish.

Last night I wanted to go to a restaurant to try the local food, but Mike said it was too expensive. We went to a cheap snack bar, and the food was awful.

Hope you're well.

Tim

Hi Lucy,

Tim and I are here in beautiful Barcelona. I'm in a self-catering apartment near the beach. It's not very comfortable, but I only go there to sleep. The first night there was a party next door, and I danced until 3a.m. Tim said it was too noisy, and he moved into a hotel downtown. He stays in his room at night and watches TV! Can you believe it – watching TV on vacation?

Yesterday we went to the Picasso Museum. Well, it was OK for about an hour, but Tim wanted to stay there all day! You know me – I like relaxing on the beach and meeting people. Yesterday, I met some great people from Madrid, and we chatted all afternoon.

Tim always wants to eat in expensive places, but I like buying food from shops and eating it on the beach. Last night, we went to a snack bar. The food was terrible.

Mike

B Who says these things? Tim (T), Mike (M) or both (TM)?

1 I don't have much money. *M*
2 A good night's sleep is important for me. ______
3 When I visit another country, I try to learn some of the language. ______
4 We don't enjoy the same things. ______
5 I love going to art galleries and museums. ______
6 I talked to some Spanish people on the beach yesterday. ______
7 I don't like eating expensive food. ______
8 The food in the snack bar wasn't good. ______

C Read the emails again and answer the questions.

1 Which is more expensive: The apartment or the hotel?
the hotel

2 Which is further from downtown: The apartment or the hotel?
______

3 Which is noisier in the evenings: The apartment or the hotel?
______

4 Which is more comfortable: The apartment or the hotel?
______

5 Who is more talkative: Tim or Mike?
______

6 Who is more serious: Tim or Mike?
______

7 Who is better at speaking Spanish: Tim or Mike?
______

8 Who is more laid back: Tim or Mike?
______

downtown / on vacation — in the city centre / on holiday

VOCABULARY

PLACES

1 **Look at the pictures and complete the puzzle. Then find the hidden words: what do you have when you go on vacation?**

1

3

4

7

1 l a k e
2
3
4
5
6
7
8
9

You have ________________!

2

6

8

9

5

GRAMMAR

SUPERLATIVES

2 **A** **Read the ads. Which vacation is good for:**

1 a family?
2 people who like relaxing?
3 people who like active vacation?

A **Luxury weekend**

A relaxing weekend at the beautiful five-star Hanover Hotel. Swim in the warm sea and relax on the beach all day! Tennis courts and bicycles are available. The perfect laid-back vacation.

(3 nights – $1,490 per person)

B **Mountain adventure**

Mountain biking in the Indian Himalayas – spend the day biking and sleep in tents at night. Prepare for temperatures of 14°F! A real adventure for the athletic vacationmaker.

(10 days – $2,490 per person)

C **Family fun**

Camp Family has everything your children need to have a good time – a lovely blue lake, an adventure playground, mini-golf and go-karts. Stay in a self-catering apartment. Sit back, relax and let us give your children the vacation of a lifetime!

(6 days – $990 per family)

B **Write sentences about the vacations using the superlative of the adjectives.**

1 expensive *The most expensive is Mountain adventure.*
2 cheap ________________
3 comfortable ________________
4 noisy ________________
5 long ________________
6 easy ________________
7 difficult ________________
8 short ________________
9 uncomfortable ________________
10 cold ________________

3 **A** **Write questions using the prompts.**

1 what / long / word in this sentence?
What's the longest word in this sentence?
2 what / short / word on this page?
____
3 which / interesting / text in units 1–6 of this book?
____
4 which / good / exercise on this page?
____
5 what / difficult / grammar point in English?
____
6 who / happy / person in your family?
____
7 who / friendly / person in your English class?
____
8 which / bad / restaurant in your town?
____

B **Answer the questions in Exercise 3A.**

athletic — sporty

LISTENING

4 A Look at the map and listen to Nick's audio diary. Does his train go to or from Moscow?

B Read the sentences and check any new words in your dictionary.

1 The Trans-Siberian train journey takes nine days. *F*
2 The compartment is for two people. ____
3 Anton doesn't speak much English. ____
4 Nick can see snow, forests, villages, and lakes out of the window. ____
5 Nick and Anton buy food from women on the train. ____
6 They drink a lot of coffee on the train. ____
7 On the last evening of the journey, Nick went to a party. ____
8 Nick loved the Trans-Siberian train journey. ____

C Listen again. Are the sentences in Exercise 4A true (T) or false (F)?

D Correct the false sentences.

1 *The Trans-Siberian train journey takes seven days.*

____
____
____
____
____
____
____

WRITING

CHECKING AND CORRECTING

5 A Read the extract from Nick's blog. Find and correct ten mistakes with:

- spelling
- the simple past
- singular/plural forms.

Hi, it's Nick again. We started the day with a surprise – but not a good one. Anton and I *went* ~~goed~~ to the dining car for brekfast, and there wasn't any food. That wasn't a big problem because I had some cookie, and we drinked some coffee, but then we went back for lunch, and it was the same situation. The waiter telled us that there's a station where they usually get food, but the food truck wasn't there.

Nobody on the train was worried about this becaus almost everybody broght their own food. A guy named Egor gaves us half of his roast chicken, and a Chinese couple gave us some bread. Peoples were so kind. Anton and I talked about how to thank them ... so I tought them some English songs, and it were really just a big party. My best day on the train!

B Write about one day on a journey. It can be a real journey or an imaginary one. Write 80—100 words. Use Exercise 5A and these questions to help you.

- Where were you?
- How did you travel?
- What happened?
- Was it a good day?

C Check your work and correct any mistakes.

VOCABULARY

PLACES

1 Add the vowels to make places in towns.

1 bl__cks
2 p__rk__ng l__t
3 __nt__rs__ct__ __ns
4 st__p l__ghts
5 c__rn__r
6 p__d__str__ __n str__ __t
7 p__rk
8 r__ __d

FUNCTION

GIVING DIRECTIONS

2 Look at the map of Dublin, Ireland, and complete the conversation. Speaker A is at Pearse Street station (START) and wants to go to the Tourist Information Office (TI).

A: Excuse me. Can you tell me the [1] *way* to the Tourist Information Office, please?

B: Sure. Go straight here, then turn [2] ________ onto Lincoln Place and then right again onto Nassau Street.

A: OK.

B: Then go [3] ________ ahead and go [4] ________ Kildare Street and Dawson Street.

A: OK, so I stay on Nassau Street.

B: Yes. [5] ________ past Grafton Street, into a small street … I forget the name … and the Tourist Information Office is on the [6] ________. You can't [7] ________ it.

A: Great. Thank you!

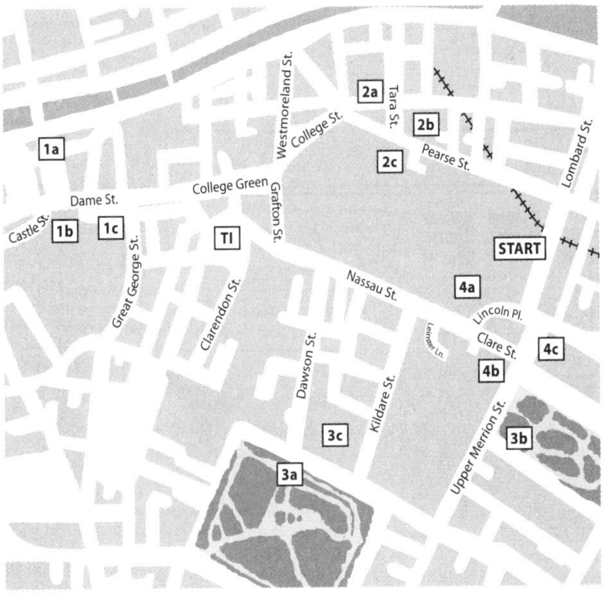

3 Read the information and look at the map in Exercise 2. Circle the correct alternatives.

Walking tours of Dublin

1 To Dublin Castle
From the Tourist Information Office, go to College Green and turn left. Go straight to Dame Street, and turn left – that's Castle Street. It's on the left and number *1a/(1b)/1c* on your map.

2 From Dublin Castle to Trinity College
Go back to Dame Street and straight to College Green and then turn left at College Street. Turn right, go straight at Pearse Street, and then turn right again. It's number *2a/2b/2c* on your map.

3 From Trinity College to St Stephen's Green
Go back to Pearse Street and turn left, then left onto College Street and then Grafton Street, and finally Nassau Street. Turn right onto Dawson Street, and go straight until the end. You can see it in front of you. It's number *3a/3b/3c* on your map.

4 From St Stephen's Green to the National Gallery
Come out of St. Stephen's Green and look for Kildare Street. Go straight, and at the end of Kildare Street, turn right, and go straight – that's Clare Street. The National Gallery is on your right, number *4a/4b/4c* on your map.

LEARN TO

CHECK AND CORRECT DIRECTIONS

4 A Look at the map and correct A's directions.

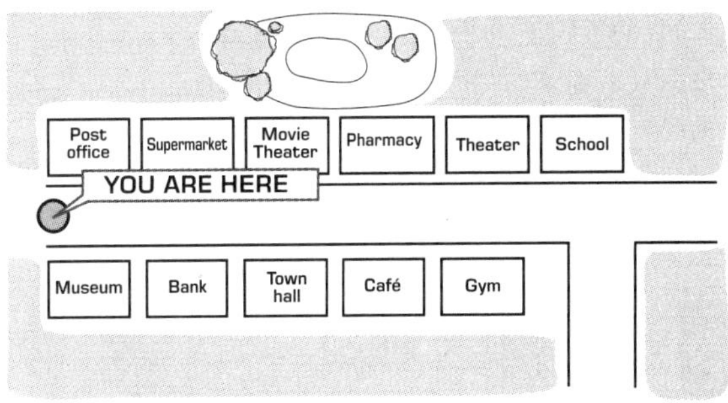

1 A: So, the park's between the movie theater and the pharmacy.
B: No, it's *behind* the movie theater and the pharmacy.

2 A: So the supermarket's between the movie theater and the pharmacy.
B: No, it's between __________.

3 A: So, the movie theater is the fourth building on the left.
B: No, it's __________.

4 A: So, the café is the fourth building on the left.
B: No, it's __________.

5 A: So, the post office is across from the bank.
B: No, it's across from __________.

6 A: So, the town hall is across from the bank.
B: No, it's __________ the bank.

B Circle the stressed words in B's answers in Exercise 4A.

1 B: No, it's (behind) the movie theater and the pharmacy.

W7.3 **C Listen and check. Then listen and repeat.**

blocks / parking lot / intersection
stop lights / straight

square / car park / crossroad
traffic lights / straight on

GRAMMAR

PRESENT CONTINUOUS

1 Write the *-ing* form of the verbs.

1 do _doing_
2 have ______
3 run ______
4 stay ______
5 swim ______
6 sleep ______
7 write ______
8 try ______
9 begin ______
10 give ______

2 A Complete the sentences with the present continuous form of the verbs in parentheses.

1 Jake _'s singing_ (sing).
2 Wesley ______ (take) a picture.
3 Jo and Dave ______ (stand) near Jake. They ______ (listen) to him.
4 Roger ______ (walk) near Jake, but he ______ (not listen) to him.
5 Megan ______ (sit) at the café. She ______ (read).
6 Paolo and Zoe ______ (chat) with each other. They ______ (not watch) Jake.
7 Lisa ______ (look) at some bags.
8 Philip ______ (sell) a bag to Kalila.

B Look at the picture and read the sentences in Exercise 2A again. Label the people in the picture.

C Write questions using the prompts.

1 what / instrument / Jake / play?
What instrument is Jake playing?
2 who / Zoe / talk to?
______
3 where / Zoe and Paolo / sit?
______
4 how many bags / Jo and Dave / carry?
______
5 who / Wesley / take / a picture of?
______
6 who / talk / on the phone?
______
7 what / Megan / read?
______
8 who / buy / bag?
______

D Look at the picture and answer the questions in Exercise 2C.

1 _He's playing the guitar._
2 ______
3 ______
4 ______
5 ______
6 ______
7 ______
8 ______

3 Put the words in the correct order to make questions. Then write short answers about you.

1 you / are / shoes / wearing
Are you wearing shoes ? *Yes, I am./No, I'm not.*

2 your / is / ringing / phone
_______________ ? _______

3 are / pen / a / with / exercise / this / doing / you
_______________ ? _______

4 room / other / the / sitting / are / people / in / any
_______________ ? _______

5 music / is / room / the / in / playing
_______________ ? _______

6 exercise / enjoying / are / this / you
_______________ ? _______

7 teacher / is / your / writing / the / board / on
_______________ ? _______

8 your / drinking / classmates / coffee / are
_______________ ? _______

VOCABULARY

VERBS + PREPOSITIONS

4 Complete the sentences with prepositions.

1 Dave's over there. He's chatting *with* Joan.
2 I'm waiting _______ the train.
3 Diana, can you take a picture _______ the class?
4 What are you listening _______?
5 We read _______ the wedding yesterday in the newspaper.
6 I can't come at the moment. I'm talking _______ the phone.
7 Ask your teacher _______ the pronunciation of this word. I can't help you, sorry.
8 When I'm on vacation, I never think _______ work.

LISTENING

W 8.1

5 A Listen and match conversations 1—5 with places a)—e).

Conversation 1	a) tennis match
Conversation 2	b) fashion show
Conversation 3	c) art gallery
Conversation 4	d) concert
Conversation 5	e) ticket office

B Listen again and underline the correct alternative for each conversation.

1 The man *really likes/doesn't like* the paintings.
2 Nellie *wants/ doesn't want* to go to the concert.
3 The woman is *in/going into* a concert.
4 Felicity says she *wants/doesn't want* to meet for a coffee.
5 *All/Some of* the people are wearing black.

WRITING

PRONOUNS

6 A Read the story. Who took Julia's phone?

B Replace the underlined nouns in the story with pronouns.

On Friday night, David, Julia and I went to the Rock Club. [1]Julia and David are fun, and I like [2]Julia and David a lot. The club was busy, but [3]David, Julia and I found a table.

Julia put her cell phone on the table, but after an hour [4]Julia saw that [5]Julia's phone wasn't there, and she was very angry. Then I had a good idea. I called [6]Julia's number, and [7]Julia, David and I heard [8]Julia's phone ringing.

David started laughing, and then [9]David took Julia's phone out of [10]David's pocket and gave [11]Julia's phone back to [12]Julia. David thought this was funny, but Julia was very angry with [13]David, so she took [14]David's phone and threw [15]David's phone out of the window! Now [16]David and Julia aren't speaking to each other.

1 *they*
2 _______
3 _______
4 _______
5 _______
6 _______
7 _______
8 _______
9 _______
10 _______
11 _______
12 _______
13 _______
14 _______
15 _______
16 _______

VOCABULARY

APPEARANCE

1 A Look at the pictures and read the sentences. Label the men in the pictures.

1 Rob has curly hair. He's tall and very slim.
2 Sam has short, straight hair, a moustache and a beard. He isn't wearing glasses.
3 Tom doesn't have a beard. He has dark hair, and he has medium build.
4 Bruce is very slim. He doesn't have short hair, but he has a beard.
5 Mike isn't very slim. He has very short, dark hair, and he's wearing glasses.
6 Will has dark, curly hair. He has a beard and a moustache, and he's a little overweight.

B Describe the women in the pictures.

1 Meg has *long, straight blond hair, and she has medium build*.
2 Jay ______________________.
3 Keira ______________________.
4 Belinda ______________________.

2 Look at the pictures and complete the crossword.

Across:

1

5
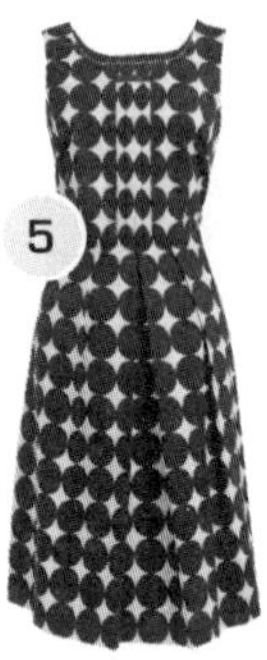
6

8

10

3

9

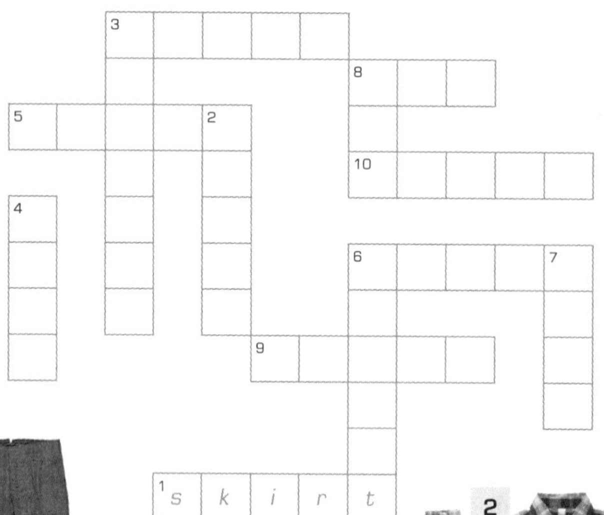

Down:

3

4

2

7

6

8
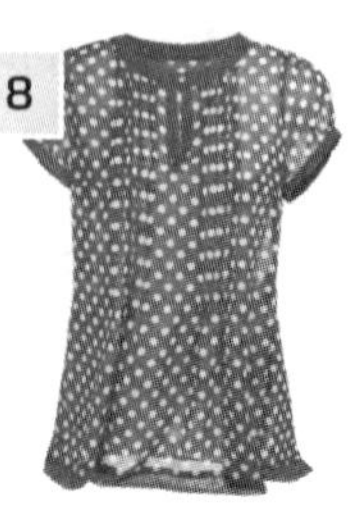

GRAMMAR

SIMPLE PRESENT AND PRESENT CONTINUOUS

3 Underline the correct alternatives.

Gerald: Hi, Bruno. It's me, Gerald. What [1]*do you do/ are you doing?*

Bruno: I [2]*have/'m having* a coffee with Carla. What about you?

Gerald: I [3]*sit/'m sitting* at my desk as usual. So you [4]*don't work/aren't working* today.

Bruno: I am, but I [5]*don't usually start/'m not usually starting* work before ten o'clock.

Gerald: How's Carla?

Bruno: OK, but she [6]*doesn't like/isn't liking* her job at the hospital.

Gerald: Oh, why not?

Bruno: Well, she [7]*works/'s working* from 11a.m. till midnight every day.

Gerald: That sounds hard. [8]*Does she look/Is she looking* for a new job?

Bruno: Yes, I think so. She [9]*looks/is looking* in the newspaper and on the internet every day.

Gerald: Really? Because [10]*I call/I'm calling* about a job opening here. Office work, not very interesting, but the money isn't bad. Perfect for Carla.

Bruno: Hey, Carla – good news, it's Gerald ...

4 Complete the conversations with the simple present or present continuous form of the verbs in parentheses.

Conversation 1

A: So who does the housework in your family?

B: We all [1]___do___ (do) it. In fact, my wife [2]__________ (cook) dinner right now, and my daughter [3]__________ (help) her.

A: And what [4]__________ you __________ (do) to help at the moment?

B: I [5]__________ (watch) TV! There are too many people in the kitchen.

Conversation 2

A: Why [6]__________ (wear) black today? You [7]__________ (usually/not wear) black.

B: What do you mean? I always [8]__________ (wear) it!

Conversation 3

A: Hi, George. It's me. Where are you?

B: I [9]__________ (stand) on the train.

A: Why? You [10]__________ (usually/not stand).

B: No, I usually [11]__________ (get) a seat, but this is a later train. Where are you?

A: I [12]__________ (wait) at the station.

B: Oh, sorry. I forgot to tell you I'm late!

READING

5 A Read the article. Are the sentences true (T) or false (F)?

1 T-shirts are 200 years old. ___F___
2 American soldiers were the first to wear T-shirts. ______
3 The most expensive T-shirts cost hundreds of dollars. ______
4 There are four different types of T-shirt. ______
5 T-shirts are popular because they are cheap. ______
6 You can change the message on an electronic T-shirt. ______

THE CHANGING T-SHIRT

It's an item of clothing many of us wear every day, and it's often the only thing we wear on the top half of our body. After its introduction over 100 years ago as underwear for American soldiers, the T-shirt is now one of the most common items of clothing.

You can find T-shirts in any clothes store, and they cost between a few dollars to a few hundred dollars. There are even "special" T-shirts that sell for thousands and thousands of dollars. And there are lots of different kinds of T-shirts: V-necks, U-necks, short-sleeved, long-sleeved, cropped T-shirts – you name it!

T-shirts are popular because they are more than just clothes: people can express themselves wearing T-shirts. A slogan on the front of your T-shirt can show people what you believe in; a T-shirt with your favorite band's logo can show people what kind of music you like; you can even wear your favorite pictures by printing them on a T-shirt.

And the latest step in the development of the most popular item of clothing in the world? Electronic T-shirts. They light up when you wear them and they can carry electronic messages that change when you program them. What's next? Texting friends through T-shirts? It might be common very soon!

B Match words from the article 1–6 with definitions a)–f).

1 underwear
2 common
3 express
4 slogan
5 logo
6 program

a) show your feelings, ideas or personality
b) give instructions to a computer, machine, etc.
c) a short, clever phrase that is easy to remember
d) clothes that you wear under your other clothes
e) a symbol for a group, organization, etc.
f) happening often; that you see, hear, etc. very often

organization organisation

VOCABULARY
TYPES OF MOVIE

1 A Add the vowels to complete the types of movie.

1 act_i_ _o_n m__v__ __s
2 h__rr__r m__v__ __s
3 sc__-f__ mov__ __s
4 m__s__c__l
5 r__m__nt__c movies
6 c__m__dy
7 dr__m__

B Match the extracts from movie reviews with the types of movie in Exercise 1A.

A
Ninety minutes in the scary world of vampires and blood ... _2_

B
Childhood friends Jessica and Tim meet after ten years, and they want to be more than just good friends ... ______

C
Gene Walker is a modern-day Fred Astaire, dancing and singing his way through the streets of Cordoba ... ______

D
New York police officer Jack Hare goes on vacation to Miami, but finds himself working to save the country from a terrorist attack ... ______

E
A farmer in France wakes up and finds that all his animals can speak ... Chinese. Lots of laughs as the farmer teaches himself Chinese to talk to the animals. ______

F
A small Indian village has a visit from space tourists – aliens from another galaxy. A surprise as the aliens have more to learn from the locals than they think ... ______

G
Sally Bonner loses her parents in a train accident. She is blind and grows up alone with no friends ... but then Edmund, her teacher, helps Sally learn to play the piano. ______

FUNCTION
RECOMMENDING

2 Put the words in the box in the correct places in the conversation. You do not need two of the words.

~~recommend~~ about (x2) I name in it kind

A: Do you want to watch a movie?

B: Sorry, I'm busy.

A: Oh. Well then, [1]can you *recommend* a good movie?

B: Hmm ... [2]What of movies do you like?

A: Horror movies, action movies ...

B: Do you like sci-fi?

A: I don't know many sci-fi movies.

B: [3]How *The Hunger Games*? Are you familiar with it?

A: [4]What's it?

B: It's about the future and the way rich people control us ...

A: [5]Who's it?

B: Jennifer Lawrence and Josh Hutcherson.

A: Oh, she's good.

B: Yeah. It's a good movie – [6]I think you'd like.

LEARN TO
LINK WORDS TO SPEAK FASTER

W8.2

3 A Listen and draw lines to show the linking.

1 Are you looking for‿a movie?
2 Is it an action movie?
3 Is anyone famous in it?
4 Do you want to watch a movie?
5 I don't have a DVD player.
6 I have it on my computer.

B Listen again and repeat.

W8.3

4 A Listen and circle the sentence you hear.

1 a) Are you looking for a movie?
b) Are you looking for a friend?
2 a) Is it an action movie?
b) Is it an interesting movie?
3 a) Is Anna Faris in it?
b) Is anyone famous in it?
4 a) Do you want to borrow a DVD?
b) Do you want to buy a DVD?
5 a) I don't have a CD player.
b) I don't have a DVD player.

B Listen again and repeat.

goes on vacation to Miami	takes a holiday in Miami
Are you familiar with it?	Do you know it?

VOCABULARY

ADJECTIVES

1 A Complete the article. Put the letters in order and write the words.

HOW DO YOU TRAVEL AROUND THE CITY?

I go to work by rollerblades. It's a [1]f*ast* (asft) way to travel, and it's very [2]h_________ (ehtlhya) because I get lots of exercise. Sometimes it feels pretty [3]d_________ (dnesaurog) with so many cars around me, and it's a little [4]i_________ (icnietnveonn) because I need to change into shoes when I go into my office. But rollerblades are a lot of fun.
Tony Jones, film producer

rollerblades

skateboard

I go everywhere by skateboard. True, it takes a long time to learn because it's [5]d__________ (idticulff) to ride one, but it's very [6]c__________ (oeneintenv) – when I go into a store, I just pick up the skateboard and carry it like a book!
Joel Williams, musician

I use my scooter all around the city. It's [7]s___________, (eafs) it's [8]e___________ (yeas) to ride, and it's more [9]c___________ (forebltaome) than rollerblades or a skateboard because balancing isn't a problem. Sometimes you see scooters with motors on them, but those are really [10]p___________ (tuinpogll). "Go green," I say!
Nanci Levine, student

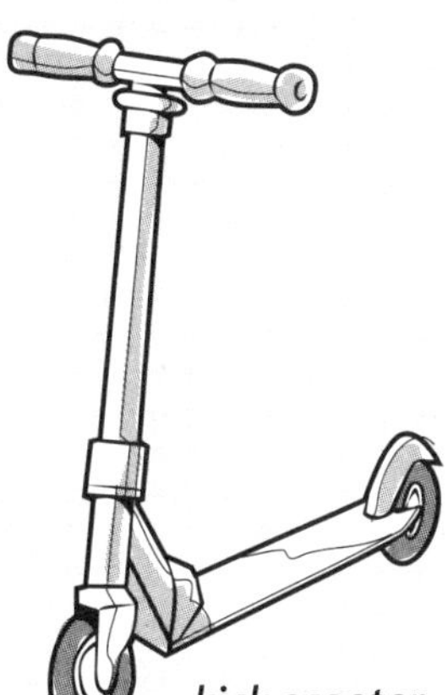

kick scooter

W 9.1 **B** Listen and check.

C Listen again and write the adjectives in the correct column for each stress pattern. Then listen and repeat.

1 O	2 Oo
fast	
3 Ooo	**4 oOo**
5 oOoo	**6 ooOoo**

READING

2 A Read the article. How does the writer feel? Choose from the words in the box.

happy relaxed angry hungry funny

NO MORE WHEELS!

A shopkeeper speaks out

"I have a small food shop downtown, and I really don't like customers coming into the shop on wheels. A businessman comes in on a kick scooter, and he thinks it's funny to do his shopping *on* the scooter. I don't think it's funny – I think it's dangerous. And the skateboarders, they're even worse. They say they ride skateboards because it's fast and convenient – you know, it's easy to pick up the skateboard when they walk into a store, but they don't pick up the skateboard, they ride it up and down my store! But the worst of all are the rollerbladers. They fly into the store; of course, they don't take off the rollerblades because it's inconvenient, and they crash into customers and knock things down. It's terrible! So now I have a new rule: No more wheels. Shoes only!"

B Read the article again. Are the sentences true (T) or false (F)?

1 The writer has a restaurant. *F*
2 He thinks the businessman is a funny person. _____
3 To the writer, kick scooters are not safe. _____
4 He thinks kick scooters are better than skateboards. _____
5 Skateboarders usually pick up their skateboards when they're in his shop. _____
6 Rollerbladers are the most dangerous, he thinks. _____

GRAMMAR

CAN/CAN'T, HAVE TO/DON'T HAVE TO

3 A Complete the conversations with the correct form of can.

1 A: Can I park (I / park) my car here?
B: No, ______. (you)

2 A: ______ (you / not ride) your bike on the sidewalk because it's too dangerous.
B: Oh. OK.

3 A: ______ (people / smoke) on the train?
B: No, ______ (they).

4 A: ______ (we / walk) to the theater?
B: Yes, ______ (we), but it's a long way.

5 A: ______ (taxis / drive) into downtown, but not cars.
B: OK, thanks.

B Complete the conversations with *can't* or *don't have to*.

Conversation 1

A: What clothes do you have to wear for the new job?
B: I don't have to wear a suit and tie, but I have to wear a white shirt, and I ______ wear jeans.

Conversation 2

A: It's late ... after midnight.
B: Yes, but we ______ get up early tomorrow. It's Saturday.

Conversation 3

A: You ______ drive down this road. It's for buses only.
B: Oh, sorry.

Conversation 4

A: I don't have any money with me.
B: It's OK. You ______ pay me now. Give me the money tomorrow.

4 Underline the correct alternatives.

A: Hey, do you want to do something tonight? I [1]*can't/<u>don't have to</u>* work.
B: Let's see ... No, I [2]*can't/don't have to* meet you tonight – I [3]*can/have to* work late.
A: Well, [4]*can we/do we have to* meet tomorrow?
B: Sorry, I [5]*can't/don't have to*, I'm busy. But I [6]*can/have to* do something on Saturday.
A: Great. We [7]*can/have to* go to that new Italian restaurant, La Spezia.
B: Hmm ... Saturday night is usually crowded. [8]*Can we/Do we have to* book a table or [9]*can we/do we have to* just go there?
A: It isn't so popular now, so we [10]*can't/ don't have to* book. And if we [11]*can't/don't have to* get a table, we [12]*can/have to* go somewhere else.
B: Great! See you on Saturday, then.

LISTENING

5 A Look at the picture of Carin Van Buren on her balancing scooter. Do you think the statements are true (T) or false (F)?

1 It's difficult to ride. ______
2 You can ride it on the pavement. ______
3 In a city, it's faster than a bus. ______
4 It's tiring to ride. ______

W 9.2

B Listen and check.

C Listen again and answer the questions.

1 Does Carin ride the scooter to work?
Yes, she does.

2 How did she travel to work before?
______

3 How long does it take to learn?
______

4 How fast can the scooter go?
______

5 Does she think a scooter is better than a bike?
______

6 Where does she leave her scooter at work?
______

7 How does she feel when people laugh at her on her scooter?
______

8 Does she like it when people stop her and ask her questions?
______

sidewalk — pavement

VOCABULARY
TRANSPORTATION COLLOCATIONS

1 A Label the pictures.

A

____

B

____

C

____

D

____

E

____

F

____

G

____

H

____

I

____

B Match sentences 1–9 with pictures A–I in Exercise 1A.

1 It has two wheels, you get on and off it, and it doesn't use gas. _C_
2 It usually has two pilots and can carry a lot of people. ____
3 It has four wheels, and you pay the driver at the end of the journey. ____
4 It has four legs and you ride it. ____
5 It has two wheels, and it uses gas. ____
6 It has hundreds of seats, but it can't go on a road. You need a ticket. ____
7 It moves on water. It can carry a lot of cars and people. ____
8 It moves on water. It can't carry a lot of people. ____
9 It has wheels, and it stops often. You pay at the start of the journey. ____

2 Complete the conversations with the correct form of the verbs in the box.

~~get off~~ go by (x2) go on take ride come by get on

1 **A:** Can you tell me the way to the Sports Center?
B: Yes, you take the number 195 bus, and you _get off_ at the third stop.
2 **A:** Did you drive here?
B: No, I ____________ bus.
3 **A:** Is this Kenji's first bike?
B: Yes, and he ____________ it everywhere.
4 **A:** What's the best way to get to the airport?
B: You can go by bus, or you can ____________ a taxi.
5 **A:** How do you go to school?
B: I usually ____________ foot.
6 **A:** How does Stefanie go to work?
B: She ____________ car.
7 **A:** Where are you?
B: I'm at the Berlin airport, and I ____________ a plane to South Africa, so I can't talk.
8 **A:** How did you travel to Paris?
B: I ____________ train.

READING

3 A Read the article and circle the correct options.

1 A *commute* is
 a) a type of transportation.
 b) the journey from home to work and back.
 c) a part of a car.

2 Jim Kendrick won $10,000 because
 a) he was the safest driver in Texas.
 b) he drove the most kilometers in one year.
 c) he traveled the furthest to work.

DO YOU THINK YOUR COMMUTE IS BAD? TRY 400 MILES A DAY!

Do you think gas prices are too high? Well, be happy that you aren't Jim Kendrick of Texas in the U.S.

Every weekday, Kendrick drives 200 miles from his home in San Antonio, Texas, to his job at AbleCargo in the port of Houston and then 200 miles back again! He leaves work at 5:00 a.m. and gets home and has dinner with his wife at 9:00 p.m.

For his daily journey, Kendrick won the competition "America's Longest Commute". His three-and-a-half-hour commute was longer than all the other people in the competition, and is a lot more than the average American commute of twenty-five minutes.

"I was surprised to win," said Kendrick, who won $10,000. "I was sure that someone else had a longer commute. But it's great – $10,000 is just enough to buy gas for another year." Why does he do it? "Well, my wife and I have a beautiful house in San Antonio, and our lifestyle is important to us. The drive also gives me a lot of energy. Sometimes, when I drive my Ford Mustang down the highway, I feel like a professional racing car driver."

How much longer does he want to do this commute? "Another five or ten years," Kendrick said. "I don't see any reason to stop. But gas prices are high, so maybe I need to look for a job closer to home."

B Read the article again and match the sentence halves. Then read the sentences and write the line number from the article where you found the information.

1 Jim won the contest because
 f – line 18

2 He was surprised to win because
 ____

3 He was happy about the money because
 ____

4 He does the commute because
 ____

5 He feels good when he drives because
 ____

6 He's thinking about changing jobs because
 ____

a) he doesn't want to change his lifestyle.
b) he spends about $10,000 a year on gas.
c) he thought someone else drove further.
d) gas prices are so high.
e) he feels like a racing car driver.
f) ~~his commute was the longest.~~

GRAMMAR

ARTICLES: *A/AN, THE,* NO ARTICLE

4 Complete the text with *a/an*, *the* or – (no article).

Jim lives in [1] *a* house near [2] ____ San Antonio, Texas. He has [3] ____ job at AbleCargo in [4] ____ Houston, Texas, in [5] ____ U.S. AbleCargo is [6] ____ shipping company, and Jim's [7] ____ engineer there. He drives seven hours every day and gets [8] ____ home at 8:30 and has [9] ____ dinner at 9:00 p.m. He likes [10] ____ fast cars, and he drives [11] ____ Ford Mustang. Jim doesn't commute on [12] ____ weekend.

5 Add *a/an* (x4) and *the* (x5) to the sentences. One sentence does not need any extra words.

1 Yes, *the* bus station is down this street on *the* left.

2 Rajiv is actor in Mumbai.

3 I don't have car, but I have motorcycle.

4 Town Hall opens at 9:30 in morning.

5 I love planes and flying. I always ask for window seat.

6 Keith often works at home in evening.

7 Is Manchester in U.K.?

8 I often go home by taxi at night.

closer to — nearer

VOCABULARY

EXCUSES

1 Complete the excuses.

1 I didn't h*e a r* my al_ _ _ cl_ _ _.
2 I lo_ _ my ke_ _.
3 My car br_ _ _ d_ _ _.
4 The traf_ _ _ was bad.
5 I got up late and m_ _ _ _ _ _ the bus.

FUNCTION

APOLOGIZING

2 A Put the words in the correct order to complete the conversation.

A	B
Oh, hi! [1] *I'm really sorry I'm late.* (late / sorry / I'm / I'm / really) I missed the train.	
	Hmm … [2] __________. (you / believe / don't / I)
No, really. [3] __________. (terrible / was / traffic / the)	
	And?
And [4] __________. (car / my / down / broke)	
	Your car, again?
And [5] __________. (my / left / I / home /at / wallet)	
	Ah, your wallet.
And … OK, I forgot about our meeting! [6] __________. (feel / this / terrible / I / about)	
	Well, [7] __________. (about / worry / don't / it)
[8] __________. (so / I'm / sorry)	
	[9] __________. (no, / fine / it's / really,)
I'm so, so …	
	That's OK!! [10] __________. (don't / but / again / happen / it / let)

W 9.3 **B Listen and check.**

LEARN TO

TELL A LONG STORY

3 A Complete the story with the words in the box.

~~first of all~~ and but so because (x2) then finally

We had a terrible day at the airport. [1] *First of all*, we arrived forty minutes late, [2] __________ we missed our train. We were worried that we might miss the plane [3] __________ they don't let you get on when you're not there on time. [4] __________, when we got to the airport, we found that the plane wasn't on time, [5] __________ we went for a coffee at the airport café [6] __________ started talking to some people. They were very interesting, and we had a nice chat. [7] __________, we got on the plane. When we found our seats, Jane looked for her bag, [8] __________ it wasn't there. It was at the café!

B Write Bruce's email using the prompts.

Dear Alexis,

I'm really sorry about last night. I know it was your birthday, but I had an unlucky evening …

First of all, I / leave / the house late because I / lose / my keys.

Then I / miss / the bus, so I / call / a taxi, but the taxi / break down / and I / wait / thirty minutes for another taxi.

After that, I / get / to the restaurant an hour late, but I / leave / your present in the taxi.

I / call / the taxi company, but they / not answer, so I / go / into the restaurant, but you / not be there.

Finally, I / go / home and / try / to call you, but you / not answer.

Now I don't know what to do. I'm really sorry.

Love,

Bruce

First of all, I left the house late because…

GRAMMAR VERB FORMS

1 A Underline the correct alternatives.

Jesse's festival blog

Jesse McCormack is a member of the rock group the Stringers. He [1]*writes/is writing* most of the band's songs and [2]*plays/is playing* lead guitar. This is his summer festival blog.

Saturday August 4

I [3]*write/'m writing* my blog today at our fourth festival this summer ... but it's the biggest, with more than 25,000 people, and we [4]*have/'re having* a great time. The atmosphere here is amazing, and people are very friendly. We usually [5]*arrive/are arriving* the day before we play, but this time we [6]*come/came* here two days ago.

Most people have tents, but in fact you [7]*don't have to/can't* sleep in a tent. You [8]*can/can't* sleep in your car. And there are the usual festival rules, for example you [9]*can/can't* use glasses for drinks – you [10]*have to/don't have to* use plastic cups. This is a good idea because sometimes people, often children, [11]*walk/are walking* around with no shoes on.

There's only one hour before we start our show. Danny [12]*talks/'s talking* to a woman from Radio One. Saul [13]*practices/is practicing* our first song. Our manager, Dave, [14]*calls/is calling* us, so I [15]*have to/can* stop now. More tomorrow!

B Complete the interview with the correct simple present or present continuous form of the verbs in parentheses.

Janna: This is Janna Towli from Radio One, and I [1]*'m talking* (talk) to Danny Wright from the Stringers. Hi, Danny.
Danny: Hi, everyone.
Janna: So Danny, [2]________________ (you / enjoy) yourself at the festival?
Danny: Yeah, it's cool.
Janna: We have some questions. First, from Luka. He asks: "[3]________________ (Jesse / write) all the songs, or [4]________________ (you / write) any of them?"
Danny: Oh, Jesse is the songwriter. I just [5]________________ (sing) the songs.
Janna: And from Viktoria: "What's your favorite Stringers song?"
Danny: Hum ... *You Never* [6]________________ (say) *"I Love You."*
Janna: OK, right. And the last question, from Abby. She asks: "What [7]________________ (Danny / wear) today?"
Danny: Me? Well, today I [8]________________ (wear) a Stringers T-shirt and jeans. My usual! Oh, there's Dave, our manager. I have to go.
Janna: Thanks for talking to us. Good luck with the show!
Danny: Thanks!

VOCABULARY ALPHABET PUZZLE

2 Complete the sentences with words beginning with the letters A–Z.

A I'm sorry I'm late. I didn't hear my *alarm* clock.
B My grandfather had a moustache and a big black *beard*.
C The train stop is near my apartment, so it's very ____________ for me.
D Riding a bike is very ____________, so you have to wear a helmet.
E The opposite of *full* is ____________.
F The White House is one of the most ____________ buildings in the world.
G I want to see the Eiffel Tower. Where do I ____________ off the bus?
H *Frankenstein* was one of the first ____________ movies. It was very scary.
I The opposite of *boring* is ____________.
J Fast food is sometimes called ____________ food.
K Do you ____________ the way to the bus station?
L The water in the ____________ is very cold. We can't swim there.
M I got up late, and I ____________ my bus.
N The children in the next room are too ____________ – I can't work.
O Do you go by car or ____________ foot?
P Cars are more ____________ than bikes. Bikes are greener.
Q ____________! The baby's sleeping.
R Can you ____________ a good DVD?
S The map says that Via Lagrange is a pedestrian ____________.
T I was late because the ____________ was bad.
U Alan's shoes are too small, so they're very ____________.
V She was born in a small ____________ in Belgium.
W The traffic is ____________ at five o'clock than at three o'clock.
X The opposite of *cheap* is e____________.
Y Hi, Liz. It's Jon. I waited for ____________ for two hours! What happened?
Z My vacations were great. We saw the Great Wall. It was ama____________!

GRAMMAR COMPARATIVES AND SUPERLATIVES

3 **Complete the text with the correct comparative or superlative form of the adjectives in the box.**

~~good~~ tall cheap hot quiet interesting slow convenient cold fast

SHANGHAI

When is the best time to go?

The 1 ___best___ months to visit are May and October, when it's 66—75°F. July and August are 2 ________ months, when it can be 82°F. November to April are 3 ________ months, when it's 37—57°F.

How can I get around?

You can travel by bus or by metro. Buses are 4 ________ than the metro, especially in the morning and evening when the traffic is bad. The metro is 5 ________ than buses, but there are only two metro lines. The 6 ________ way to travel around the city is by taxi because there are lots – they go everywhere, and they aren't very expensive.

I only have one day! What can I see?

Visit 7 ________ building in China, the 1614-feet Shanghai World Financial Center. The floor is glass, and it feels like walking in the sky. Walk along the Bund, next to the river – it's very central, but it's a lot 8 ________ than the noisy city downtown. And visit the Shanghai Museum – most visitors to the city say this is 9 ________ thing to see in Shanghai.

Where can I stay?

Shanghai has hundreds of hotels, and there are many two-star and three-star hotels for travelers on a budget – of course, these are 10 ________ than the 4-star luxury hotels. Check the internet for recommendations from other travelers.

FUNCTION RECOMMENDING; GIVING DIRECTIONS

R3.1

4 **A** **Listen to the conversations and circle the correct option.**

Jurgen recommends a restaurant to Greg, but

a) Greg doesn't understand and takes the wrong street.
b) He gives bad directions, and Greg doesn't find the restaurant.
c) Greg decides to stay home and eat pizza.

B **Listen again. Are the sentences true (T) or false (F)?**

1 It's Jurgen's wife's birthday. ___F___
2 Greg and his wife like Chinese food. ______
3 Jurgen recommends a Chinese restaurant. ______
4 The restaurant is near the movie theater. ______
5 Greg and his wife find the restaurant. ______
6 They have pizza at the restaurant. ______

C **Listen again and complete the sentences.**

1 What kind of food ___do you like___?
2 Do you think my wife ________?
3 Can you tell ________?
4 Go down Mason Street past the pharmacy ________.
5 Then go straight ________ 200 meters.
6 Oh, no – I'm so ________.
7 I feel terrible ________.
8 Don't worry ________.

GRAMMAR ARTICLES

5 **Complete the text with *a/an*, *the* or – (no article).**

POLAND – DAY 7

The best way to see 1 ___the___ city of 2 ______ Krakow is in 3 ______ Trabant – the classic eastern-European car. The tour starts at 9:00 a.m. 4 ______ downtown, where you meet your tour guides Irek and Kasia. Irek is 5 ______ college student, and Kasia is 6 ______ history teacher, and together they know Krakow better than most professional guides. You start the tour on 7 ______ foot and visit Cloth Hall in 8 ______ center of Grand Square. You then go by 9 ______ car and visit Nowa Huta and the Jewish quarter. Lunch is at 10 ______ restaurant near the castle. 11 ______ Polish food is quite rich, so try not to eat too much! In 12 ______ afternoon, Irek and Kasia can show you Wawel Castle or take you back to your hotel.

CHECK

Circle the correct option to complete the sentences.

1 Sitting on the beach is __________ working.
a) relaxing than b) better than c) more nice than

2 There was a bridge over the __________.
a) desert b) river c) mountain

3 I __________ my MP3 player.
a) listening to b) 'm listenning to c) 'm listening to

4 What __________ like?
a) does Jon look b) Jon does look c) Jon looks

5 A: Do I __________ the bus here for the museum?
B: No, at the next stop.
a) go by b) ride c) get off

6 I didn't get a seat because the bus was __________.
a) comfortable b) uncomfortable c) crowded

7 Sorry I'm late. I __________ my train.
a) lost b) missed c) left

8 A: What __________?
B: I'm working on the computer.
a) you are doing b) are you doing c) do you doing

9 I don't think __________ this DVD. It's too scary.
a) you'd like b) you like c) you recommend

10 My wife works __________. She's a writer.
a) at home b) at the home c) home

11 __________ to the airport by bus?
a) You can go b) Do you can go c) Can you go

12 Go __________ until the end of the street.
a) straight b) straight at c) strait on

13 It was difficult to walk in the __________ because of all the trees.
a) mountain b) forest c) village

14 The children __________ very well at the moment.
a) aren't feeling b) don't feeling c) aren't feel

15 He __________ slim with short black hair.
a) 's got b) 's c) has

16 Spanish is __________ than English.
a) easyer b) easier c) more easy

17 Children __________ pay. It's free for them.
a) don't have to b) can't c) haven't to

18 A: I laughed a lot at this DVD. It's very funny.
B: Oh, so it's a __________.
a) drama b) musical c) comedy

19 A: Is there a post office near here?
B: Yes, go down here, and it's __________.
a) on the left b) on left c) the left

20 I always go by subway because it's fast and __________.
a) convenient b) polluting c) dangerous

21 It's __________ hotel in Saudi Arabia.
a) the bigger b) the bigest c) the biggest

22 The sign says "No Parking", so you __________ park here.
a) have to b) don't have to c) can't

23 My grandmother is __________.
a) in sixties b) in her sixties c) in the sixties

24 A: Do you often call your parents?
B: Yes, I talked to __________ last night.
a) them b) him and her c) they

25 __________ is good for you.
a) Milk b) The milk c) A milk

26 Who is __________ player on the soccer team?
a) most bad b) the worst c) the baddest

27 __________, the train arrived. It was four hours late.
a) First of all b) After c) Finally

28 Leonie __________ black.
a) always is wearing b) is wearing always
c) always wears

29 A: Where's the tourist information center?
B: You __________ left and walk for about five minutes.
a) take b) turn to c) turn

30 A: Do you have __________?
B: No, I don't, but I have two brothers.
a) a sister b) the sister c) sister

RESULT /30

GRAMMAR

BE GOING TO; WOULD LIKE TO

1 A Look at the table and complete the sentences with the correct form of *be going to* or *would like to*.

	Plans for next week	Plans for next year	Wishes for the future
Jim, U.S.	start new job at the bank – Monday	look for a new apartment not stay at parents' house	be very rich
Hiro, Japan	have haircut – Tuesday	go to college	work in TV
Tom and Kim, Ireland	visit daughter Lynn and family – Saturday/ Sunday	not go on vacation	move closer to Lynn

Jim

Hiro

Tom and Kim

1 Jim's *going to start* his new job at the bank on Monday.
2 He ______ for a new apartment next year.
3 He ______ at his parents' house.
4 He ______ very rich.
5 Hiro ______ a haircut on Tuesday.
6 She ______ to college next year.
7 She ______ in TV.
8 Tom and Kim ______ their daughter on the weekend.
9 They ______ on vacation next year.
10 They ______ closer to their daughter.

B Write questions about the people in Exercise 1A using the prompts. Use be going to or would like to.

1 which bank / you / work at, Jim?
Which bank are you going to work at, Jim?
2 where / you / look for / a new apartment, Jim?
______
3 when / you / go / to college, Hiro?
______
4 why / like / work / in TV, Hiro?
______
5 how / you / travel, Tom and Kim?
______
6 why / like / move / closer to your daughter, Tom and Kim?
______

C Match answers a)–f) with questions 1–6 in Exercise 1B.

a) Because I want to be famous. *4*
b) We're going to go by train. ______
c) Downtown. ______
d) We'd like to see our grandchildren more. ______
e) In September next year. ______
f) At HACB bank. ______

2 Put the words in the correct order to make questions. Then write short answers about you.

1 TV / you / to / evening / watch / are / this / going
Are you going to watch TV this evening?
Yes, I am./No, I'm not.
2 like / work / would / TV / to / you / in
______?
______
3 weekend / you / family / see / next / are / to / going / your
______?
______
4 for / English / to / useful / be / you / is / going
______?
______
5 like / new / would / phone / a / you / buy / to / cell phone
______?
______
6 your / study / classmates / year / you / going / English / next / to / are / and
______?
______
7 in / like / live / country / you / to / would / another
______?
______
8 home / your / like / now / to / go / would / classmates
______?
______

READING

3 A Read the article and circle the best title.

a) Lottery winners around the world

b) Jobless man wins lottery

c) Lottery winner starts organization to help people

When Juan stopped to buy a lottery ticket last week, he didn't have a job or enough money to pay the bills. These were his last few coins. He picked seven numbers, and then asked another customer to pick the last number. "I'll never win, anyway," he thought. But he was wrong – he won $1.2 million!

First of all, he paid all his bills, and then he went to buy two – yes, two – really, really expensive cars. But Juan isn't going to drive them – he never learned to drive because he didn't have enough money to buy a car before. He bought them for his children, Carla and Paolo.

Winning the lottery isn't going to change Juan. He and his wife aren't going to spend their money without thinking. First, they are going to buy homes for their children, and then they are going to take a long vacation in America. After that, Juan is going to start an organization to help people without jobs because he was also unemployed and knows how hard it is.

B Read the article again and answer the questions.

1 How much money did Juan have when he bought the ticket?

A few coins.

2 Did he think he could win the lottery?

______

3 How much money did he win?

______

4 Who is going to drive the cars?

______

5 Does he want to change his life?

______

6 Who are Juan and his wife going to buy homes for?

______

7 Who does Juan want to help with his organization?

______

VOCABULARY

PLANS

4 A Complete the puzzle with the words in the box and find the message.

~~time off~~ married stay clubbing learn vacation start move some work go for

I
1 t a k e *t i m e o f f*
2 _ _ _ _ _ a w a l k
3 d o _ _ _ _ _ _ _ _
's
4 g o o n _ _ _ _ _ _ _ _
5 g o _ _ _ _ _ _ _ _
6 _ _ _ h o m e
7 g e t _ _ _ _ _ _ _
8 _ _ _ _ _ a n e w j o b
e
9 _ _ _ _ _ t o s w i m
10 _ _ _ _ i n

Message: ______!

B Complete the words in the conversations.

Conversation 1

A: What are you going to do this weekend?

B: I'm going [1]jo*gging* on Saturday morning, and then at night I'm going to meet Bob, and we're going for a [2]dr______ in the bar.

Conversation 2

A: So, what are your plans?

B: Well, we're going to get [3]ma______ next year, and we'd like to [4]mo______ to another country – maybe Spain. We'd like to [5]ge______ a house there, and start a [6]fa______ – maybe have three or four children.

Conversation 3

A: What's your son going to do?

B: He's going to stay with some [7]fr______ in São Paulo. He wants to do a [8]co______ and [9]le______ Portuguese, and then he'd like to get a [10]jo______ with a computer company in Brazil.

Conversation 4

A: What are you going to do with your lottery money?

B: First, I'm going to [11]ta______ a break! I'm going to [12]g______ on a long vacation – and [13]st______ in a five-star hotel, of course!

Conversation 5

A: Are you going to have a [14]pa______ and invite all your friends?

B: Of course! And then I'm going to go [15]sh______ in Paris to buy some fantastic designer clothes.

learned learnt

VOCABULARY

PHRASES WITH *GET*

1 A Add the vowels to complete the phrases.

1 Marco got *sunburned* (brnsd), so he
2 I got ________ (thrsty), so I
3 Adrian got ________ (trd) at school, so he
4 They got ________ (wt), so they
5 Ed and Leo got ________ (hngry), so they
6 I got very ________ (ht), so I
7 Helena got ________ (lst), so she
8 We got ________ (cld), so we
9 Ferdi got ________ (stng) by a bee, so he
10 Alice was cold, so to get ________ (wrm), she

B Match a)–j) with 1–10 in Exercise 1A to make sentences.

a) was an hour late for the meeting. ____
b) put some lotion on his finger. ____
c) had a second breakfast. ____
d) went to sleep in the break. ____
e) changed into dry clothes. ____
f) took a hot shower. ____
g) went for a drink with Carson. ____
h) put on our coats. ____
i) stayed indoors for the next two days. *1*
j) took off my sweater. ____

C Listen and write the words in the correct column.

1 /ʌ/ e.g. *cup*	2 /ɒ/ e.g. *job*	3 /e/ e.g. *red*
	hot	
4 /ɜː/ e.g. *her*	**5 /ɔː/ e.g. *four***	**6 /əʊ/ e.g. *go***

2 Look at meanings 1–4 of *get* in the table. Then write the words below in the correct column.

1 become	2 arrive	3 buy	4 obtain
get … *hungry*	get …	get …	get …

to school | hungry | a new computer | some help | a present for a friend | to work | a new car | home | a glass of water | a job | lost | tired

LISTENING

3 A Listen to four people who survived in difficult situations. Match speakers 1–4 with places a)–d).

Speaker 1	a) jungle
Speaker 2	b) mountain
Speaker 3	c) desert
Speaker 4	d) sea

B Listen again and circle the correct options.

1 Speaker 1 ____
a) ate fish.
b) drank seawater.
c) was cold.

2 Speaker 1 ____
a) got sunburned.
b) got tired.
c) saw a lot of sharks.

3 Speaker 2 ____
a) got cold.
b) walked all day.
c) got very thirsty.

4 Speaker 2 ____
a) saw lots of insects.
b) had food with her.
c) sometimes took her shoes off.

5 Speaker 3 ____
a) was on the mountain for three nights.
b) got lost because of the snow.
c) made a fire.

6 Speaker 3 ____
a) slept on the ground.
b) got hungry.
c) stayed warm.

7 Speaker 4 ____
a) got very hungry.
b) got thirsty.
c) didn't get bored.

8 Speaker 4 ____
a) had some food with her.
b) ate plants.
c) ate insects.

lotion / took a shower — cream / had a bath

GRAMMAR

WILL, MIGHT (NOT), WON'T

4 Complete the sentences with *will* or *won't* and the verbs in the box.

~~get~~ be (x2) miss win come know love

1 Wear your coat, or you*'ll get* cold.
2 Do you think Brazil ______ the World Cup?
3 It's very late. I'm sure the store ______ open.
4 I don't want to go to the party! I ______ any people there.
5 Come on! We ______ the train.
6 Read this book. I'm sure you ______ it.
7 Oh, no! I'm late again. The boss ______ happy.
8 You can invite Alain, but he ______. He doesn't like jazz music.

5 Underline the correct alternatives.

SURVIVE
IN THE CITY

People always talk about survival in the jungle, at sea, etc., but I'll tell you a really dangerous place: The city! Here are my tips for survival.

- Don't drive. Traffic is usually terrible, and you [1]*might not/'ll/won't* spend more time in your car than seeing the city.
- Ask people for help – most people [2]*will/might/won't* be happy to stop and help you.
- Don't stand in the street with a map in your hand and a camera around your neck. People [3]*will/might not/won't* know you're a tourist. That's not a problem, but someone [4]*will/might/might not* come and take your money.
- Wear normal clothes, not expensive ones. With expensive clothes, people [5]*will/might not/won't* think you have lots of money and yes – they [6]*'ll/might/won't* take it away from you!
- Carry an umbrella. It often rains, and with an umbrella you [7]*'ll/might/won't* get wet.
- Don't stay out too late, or it [8]*'ll/might/might not* be easy to find a bus or a taxi.
- Give waiters a good tip, maybe 20%. You [9]*'ll/might/might not* go back to the same restaurant, and the waiter [10]*will/might not/won't* forget you!

W10.3

6 Listen and number each pair of sentences in the order you hear them.

1 a) You'll get cold *2*
b) You get cold. *1*
2 a) We'll miss the train. ______
b) We miss the train. ______
3 a) I'm sure you'll hate it. ______
b) I'm sure you hate it. ______
4 a) They'll know you're a tourist. ______
b) They know you're a tourist. ______
5 a) I'll stay at home. ______
b) I stay at home. ______
6 a) I'll never go out. ______
b) I never go out. ______

WRITING

TOO, ALSO, AS WELL

7 Are *too*, *also* and *as well* in the correct place? Check (✓) three correct sentences. Correct the wrong sentences.

1 The bus is a good way to travel, and the subway is too good. *too*
2 If you buy a travel card for the subway, you can also use it on the bus.
3 You can ask storekeepers for help – they're very friendly, and they'll know the city as well.
4 It's generally a safe city, but it can be dangerous also to walk alone late at night in some areas.
5 It isn't a good idea to carry a lot of money, and leave your expensive watch too at home.
6 You can get delicious food in cafés and as well in street markets.
7 Don't walk too far, and also wear comfortable shoes – then you won't get tired.
8 At night, taxis are as well convenient, but they're expensive.

8 Write a short text giving advice for a visitor to your town or city. Use *too*, *also*, *as well* and these phrases to help you. Write 80–100 words.

The ... is a good way to travel ...
It's a good idea to carry ...
You can ask ... for help, and you can ask ...
It can be dangerous to ...

subway or metro / storekeepers — underground / shopkeepers

VOCABULARY

ART AND CULTURE

1 Put the letters in the correct order to make words connected with art and culture. Then write them in the correct place in the crossword.

IMEVO	M*OVIE*
INATPIGN	P________
RWGIAND	D________
AORPOGHHTP	P________
TESAUT	S________
EHIXTOINIB	E________
EACND EPNAMRCEOFR	D________
OCCTNER	C________
LPYA	P________

FUNCTION

MAKING SUGGESTIONS

2 Complete the conversation with the words in the box. There are two extra words.

~~why~~ do how don't about let's have stay

Tim: Gordon, 1 *why* don't we do something different this evening?
Gordon: I don't know. Do you have any ideas?
Tim: How [2] ________ going to a concert?
Gordon: Hmmm ... That might be difficult. We don't like the same music. You like rock, I like hip hop.
Tim: Oh. That's true. [3] ________ you want to invite some friends over?
Gordon: I don't really feel like doing that.
Tim: OK then. Why [4] ________ we [5] ________ home and watch TV?
Gordon: That's a good idea. What's on?
Tim: Let me see ... Uh, *Prometheus* by Ridley Scott.
Gordon: Great!
Tim: And [6] ________ popcorn, too.
Gordon: Sounds good!

LEARN TO

RESPOND TO SUGGESTIONS

3 A Correct the mistakes in suggestions 1–5 and responses a)–e).

1 Let*'s* go shopping. *e*
2 How about go for a bike ride? ____
3 Why don't we going to an art gallery? ____
4 What about staying at home and cook something? ____
5 Who about making spaghetti and meatballs? ____

a) It's not for. Looking at paintings is boring!
b) I don't really feel like do that. I'm too tired.
c) That a good idea. You make the meatballs; I can make the pasta.
d) Wonderful! What we eat?
e) That isn't very good idea. I have not much money.

B Match the suggestions with the responses in Exercise 3A.

Do you want to...? Great! or Wonderful! | Shall we...? Brilliant!

VOCABULARY

THE BODY; HEALTH

1 A Find twelve words for parts of the body in the puzzle.

N	M	O	E	L	B	O	W
O	T	H	U	M	B	I	V
S	L	E	G	U	T	M	B
E	K	N	E	E	O	O	A
P	H	E	A	D	E	U	C
E	E	N	E	C	K	T	K
S	T	O	M	A	C	H	C
W	E	H	A	N	D	I	N

W11.1

B Listen and repeat.

C Listen again and write the words in the correct column.

1 /e/ e.g. *red*	2 /æ/ e.g. *happy*
3 /iː/ e.g. *meat*	**4 /əʊ/ e.g. *no***
	elbow
5 /ʌ/ e.g. *fun*	**6 /aʊ/ e.g. *now***

2 Put the letters in the correct order to make health problems. Start with the underlined letter.

1 I have a *cold*, so I must stay in bed today. (dclo)
2 My leg ________. (shutr)
3 I have a bad ________. (chadeeha)
4 I have a ________ ________. (rose trahot)
5 I have a ________. (nrnuy osne)
6 I have an awful ________. (cahastcehom)
7 I have a ________. (metterupare)
8 I have a ________. (gucoh)

GRAMMAR

SHOULD/SHOULDN'T

3 Read the leaflet about travel health. Check any new words in your dictionary. Then complete the leaflet with *should/shouldn't* and the words in parentheses.

TRAVEL HEALTH: BEFORE YOU GO

We answer your FAQs (frequently asked questions) about health on vacation:

[1] *Should I see* (I/see) my doctor before I go on vacation?
Yes, [2] ________ (you/speak) to your doctor or your local travel center about six weeks before you leave.

[3] ________ (I/get) any vaccinations?
Your doctor or nurse can give you information, or you can check on the internet. [4] ________ (you/not have) a lot of vaccinations together, so start early.

What else [5] ________ (I/do)?
[6] ________ (you/visit) your dentist as well because dentists can be very expensive in other countries. [7] ________ (you/take) a Traveler's First Aid Kit with sunblock, bandages and painkillers, but [8] ________ (you/not open) these before you travel. Officials at the airport might ask to check them.

Any other advice?
Well, [9] ________ (you/not travel) when you have a bad earache or a cold. And it's important to relax, but [10] ________ (you/not drink) alcohol or coffee in the airport or on the plane because they'll make you feel worse.

4 Complete the conversation with *should/shouldn't* and the verbs in the box. Add the correct pronouns (*I* or *you*).

go (x2) watch sleep do (x2) change eat

A: I'm going to fly to Japan soon, and I'm worried about the time difference, you know, getting tired after the journey.
B: Oh yes, jet lag can be difficult. [1] *You should go* to bed early for two or three nights before you travel.
A: What else [2] ________?
B: When you're on the plane, [3] ________ all the food they bring; it's too much. And [4] ________ your watch to Japanese local time.
A: And [5] ________ on the plane?
B: Yes, you need to rest, so [6] ________ all the movies or stay awake the whole time. It's a long journey! What time do you arrive?
A: At two in the afternoon.
B: You'll be very tired, but [7] ________ to bed. [8] ________ some exercise. It's a good idea to go for a walk and then wait and sleep when it's dark.
A: Thanks. That's good advice.

sunblock / bandages — sun cream / plasters

Walking – the perfect sport?

Forget about tennis, swimming, skiing and jogging. Walking is the easiest and cheapest way to stay fit. It's free, you don't need special clothes or equipment, you don't need a trainer or a special place. Anybody can do it any time: young people, older people, alone or in groups.

OK – perhaps it's not really a sport, but it is the most popular physical activity and one of the best ways to stay healthy. What are the benefits? Walking is good for your heart and your legs; regular walkers say they sleep better and feel happier, and smokers say they don't smoke so much.

Maybe you don't have very much time, so here are some ideas to help you start walking:

- Walk, don't drive, to the local store. If you have a lot to carry, take a small backpack.
- If you have children, walk with them to and from school.
- Get off the bus or train a stop or two early. This will give you some extra daily exercise – and it's cheaper, too!
- Take a walk on your lunch hour at school or work.
- Once a week take a longer walk, and go on a completely new route; this helps to keep things interesting.

There are walkers' clubs all over the world. Join one – walking is a great way to meet people and make new friends!

READING

5 A Read the article and number topics a)–d) in the order that you read about them.

a) Why is walking better than other sports? ___1___
b) How can you find time for walking? ______
c) Who can you walk with? ______
d) Why is walking good for your health? ______

B Read the article again and check (✓) the ideas it talks about.

1 Walking isn't expensive. ___✓___
2 You have to wear good walking shoes. ______
3 Age isn't important. ______
4 Walking is good for headaches. ______
5 You should go shopping on foot. ______
6 Get up earlier in the morning, and do some extra exercise every day. ______
7 Take a different walk every week so you don't get bored. ______
8 You can meet people more easily when walking. ______

C Find words 1–7 in the article. Then match them with definitions a)–g).

1 equipment	a) with no other people
2 a trainer	b) a bag that you carry on your back
3 alone	c) connected to your body
4 physical	d) the things you use for an activity, e.g. a machine in the gym
5 benefits	e) a way from one place to another
6 a backpack	f) good things
7 a route	g) a teacher

D Cover the article and try to complete the sentences. Then look at the article and check your answers.

Maybe you don't have very much time, so here are some ideas to help you start walking:

- Walk, don't drive, 1 ____________ the local store. If you 2 ____________ a lot to carry, take a small backpack.
- If you 3 ____________ children, walk 4 ____________ them to and 5 ____________ school.
- Get off the bus or train a stop or two early. This will give you some extra daily exercise – and it's cheaper, 6 ____________!
- Take a walk 7 ____________ your lunch hour 8 ____________ school or work.
- Once a week 9 ____________ a longer walk, and go on a completely new route; this helps to keep things interesting.

There are walkers' clubs 10 ____________ over the world. Join one – walking is a great way to 11 ____________ people and 12 ____________ new friends!

VOCABULARY

COMMUNICATION

1 A Complete the diagrams with the verbs in the box.

~~start~~ ~~finish~~ forget get send have answer (x2) turn on exchange remember turn off

1 _start_ / _finish_ / ______ → a conversation

2 ______ / ______ / ______ → a text message

3 ______ / ______ / ______ → names and numbers

4 ______ / ______ / ______ → your phone

B Complete the sentences with the verbs in Exercise 1A.

1 Sorry, I have to go now. Can we _finish_ the conversation now and talk again later?
2 I'll ______ you a text message when I get home.
3 I'm sorry, I don't ______ your name – I have a terrible memory.
4 Please ______ your phone. The play is starting.
5 I can't ______ his text message now – I'm busy. I'll do it later.
6 Good to see you again! Let's ______ numbers so we can talk again soon.
7 The two of you need to ______ a conversation – you should talk about this.
8 Please ______ your phone – it's ringing, again! And tell your friend that you are in a meeting and can't talk right now!
9 I always ______ my cell phone number. I have to write it down.
10 I didn't want to talk about this. I didn't ______ the conversation – you did.
11 The play's over – you can ______ your phone now.
12 When did you ______ this text message from Ewan? What does it say?

LISTENING

W11.2

2 A Listen to a radio program about time management. Number the problems in the order you hear about them.

multi-tasking	______	______
forgetting things you have to do	______	______
staying late to finish work	______	______
doing what you like doing first	______	______
starting work without planning	_1_	_d_
keeping two or three lists of things to do	______	______

B Listen again and match the problems in Exercise 2A with solutions a)–f).

a) Write a to-do list.
b) Do one thing, then do another thing.
c) Don't try to finish something if you are tired.
d) Make time to plan your day and week.
e) Make only one list.
f) Put the important things at the top of your list.

C Complete the guide for the radio program with the words in the box. There are two extra words.

~~professor~~ multi-task same hour use time management improve make

Working Week

with Patti Fry
5:30 p.m.–6:30 p.m.

In today's Working Week, Patti Fry talks to [1]_Professor_ Emma Fields and asks why some people [2]______ their time better than others. She also asks how to [3]______ our time at work by using different [4]______ techniques. Emma gives us some useful ideas for working better. One of them is: Don't [5]______ – do one thing first, then another. Doing two or more things at the [6]______ time isn't such a good idea.

GRAMMAR

ADVERBS OF MANNER

3 Underline the correct alternative.

1 **A:** Your mom drives really *slow/slowly*.
B: Yes, well you know that *slow/slowly* drivers don't have many accidents.

2 **A:** Jeff is quite *lazy/lazily* about doing tasks around the house.
B: That's true, he does them *lazy/lazily*, but he does them in the end!

3 **A:** The teacher talks very *quiet/quietly*.
B: Yes, and the students aren't *quiet/quietly*, so it's difficult to hear.

4 **A:** I found the store *easy/easily*, thanks to your clear directions.
B: Well, in fact, it's pretty *easy/easily* to find.

5 **A:** Our team played *bad/badly*, and we lost the match.
B: That's surprising, I thought the other team was *bad/badly*.

6 **A:** You're so *energetic/energetically* when you get up in the morning. How do you do it?
B: I read somewhere that if you get up *energetic/energetically*, you'll feel good all day.

7 **A:** You came in pretty *noisy/noisily* last night.
B: Sorry, I didn't mean to be so *noisy/noisily*.

8 **A:** This exercise isn't very *hard/hardly*.
B: No? Well, work *hard/hardly* to the end because the second part is difficult.

4 A Complete the sentences with adverbs formed from the adjectives in parentheses.

1 You have to drive _carefully_ (careful) and ________ (safe). You can't drive ________ (dangerous) or ________ (fast).

2 You have to work very ________ (hard) and often very ________ (late) at night, but you get long summer vacations. You don't have to speak ________ (loud), but it helps.

3 You should eat ________ (healthy) and go to bed ________ (early). You don't have to walk or run ________ (fast), but you have to see ________ (clear).

4 You don't have to read music ________ (perfect), but it helps. You have to sing ________ (good), but you don't have to sing ________ (loud).

B What jobs are the sentences in Exercise 4A about? Underline the correct alternative.

1 a bus driver / a racing driver
2 a teacher / a politician
3 a soccer player / a golfer
4 a jazz singer / an opera singer

5 Complete the adjectives and adverbs in the conversations.

Conversation 1

A: Are you OK?
B: No, I don't feel very w_ell_. Can I lie down somewhere?
A: Yes, over here.
B: I'm really tir________. I slept terri________ last night.

Conversation 2

A: This room's very comf________.
B: Yes, but it's pretty noi________. I can hear the people downstairs.
A: Well, we don't have to stay here all evening. I'm hun________.
B: Yes, we can eat che________ in the café tonight, and then we can go to that exp________ Italian restaurant tomorrow.

Conversation 3

A: I sing very ba________.
B: No, you don't. You sing beau________.
A: Thank you. That's ki________ of you.

WRITING

ADVERBS IN STORIES

6 A Write the adverbs.

1 slow _slowly_
2 quick ________
3 angry ________
4 nervous ________
5 careful ________

B Complete the joke with the adverbs from Exercise 6A.

A man walked [1] _nervously_ into the dentist's office. The dentist looked [2] ________ at the man's teeth and then said, "I have to take one tooth out. I can do it [3] ________ – it'll only take five minutes and it'll cost $100."

"A hundred dollars for five minutes' work!" the man said [4] ________. "That's too expensive!"

"Well," answered the dentist, "I can do it [5] ________ if you want!"

pretty / soccer player — rather / footballer

VOCABULARY
VERBS OF MOVEMENT

1 Complete the conversations with the verbs in the box.

~~carry~~ drop lift stand cross push lie pick up

1 A: I'll take these dishes.
B: Don't _carry_ all of them. You'll __________ them!

2 A: Don't __________ the road now – the crossing light is still red.
B: Sorry, I didn't look.

3 A: And then my car just stopped.
B: So what did you do?
A: Lee helped me to __________ it – and a couple of minutes later, it started again.

4 A: Don't worry, I'll be OK. Oh, no!
B: What's wrong?
A: This box is too heavy. I can't __________ it!
B: I can __________ it __________ for you.

5 A: Don't __________ in the sun for too long. You'll get sunburned.
B: Twenty minutes is not too long – I'll be fine.

6 A: Hi, Jenny. It's me.
B: Hi, Frank. Where are you?
A: I'm on the train. It's really crowded, so I have to __________.

FUNCTION
OFFERING TO HELP

2 A Put 1–4 and a)–d) in the correct order to make sentences.

1 my / problem / MP3 / there's / a / player / with
There's a problem with my MP3 player. ____

2 favorite / was / that / my / vase
__________________. ____

3 tired / really / I'm
__________________. ____

4 in / cold / here / it's
__________________. ____

a) coffee / let / you / a / make / me
__________________.

b) look / me / let
__________________.

c) you / I'll / buy / one / another
__________________.

d) I / window / Can / close / the
__________________?

B Match sentences 1–4 in Exercise 2A with offers a)–d).

3 A Read Jim's "To do" list. Then complete the conversation.

TO DO
- call Noriko in Tokyo
- email Moscow office
- get flowers for Ellie – send them to hospital
- meet Anne at airport (5:30)

Ruth: Are you OK, Jim?
Jim: No. I have to meet Anne at 5:30 and look at this list!
Ruth: [1] _Let_ me _help_. I'm not busy at the moment.
Jim: Oh, can you? Thanks!
Ruth: No problem. [2] ________ I ________ Noriko?
Jim: Yes, please.
Ruth: And then I [3] ________ ________ the Moscow office.
Jim: Can you tell them I'll call tomorrow?
Ruth: OK. And I [4] ________ ________ some flowers for Ellie. I'm going to the hospital to see her tonight anyway.
Jim: Fantastic! [5] ________ me ________ you the money.
Ruth: It's OK. Give it to me tomorrow.
Jim: Thanks a lot. I [6] ________ ________ the same for you any time!

W11.3 **B Listen and check. Then listen and repeat the offers of help.**

LEARN TO
THANK SOMEONE

4 Circle the correct option.

1 A: Are you OK? Let me carry that.
B: a) Yes. b) No problem. (c) Thanks a lot.)

2 A: Should I speak to Mr. Chen for you?
B: a) That's kind of you. b) You're welcome. c) It's a problem.

3 A: I'll drive you home.
B: a) You're welcome. b) Should I do it? c) Thanks. I'm very grateful.

4 A: Thank you very much.
B: a) Yes. b) You're welcome. c) Your welcome.

5 A: Is this seat free?
B: Sure.
A: a) Thanks a lot. b) No problem. c) You're welcome.

6 A: I'll buy lunch.
B: a) Really? Please. b) Really? Sure. c) Really? Thanks.

What's wrong? What's the matter?

VOCABULARY

EXPERIENCES

1 A Underline the correct alternative.

1 I'm very excited. I'm going to *do/be* in a play.
2 Look, we can *ride/drive* an elephant on a forest tour on Wednesday.
3 Let's *climb/do* Mount Bromo – it's a live volcano.
4 Are you really going to *make/do* the bungee jump?
5 Harry *met/saw* his new friend Ali on a train journey across Pakistan.
6 On Saturdays, we go *to/play* a soccer game – we love watching sports.
7 *Sleeping/Meeting* outside? No, thank you – camping's not for me!
8 Come on, let's sit over there and *look/watch* the sun rise.

W12.1

B Listen and write the phrases in the correct column for each stress pattern.

1 ooO	2 oooO
	be in a play
3 ooOo	**4 ooOoo**

C Listen again and repeat.

WRITING

LINKERS REVIEW

2 Complete the email with the words in the box.

~~so~~ but and then because too or first finally as well

Dear Mom and Dad,

We're having a great time. There's lots of snow, [1] *so* skiing down the mountain is perfect. The ski slopes are near [2] ___________ you can go ice-skating [3] ___________. The hotel's beautiful – a little noisy, [4] ___________ there's a big group staying here, [5] ___________ it's a lovely old building in the center of the village.

There are some famous people here. [6] ___________, Karen met Justin Davies (he's a pop star, Mom!) at breakfast, and [7] ___________ I saw Emma Bower, the pianist, on the ski slope. [8] ___________, at night, we did karaoke with Ercol Blonde, the rock star from the 80s!

The food's great, [9] ___________ – really tasty! Speaking of food, it's dinner in five minutes, so I've got to go now. I hope you're all OK. I'll call [10] ___________ email you again tomorrow!

Love, Janis

GRAMMAR

PRESENT PERFECT

3 Write the past participle of the verbs.

1 be *been*
2 climb ___________
3 do ___________
4 travel ___________
5 have ___________
6 ride ___________
7 drink ___________
8 play ___________
9 meet ___________
10 fly ___________

4 A Look at the table and complete the sentences. Use the present perfect form of the verbs.

	Ethan	Amy	Tom and Lily
go to South America	✓	✗	✓
see Red Square	✗	✓	✓
eat Mexican food	✗	✓	✗
visit the Louvre gallery in Paris	✗	✗	✓
swim in the Black Sea	✓	✗	✗

1 Ethan *has been* to South America.
2 Amy ___________ to South America.
3 Tom and Lily ___________ to Red Square.
4 Ethan ___________ to Red Square.
5 Amy ___________ Mexican food.
6 Tom and Lily ___________ Mexican food.
7 Tom and Lily ___________ to the Louvre gallery in Paris.
8 Amy ___________ in the Black Sea.

B Complete the questions. Use the present perfect form of the verbs.

1 *Has* Ethan *swum* in the Black Sea?
2 ________ Ethan and Amy ________ to the Louvre gallery in Paris?
3 ________ Lily ________ Mexican food?
4 ________ Amy ________ to Red Square?
5 ________ Tom and Lily ________ to South America?
6 ________ Tom ________ in the Black Sea?

C Write short answers to questions 1–6 in Exercise 4B.

1 *Yes, he has.*
2 ___________
3 ___________
4 ___________
5 ___________
6 ___________

I've got to go — I must go

READING

5 A Read Jim's travel blog and write the correct day under each picture.

A

Day 1 ________

B

____

C

____

D

____

E

____

Day 1

We arrived in Piraeus early this morning. Liz has never seen the Parthenon. I've been to Athens once before, so I'm going to be her tour guide. We're going there tonight!

In the afternoon, we went by train from Piraeus into the city of Athens and walked up to the Parthenon – amazing!

Day 2

Back to Athens again, and this time we found a restaurant in the Plaka area. We've eaten Greek food many times back in New Zealand, but this is real Greek food! This is the first time in my life that I've tried octopus, and it was delicious!

Day 3

We stayed overnight in Athens and then took a bus down to Cape Sounion in the afternoon to visit the Temple of Poseidon. We've seen many sunsets in our lives, but this was the most beautiful – the sun going down into the Aegean Sea.

Day 4

We left Piraeus early this morning and sailed for twenty hours to the island of Santorini. We arrived in the old port late in the evening. Tomorrow morning, we're going up to the village – by donkey! I've ridden horses, camels, and elephants, but I've never ridden a donkey!

Day 5

Donkey disaster! I'm writing this from a hospital bed in Athens. We started our donkey ride this morning, and I made a big mistake: I walked behind the donkey, and it kicked me in the stomach! There was no hospital on the island, so they took me by helicopter to Athens. I've broken three bones ... and I still haven't ridden a donkey. But I have flown in a helicopter!

B Read the blog again. Are the sentences true (T) or false (F)?

1 Jim and Liz walked from Piraeus to Athens. *F*
2 Jim hasn't eaten Greek food before. ____
3 Jim liked the octopus. ____
4 They watched the sunrise near the Temple of Poseidon. ____
5 Jim and Liz traveled to Santorini by boat. ____
6 Jim enjoyed riding the donkey. ____
7 Jim flew back to Athens. ____
8 Now he's back home in New Zealand. ____

C Correct the false sentences.

Jim and Liz went to Athens by train.
____
____
____
____

6 A Imagine it's before Jim's vacations. Read the blog again and write short answers to the questions.

1 Has Liz ever seen the Parthenon? *No, she hasn't.*
2 Has Jim ever been to Athens? ____
3 Has Jim ever eaten octopus? ____
4 Have Jim and Liz ever seen a sunset? ____
5 Has Jim ever ridden a donkey? ____

B Now imagine it's after Jim's vacations. Read the questions in Exercise 6A again and write short answers.

1 *Yes, she has.*
2 ____
3 ____
4 ____
5 ____

LISTENING

1 A Match activities 1–8 with pictures A–H.

1 go on a roller coaster ___B___
2 get lost ______
3 be on TV ______
4 sing in a karaoke club ______
5 go to the movie theater alone ______
6 fly in a helicopter ______
7 swim in a lake ______
8 drive in bad weather ______

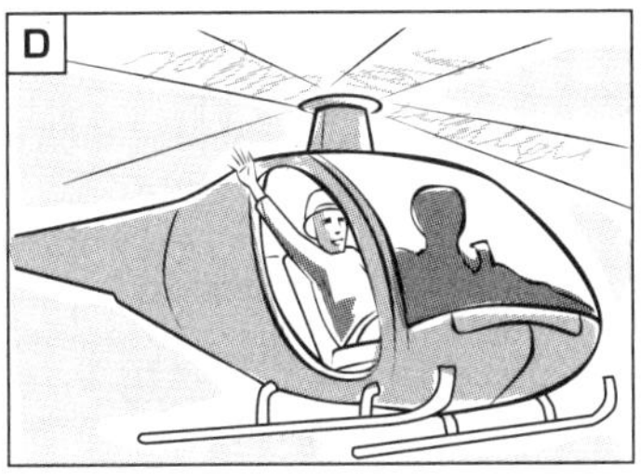

B Complete the quiz with the past participle of the verbs in parentheses.

FEAR OR FUN?

Have you ever ...

1 ___been___ on a roller coaster? (go)
2 ______ lost in a city? (get)
3 ______ on TV? (be)
4 ______ in a karaoke club? (sing)
5 ______ to the movie theater alone to see a movie? (go)
6 ______ in a helicopter? (fly)
7 ______ in a lake? (swim)
8 ______ in really bad weather? (drive)

C Listen to four conversations. Which situations from Exercise 1B do the people talk about?

Conversation 1 ___6___
Conversation 2 ______
Conversation 3 ______
Conversation 4 ______

D Listen again. Write when the person did the activity.

Conversation 1 ___five years ago___
Conversation 2 ______
Conversation 3 ______
Conversation 4 ______

GRAMMAR

PRESENT PERFECT AND SIMPLE PAST

2 Underline the correct alternatives.

Conversation 1

A: [1]*Did you ever fly/Have you ever flown* in a helicopter?

B: No, I [2]*didn't/haven't*. [3]*Did/Have you?*

A: Yes, I [4]*did/have*. Just once, when I [5]*went/'ve been* helicopter skiing, five years ago.

Conversation 2

A: [6]*Have you ever sung/Did you ever sing* in a karaoke bar?

B: No, but I [7]*sang/'ve sung* at a party. It [8]*was/'s been* last year sometime. No, two years ago. At a birthday party.

A: What [9]*did you sing/have you sung?*

B: I can't remember ... Oh, yes – I did it "My way."

Conversation 3

A: [10]*Did you ever drive/Have you ever driven* in really bad weather?

B: Yes. I [11]*drove/'ve driven* up to Montana to visit my grandparents in 2007, and it just [12]*snowed/has snowed* non-stop.

3 Complete the conversations with the present perfect or simple past form of the verbs in parentheses.

Conversation 1

A: [1]*Have you ever ridden* (you / ever / ride) a horse?

B: Yes, I have. I [2]__________ (ride) one in Argentina last year.

A: [3]__________ (you / like) it?

B: Yes, it [4]__________ (be) fun, but the horse [5]__________ (not go) very fast.

Conversation 2

A: Does Emilio go everywhere by motorcycle?

B: Yes, he does.

A: [6]__________ (he / ever / hurt) himself?

B: Yes, he [7]__________ (break) his arm twice.

A: Really? How [8]__________ (he / do) that?

B: Both times the weather [9]__________ (be) bad, and he [10]__________ (fall) off the bike.

VOCABULARY

PREPOSITIONS

4 Look at the map and complete the directions with the prepositions in the box.

through (x2) down up under toward away from across over into

Get off the train and walk [1] *through* the station and [2]__________ the steps. There's a big square in front of the station with a clock tower on the other side. Walk [3]__________ the square [4]__________ the clock tower. Walk past the clock tower and go straight until you see a bridge going [5]__________ the road. Walk [6]__________ the bridge, and soon you'll see a shopping mall on your left. It's called WhiteWays. Walk [7]__________ the shopping mall, and at the other side, you'll come out on Kirkby Street. Walk along Kirkby Street [8]__________ the shopping mall. Then turn right onto Sedgefield Road. My apartment is in number thirty-five. The door's usually open, so just come [9]__________ the hall. Walk [10]__________ the stairs to the first floor. My door is the blue one.

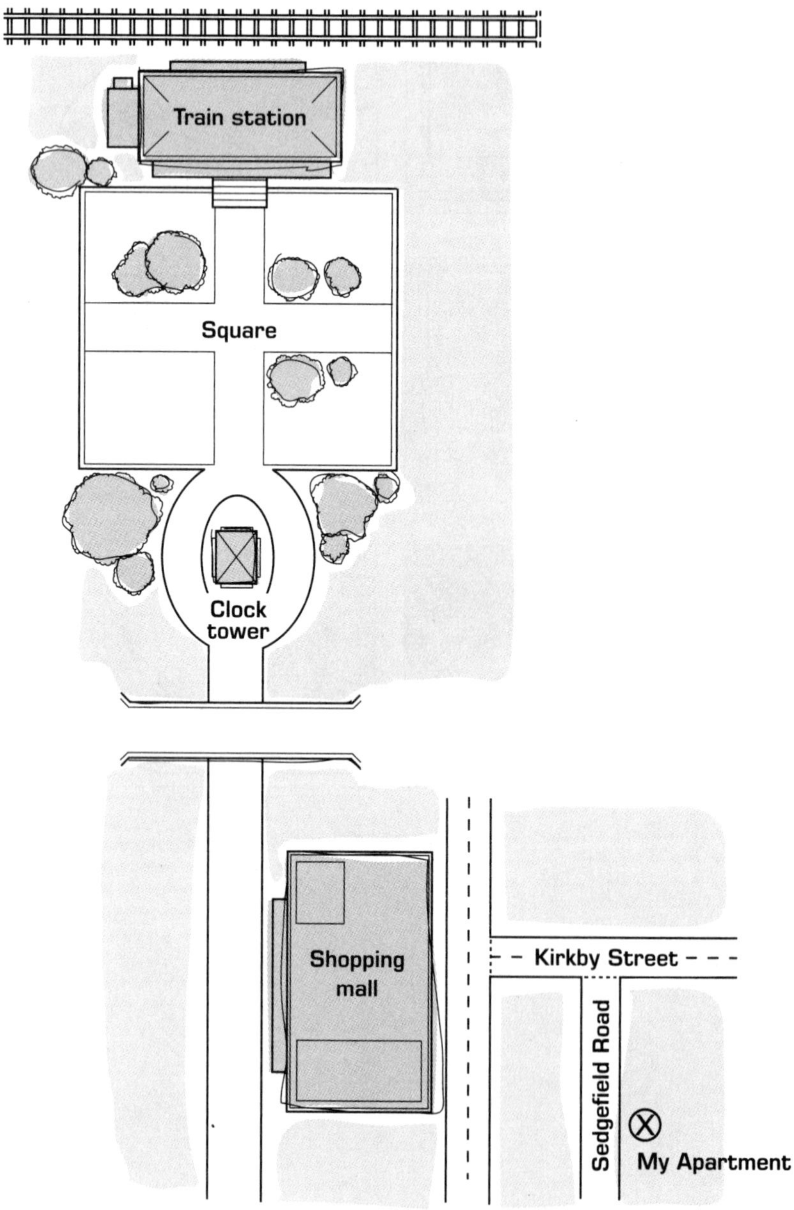

VOCABULARY
CALLING EXPRESSIONS

1 Complete Susie's answering machine messages with verbs in the correct form.

1 This is Lisa from the health clinic. I l*eft*______ a message on your answering machine yesterday. Can you c__________ the clinic, please?
2 Hi, Susie. It's Meg. Can you c__________ me back? I'm at home this evening.
3 Hi. It's me, Bernie. Did you t__________ a message for me last night from Simon?
4 Hello. This is Sports Mad. Can you c__________ us, please? There's a problem with your tennis shoes.
5 Hi, Susie. It's Fallon. I got your message, and I'm c__________ you back.
6 Hi, it's me again. I know you're there! A__________ the phone!

FUNCTION
PHONE CONVERSATIONS

2 Find and correct mistakes in six of the sentences. Check (✓) the two correct sentences.

1 Just ask ~~she~~ *her* to call me.
2 Could you say me the number?
3 OK, I call you back.
4 Could I leave a message to her?
5 Let me check that.
6 Hi, Frank. I'm Sally.
7 Good morning. Could I chat to Mr. Suriano, please?
8 Just a moment.

3 Write telephone conversations using the prompts.

Conversation 1

A: could / call / me / back, please?
____
B: Of course. / can / you / give / number?
____
A: yes, / it / 389-642-1566
____
B: let / check / that. / 389-642-1566
____
A: that / right
____

Conversation 2

A: Hi, Xavier. This / Bea
Hi, Xavier. This is Bea.
B: Hi, Bea. How / you?
____
A: I / OK. Michelle / there?
____
B: Yes, but she / sleep
____
A: I / leave / message / her?
____
B: Of course.
A: just ask / to call / me
____
B: OK. Bye.

Conversation 3

A: Hello. / I / speak / the manager, please?
B: just / moment. I / sorry, he / busy / moment. / call / back later?
____
A: it / very important
____
B: I / take / message?
____
A: no thanks / I / call back later
____

LEARN TO
SAY TELEPHONE NUMBERS

4 A Write the telephone numbers in words. Put a comma between number groups.

1 3234996705 *three two three, four double nine, six seven oh five*
2 4896916615 ____________________
3 0757281867 ____________________
4 6232889470 ____________________
5 9897766112 ____________________
6 0870 533899 ____________________

W12.3 **B Listen and check. Then listen and repeat.**

answering machine / call — answerphone / ring

GRAMMAR VERB FORMS

1 A Complete the article with the correct form of the verbs in parentheses. Use the simple past, the present perfect, *would like* to or *be going to*.

Irish nurse Liz Johnson works with the international aid agency, Médecins Sans Frontières (MSF). She talked to us about her experiences.

"About seven years ago, I [1] saw (see) a TV program about MSF, and I [2] ____________ (decide) to work for them. I [3] ____________ (join) MSF three months later."

"I love my work. I [4] ____________ (go) to a lot of different places in the world, and I [5] ____________ (meet) some amazing people: doctors, nurses, helpers and patients. In fact, four years ago in Sudan, I [6] ____________ (meet) my husband, Jacques, a French doctor. We now travel and work together. I'm very proud of him."

Last week, Liz and Jacques [7] ____________ (return) to France after six months work in Haiti. What are their plans for the future? " We have some definite plans: Jacques [8] ____________ (speak) at a big MSF meeting next week, and then we [9] ____________ (have) a one-week vacation in Spain. After that, we aren't sure. Next, we [10] ____________ (open) a hospital, but we don't know in which country."

B Put the words in the correct order to make questions for Liz.

1 did / decide / you / for / when / to / MSF / work
When did you decide to work for MSF ?

2 you / to / a / have / been / lot / different / of / countries
____________________?

3 meet / you / husband / did / when / your
____________________?

4 to / Jacques / going / week / where / speak / is / next
____________________?

5 do / you / like / to / next / would / what
____________________?

C Now imagine you are Liz. Answer the questions.

1 About seven years ago.
2 ____________________
3 ____________________
4 ____________________
5 ____________________

VOCABULARY REVISION

2 A Add vowels to the words in each group.

1
f i n a lly
_ s w _ ll
b _ c _ _ s _
_ l s _
first

2
h _ _ d _ ch _
s _ r _ thr _ _ t
t _ mp _ r _ t _ r _
c _ _ gh
____

3
thr _ _ gh
t _ w _ rd
_ w _ y fr _ m
_ _ t _ f
____

4
h _ ngry
th _ rsty
s _ nb _ rn _ d
l _ st
____

5
dr _ w _ ng
c _ nc _ rt
_ xh _ b _ t _ _ n
st _ t _ _
____

6
c _ rry
dr _ p
p _ ck _ p
____

7
sh _ _ ld _ r
kn _ _
f _ ng _ r
_ lb _ w
____

B Match headings a)–g) with groups 1–7 in Exercise 2A.

a) linkers 1
b) the body ______
c) health ______
d) art and culture ______
e) prepositions of movement ______
f) verbs of movement ______
g) words that go with *get* ______

C Add the words in the box to the groups in Exercise 2A. There are two extra words.

~~first~~ stung conversation into runny nose dance performance neck text message push

In English, MSF is known as Doctors Without Borders.

GRAMMAR *SHOULD/WILL/MIGHT*

3 A Read the text. Who has these problems? Daniel (D), Rebecca (R) or both (DR)?

1 wants to change jobs ___R___
2 works too much ______
3 lives unhealthily ______
4 doesn't have any friends ______
5 is bored with work ______
6 has money problems ______

life coaching*

Improve your life and reach your dreams ...

Read about two of our customers and how life coaching has helped them:

Daniel is a successful businessman, but he finds it difficult to make friends, so on weekends he stays at home and spends a lot of time alone on his computer. On weekdays, he often stays in the office late. He's also overweight and says he's never done much exercise. He'd like to become healthier and go out and meet people, maybe find a girlfriend, but he doesn't know where to start.

Rebecca loves dancing and she teaches a dance class once a week. She works for an electronics company, but she doesn't like her job. She thinks it's boring and works long hours, but she needs the money because her rent is very high. She'd like to teach dance all the time, but she doesn't know how to start.

*coaching = training, teaching

B Read the life-coaching advice and underline the correct alternatives.

"**Daniel** [1]*should/'ll* look for activities he can do with other people. He [2]*should/shouldn't* join a club or group, for example a walking club or a cooking group because then he [3]*'ll/might* meet people who enjoy the same things. When he's with other people, he [4]*should/shouldn't* ask them lots of questions, and he [5]*should/shouldn't* show interest in their answers. People love talking about themselves, and they [6]*'ll/won't* think he's a great guy! Who knows? He [7]*'ll/might* find a girlfriend one day!

"**Rebecca** [8]*shouldn't/might not* wait any more. She's in the wrong job. She [9]*should/'ll* contact the Association of Dance Teachers – she can find them on the internet, and they [10]*might/'ll* give her advice about starting a new business. At the moment, she [11]*won't/shouldn't* leave her job. The best thing is to work part-time, but her company [12]*might/might not* agree. She [13]*should/shouldn't* start teaching more classes – lots of people want to learn to dance, and I'm sure she [14]*won't/might not* find it difficult to reach her dream.

VOCABULARY PLANS

4 Find twelve verb phrases for future plans in the puzzle.

W	T	R	G	R	W	Y	H	T	H
H	O	V	E	A	B	H	I	A	D
A	I	S	T	A	Y	I	N	K	O
V	U	G	M	V	G	D	M	E	S
E	G	O	A	N	O	O	O	A	O
A	O	S	R	G	J	A	V	B	M
B	F	H	R	G	O	C	E	R	E
A	O	O	I	G	G	O	H	E	W
R	R	P	E	I	G	U	O	A	O
B	A	P	D	C	I	R	M	K	R
E	W	I	L	R	N	S	E	V	K
C	A	N	A	Z	G	E	B	E	T
U	L	G	E	T	A	J	O	B	B
E	K	Q	S	C	K	X	L	L	X
G	O	F	O	R	A	M	E	A	L

FUNCTION CALLING, OFFERING AND SUGGESTING

5 A Complete the conversation.

A: "Could I [1]s*peak* to Susie Dee?"
B: "She's not at [2]h________. She's back at three. Could you [3]c________ her back tonight?"
A: "I'll [4]l________ a message. Is that all right?"
B: "Just a [5]m________, I need a pen."
A: "She has my [6]n________. My name's Ben."
B: "[7]L________ me check – your name is Jack?"
A: "Oh, never mind – I'll [8]c________ her back."

A: "Well, hello Susie! How are you?"
C: "I'm fine. What [9]w________ you like to do?"
A: "Why [10]d________ we meet and have a chat?"
C: "I don't really [11]f________ like doing that."
A: "Then how [12]a________ a walk together?"
C: "[13]S________ good. Let me check the weather. It's going to rain – that's not ideal."
A: "So [14]l________ stay in and cook a meal!"

R4.1 **B Listen and check.**

CHECK

Circle the correct option to complete the sentences.

1 You dance ____________.
a) beautiful b) good c) well

2 A: It's Estelle's birthday on Saturday.
B: Yes, ____________ her a camera. I ordered it last week.
a) I'm going to give b) I'd like to give c) I give

3 A: Should I tell Felipe?
B: ____________.
a) Yes, you should tell. b) No, you shouldn't.
c) Yes, you shouldn't.

4 Mack ran quickly ____________ Anya and said, "I'm so happy to see you!"
a) away from b) towards c) across

5 Jan ____________ to Germany.
a) never has been b) was never c) has never been

6 I have ____________.
a) the headache b) a cough c) my sore throat

7 Have you ever ____________ in a lake?
a) swim b) swam c) swum

8 A: Oh, no! A snake!
B: Don't be afraid. I'm sure it ____________ you.
a) won't hurt b) 'll hurt c) might not

9 Hi, ____________ Fabio. Is Luigi there?
a) I'm b) this is c) is this

10 A: I feel worse today.
B: You ____________.
a) should to go home b) shouldn't go to bed
c) should go to bed

11 A: Where ____________ in Malta?
B: At the Carlton Hotel.
a) you're going to stay b) are you going to stay
c) you would like to stay

12 They ____________ yesterday.
a) 've been fishing b) 've gone fishing
c) went fishing

13 Peter's very ____________ today.
a) seriously b) quiet c) noisily

14 We ____________ a great barbecue – about twenty people came.
a) went b) had c) got

15 A: Tom Grady has a temperature, and he ____________ says his arms and legs hurt.
B: I'll call his mother. I think he's got flu.
a) also b) too c) as well

16 He jumped out of ____________.
a) a helicopter b) a bridge c) an elephant

17 It's not easy for me to ____________ a conversation in Spanish.
a) make b) have c) do

18 I always carry lots of water with me so I don't get ____________.
a) dry b) thirsty c) hungry

19 Sorry, I can't talk at the moment. Can I ____________ in half an hour?
a) leave a message b) take a message
c) call you back

20 I love *The Great Gatsby*. I ____________ it about ten times.
a) saw b) see c) 've seen

21 My ____________ hurts.
a) shoulder b) flu c) temperature

22 You have to go ____________ passport control and security.
a) out of b) through c) into

23 He drove ____________ through the city.
a) fastly b) slow c) fast

24 A: What should we do tonight?
B: ____________ stay in and watch a DVD.
a) Let's b) Why we don't c) How about

25 A: Did Jake invite you to his wedding?
B: Yes, but I ____________ go because it's in Canada, and it's very expensive to fly there.
a) might b) might not c) 'll

26 ____________ that for you?
a) Let me carry b) Do you want me to carry
c) I'll carry

27 Have you ever been to China?
a) No, I haven't. b) Yes, I have been to.
c) Yes, I have gone.

28 We ____________ get married!
a) going to b) 're going to c) 're going

29 I hurt my ____________ yesterday, and I can't walk.
a) thumb b) finger c) toe

30 I ____________ around the world.
a) 'd like to travel b) 'm like to travel c) like travel

RESULT	/30

UNIT 7 RECORDING W7.1

empty
noisy
cheap
boring
uncomfortable
slow
expensive
quiet
fast
comfortable
crowded
interesting

UNIT 7 RECORDING W7.2

Hello. It's 9:48 a.m. on Monday December the second. I'm Nick Young, and I'm on the Trans-Siberian train. Welcome to my audio diary. First of all, some facts: The Trans-Siberian is the longest train journey in the world. It's five thousand seven hundred and seventy eight miles and takes seven days. So, this is day one. We left the city an hour ago, and I'm here in my compartment. It's very comfortable, with two beds, one for me and one for Anton. Anton's from Sweden, and he's very friendly. He doesn't speak much English, but that's not a problem.

...

Hi, Nick here. It's day three, and we're in Siberia. Out of the window you can see snow and forests and small villages for mile after mile. It's beautiful. About every two hours the train stops at a small station, and there are women selling bread, fish, fruit or vegetables. We often buy food for lunch or dinner. When we get back on the train, we chat and read and have more cups of tea. Then we have lunch and then dinner, and then we go to bed. It's all very relaxing.

...

Hi there. This is my last audio diary on this journey. In one hour, we get into Vladivostok station! Last night, the Russian lady in the carriage next door had her fiftieth birthday party. It was crowded, but we had a good time! So what do I think about the Trans-Siberian train? Fantastic! And my best memories? Great dark forests, small Russian villages, and some good new friends. I really think this is the best journey of my life!

UNIT 7 RECORDING W7.3

1 **A:** So, the park's between the movie theater and the pharmacy.
B: No, it's behind the movie theater and the pharmacy.

2 **A:** So, the supermarket's between the movie theater and the pharmacy.
B: No, it's between the movie theater and the post office.

3 **A:** So, the movie theater is the fourth building on the left.
B: No, it's the third building on the left.

4 **A:** So, the café is the fourth building on the left.
B: No, it's the fourth building on the right.

5 **A:** So, the post office is across from the bank.
B: No, it's across from the museum.

6 **A:** So, the town hall is across from the bank.
B: No, it's next to the bank.

UNIT 8 RECORDING W8.1

1 Hello? Oh, hi, Rob. No, we're at the new exhibition at the National Gallery, and we're looking at the Klimt paintings. Yeah, they're fantastic. OK, see you later.

2 Nellie, it's me, Russ. Hi, yeah, we're in line to buy tickets for the concert. Do you want to come? I can get you a ticket. Two? Oh, who's your new friend? Right. See you soon.

3 Hi. Oh, look, I can't talk now – we're just going into a concert. It's the Mozart. Yes, the *Requiem*. Sorry, I have to go.

4 Hi, Felicity. Fine, thanks. Listen, do you want to have a coffee later? After the game – maybe around four o'clock. Yeah, it's Nadal again – he's amazing! Oh, you're watching the game on TV? Right, see you at four.

5 Zsuzsa, I just had to call you. The new designs, they're fantastic – everything's black and white, you know. Kate's wearing white and Fabio's in all-black – black jeans, a black sweater and black jacket. OK, yeah, I'll take some pictures. Talk to you later.

UNIT 8 RECORDING W8.2

1 Are you looking for a movie?
2 Is it an action movie?
3 Is anyone famous in it?
4 Do you want to watch a movie?
5 I don't have a DVD player.
6 I have it on my computer.

UNIT 8 RECORDING W8.3

1 Are you looking for a friend?
2 Is it an action movie?
3 Is anyone famous in it?
4 Do you want to buy a DVD?
5 I don't have a CD player.

UNIT 9 RECORDING W9.1

1 fast
2 healthy
3 dangerous
4 inconvenient
5 difficult
6 convenient
7 safe
8 easy
9 comfortable
10 polluting

UNIT 9 RECORDING W9.2

R = Reporter C = Carin

R: We're in Amsterdam, the Netherlands, and we're talking to Carin van Buren. Carin's riding a kind of scooter with a motor. Carin, what is this, um, machine called?
C: It's a balancing scooter.
R: And do you ride it around the city?
C: Yes, I use it to go to work. Before this year, I went to work by bike or sometimes by bus. Then I saw a balancing scooter on the internet and thought, "That looks good," and I bought one!
R: Is it difficult to ride?
C: No, it's actually very easy.
R: And how long does it take to learn to ride?
C: It takes about two hours. Yes, it took me two hours.
R: Can you ride it on the sidewalk here?
C: No, you can't. You have to ride it on the road or you can use the bike paths.
R: And how fast does it go?
C: The maximum speed is fifteen miles an hour, but I usually go slower than that.
R: Do you feel safe on it?
C: Yeah – yes, I do. I always wear a helmet. The scooter doesn't go very fast, and it's easy to stop.
R: And is it better than traveling by bus or bike?
C: I think so. By bus it took about forty-five minutes to go to work, and now it takes me twenty minutes by scooter. And it's better than a bike because I'm not hot when I arrive at work.

R: Where do you leave your scooter at work?
C: I take it into my office, and I leave it near my desk.
R: Really?
C: Yeah, it isn't a problem.
R: Is it tiring to ride?
C: Yes, it *is* quite tiring. You can't really relax.
R: Is there anything else you don't like about the scooter?
C: Sometimes people laugh at me, and I feel quite stupid. Oh yes, and people often stop me and ask questions about it! I don't like that.

UNIT 9 RECORDING W9.3

A: Oh, hi. I'm really sorry I'm late. I missed the train.
B: Hmm … I don't believe you.
A: No, really. The traffic was terrible.
B: And?
A: And my car broke down.
B: Your car, again?
A: And I left my wallet at home.
B: Ah, your wallet.
A: And … OK, I forgot about our meeting! I feel terrible about this.
B: Well, don't worry about it.
A: I'm so sorry.
B: No, really, it's fine.
A: I'm so, so …
B: That's OK! But don't let it happen again.

Review 3 RECORDING R3.1

G = Greg J = Jurgen

G: Hey, Jurgen. It's my wife's birthday tomorrow. Can you recommend a good restaurant?
J: Well, what kind of food do you like?
G: We both like Chinese food and, uh, French food.
J: There's a good restaurant called Bouchon in town. It serves French food.
G: Do you think my wife would like it?
J: Yes, I think so. It's quite romantic.
G: Where is it?
J: It's in a small street near the movie theater.
G: Can you tell me the way?
J: From the movie theater, you go down Mason Street past the pharmacy and turn left.
G: Left at the pharmacy. OK …
J: Then go straight ahead for about two hundred meter – Bouchon is on the right. It isn't far.
G: Great – thanks!
…
J: Hi, Greg. Did you find the restaurant?
G: No!
J: Oh? Why?
G: Your directions were all wrong! You said to turn *left* at the pharmacy.
J: Oh, no!
G: And we did, but it took us completely the wrong way!
J: Oh, no – I'm so sorry. I always mix up left and right.
G: Hm. My wife was really angry.
J: I feel terrible about this.
G: In the end, we went home and ordered pizza!
J: Oh, no!
G: Ah, well. Maybe next year! Don't worry about it, really.

UNIT 10 RECORDING W10.1

hot, thirsty, warm, wet, lost, stung, cold, hungry

UNIT 10 RECORDING W10.2

1 Well, the most difficult thing was that there was so much water, but I was so thirsty. Food wasn't a big problem because I caught fish and ate them. Of course, I got sunburned after the first day because I had nothing to put on my head. And I was afraid of sharks. Once I saw one, but it just swam around the raft for a few minutes, and then it went away.

2 I felt very small and very tired. I walked all night, very slowly because of the sand, and I tried to stay cool in the daytime, but it was so hot. On the second day, I found some water – that was very lucky – but then I wanted to walk more, not just stay by the water. I wanted to try to find my way back to the town. I had food with me, so I didn't get hungry – just very thirsty. Once I saw a snake, and I was afraid that one might go into my shoe, so I never took my shoes off.

3 There was snow everywhere. Everything was white, and that's why I got lost – I didn't see the path. I was up there only one night, but it was the longest night of my life. The most important thing was staying warm. I didn't have enough clothes with me, so I got terribly cold. I wanted to make a fire, but everything was wet. I slept on the ground and got colder. I didn't think about food – I wasn't really hungry, but just so thirsty! It was difficult, very difficult.

4 There was water, so I didn't get thirsty. And I didn't get too hungry because I knew what kind of plants to eat. Of course, I got very lost – I walked day and night – but you know, you can never, ever get bored there. There are so many different types of plants and animals and insects – it was beautiful. So yes, I felt tired and lost, but not bored.

UNIT 10 RECORDING W10.3

1 You get cold.
You'll get cold.
2 We'll miss the train.
We miss the train.
3 I'm sure you'll hate it.
I'm sure you hate it.
4 They know you're a tourist.
They'll know you're a tourist.
5 I stay at home.
I'll stay at home.
6 I'll never go out.
I never go out.

UNIT 11 RECORDING W11.1

elbow, thumb, leg, knee, head, neck, stomach, hand, nose, toe, mouth, back

UNIT 11 RECORDING W11.2

P = Presenter E = Emma

P: Hello and welcome to *Working Week*, where we take a look at the world of work. This week, we're looking at time management. We all know there are twenty-four hours in a day, but some people are just much better at using these than other people. In today's program we'll look at ways to improve the time we spend at work – things we should do and things we shouldn't. Professor Emma Fields from the Institute of Work Psychology joins us today. Emma, what are the good and bad time management techniques?
E: Well, the first thing you have to do is to make sure you have time to plan. Most of us start work without organizing our week and days first. You should always give yourself some planning time. Secondly, make sure you don't forget your plans – write a to-do list for the day and for the week. We all try to keep too much in our heads, and of course, we forget things. It's better to make a list and make only one list – some people make two or three different lists, and that doesn't help. Thirdly, put

the most important things at the top of the list and do them first. A lot of people do the things they like doing first, not the important things. Fourthly, don't multi-task – do one thing, then do another thing. When you multi-task, you work more slowly – each task takes more time. And you often make mistakes when you do two or more things at the same time. Finally, work smarter, not harder. We all spend extra time in the office trying to finish something. But is that last hour on Friday the best time to do it? When you are tired and not concentrating? If you're smart, you'll make time for the task on Monday morning – you'll do it better and more quickly then.

UNIT 11 RECORDING W11.3

A: Are you OK, Jim?
B: No. I have to meet Anne at 5:30 and look at this list!
A: Let me help. I'm not busy at the moment.
B: Oh, can you? Thanks!
A: No problem. Should I call Noriko?
B: Yes, please.
A: And then I'll email the Moscow office.
B: Can you tell them I'll call tomorrow?
A: OK. And I'll get some flowers for Ellie. I'm going to the hospital to see her tonight anyway.
B: Fantastic! Let me give you the money.
A: It's OK. Give it to me tomorrow.
B: Thanks a lot. I'll do the same for you any time!

UNIT 12 RECORDING W12.1

be in a play, ride an elephant, climb Mount Bromo, do a bungee jump, meet a new friend, go to a game, sleep outside, watch the sun rise

UNIT 12 RECORDING W12.2

1
A: Have you ever flown in a helicopter?
B: No, I haven't. Have you?
A: Yes, I have. Just once, when I went helicopter skiing – five years ago.
B: That sounds interesting. What's helicopter skiing?
A: A helicopter takes you up the mountain, and you ski from there.
B: And how was it?
A: It was fun. I enjoyed it.

2
A: Matt, have you ever sung in a karaoke club?
B: No, but I've sung at a party. It was last year sometime. No, two years ago. At a birthday party.
A: What did you sing?
B: I can't remember ... Oh, yes – *I did it my way*. It was fun. I can't sing, but it was a good laugh. Why are you asking?
A: I'm going to a karaoke club tonight, and I'm feeling very nervous about it.
B: You'll be all right. Just relax and enjoy it!

3
A: What's wrong?
B: I have to drive to San Francisco tomorrow, and look at the rain! Have you ever driven in really bad weather?
A: Yes. I drove up to Montana to visit my grandparents in 2007, and it just snowed non-stop – it was impossible to see the road ahead.
B: Sounds dangerous.
A: Yes, so I stopped and stayed overnight in a hotel. After that, I always visit them by train!
B: Yeah, that's a good idea. Maybe I'll go by train.

4
A: Look at this picture. It looks scary! Have you ever been on a roller coaster like that?
B: Yes, when I was about nineteen, in Munich. A friend of mine took me on a really big roller coaster.
A: Were you afraid?
B: No. After ten seconds I closed my eyes and didn't open them until it stopped!

UNIT 12 RECORDING W12.3

1 three two three, four double nine six, seven oh five
2 four eight nine, six nine one, double six one five
3 oh seven five, seven two eight one, eight six seven
4 six two three, two double eight nine, four seven oh
5 nine eight nine, double seven double six, double one two
6 oh eight seven oh, five double three, eight double nine

Review 4 RECORDING R4.1

A: Could I speak to Susie Dee?
B: She's not at home. She's back at three.
Could you call her back tonight?
A: I'll leave a message. Is that all right?
B: Just a moment, I need a pen.
A: She has my number. My name's Ben.
B: Let me check ... your name is Jack?
A: Oh, never mind – I'll call her back.
A: Well, hello Susie! How are you?
C: I'm fine. What would you like to do?
A: Why don't we meet and have a chat?
C: I don't really feel like doing that.
A: Then how about a walk together?
C: Sounds good. Let me check the weather.
It's going to rain – that's not ideal.
A: So let's stay in and cook a meal!

Photo acknowledgments

The publisher would like to thank the following for their kind permission to reproduce their photographs:

(Key: b-bottom; c-centre; l-left; r-right; t-top)

123RF.com: Graça Victoria 53 (E), 27/3, 27/8, 28 (Apple), 28 (Cheese), 28 (Chicken), 28 (Milk), 28 (Orange Juice), 28 (Pear), 43/1, 43/2, 43/3, Stefano Cavoretto 27/4, djem 53(H), Jennifer Keddie de Cojon 10, Maksym Yemelyanov 27/7; **Alamy Images:** Media Works Private limited 18b, Rory Buckland L 24, Robert Fried 32t, Hangon International Photobank 42, Robin Weaver 52, Natalie Jezzard 56, MBI 60, Horizons WWP 74, **Fotolia.com:** Lilyana Vynogradova 6tr, Martin Turzak 6tc, sugar0607 6tl, larisa13 6b, WavebreakMediaMicro16, Kimberly Reinick 27/1, Brent Hofacker 31, julialine802 43/7, cristi180884 48/3, zakaz 48/7, fotomatrix 48/8 (Blouse), Alexandra Karamyshev 48/1, 48/4, 48/5, OlegDoroshin 48/9, Popova Olga 48/10, eugenesergeev 53 (B), underworld 53 (C), **Getty Images:** Stephen Mallon/The Image Bank 12, Mark Bowden/Vetta 15, Ian Cook / The LIFE Images Collection 35, SD Productions/Photodisc 36, Stone / Michelle Pedone 41, Ghislain & Marie David de Lossy/The Image Bank 54, Jupiterimages 65; **Pearson Education Ltd:** Gareth Boden 32b, MindStudio 44; **Rex Features:** Action Press 34t, Erik C. Pendzich 34b; **Shutterstock.com:** Andresr 19t, IR Stone 25, KKulikov 27/2, Pablo Eder 27/5, Jiri Hera 27/6, Thaagoon 27/9, Peter Gudella 27/10, chikapylka 28 (Pepper), 6493866629 28 (Bread), Bola_BR 28 (Garlic), Freer 28 (Potato), Alex Staroseltsev 28 (Salmon), Narodenko 28 (Banana), Elena Schweitzer 28 (Butter), motorolka 28 (Broccoli), Kuzma 28 (Strawberry), Maks nickichen 43/4, Vladimir Wrangel 43/5, BlueOrange Studio 43/6, Somchai Som 43/8, Alexey Stiop 43/9, michaeljung 48(A), Maxriesgo 48(B), 48(C), Juniart 48(D), Djomas 48(E), Studioloco 48(F), Kaarsten 48(G), Stockyimages 48(H), wong yu liang 48(I), Hogan Imaging 48(J), Karkas 48/2, Shebeko 48/3(Jumper), Karkas 48/6, 48/6 (Jacket), terekhov igor 48/8, Surrphoto 49, Vibrant Image Studio 53 (A), Shout It Out Design 53(D), Binkski 53(F), Oleksiy Mark 53 (G), Elena Elisseeva 53 (I), Pkchai 59c, Goodluz 59r, violetblue 59l, bikeriderlondon 63, Anton Gvozdikov 66b, Robert Kneschke 66t; **SuperStock:** Blend Images 20, Radius 62.

Every effort has been made to trace the copyright holders and we apologize in advance for any unintentional omissions. We would be pleased to insert the appropriate acknowledgment in any subsequent edition of this publication.